Oracle 11*g* Streams Implementer's Guide

Design, implement, and maintain a distributed environment with Oracle Streams

Ann L. R. McKinnell

Eric Yen

BIRMINGHAM - MUMBAI

Oracle 11*g* Streams Implementer's Guide

First published: January 2010

Production Reference: 1130110

Published by Packt Publishing Ltd.
32 Lincoln Road
Olton
Birmingham, B27 6PA, UK.

ISBN 978-1-847199-70-6

www.packtpub.com

Cover Image by Ann L.R. McKinnell (ann.mckinnell@apgtech.com)

Credits

Authors
Ann L. R. McKinnell

Eric Yen

Reviewer
Shekar Kadur

Lavanya Kompella

Acquisition Editor
James Lumsden

Development Editor
Dilip Venkatesh

Technical Editors
Neha Damle

Arani Roy

Copy Editor
Sanchari Mukherjee

Indexer
Rekha Nair

Production Editorial Manager
Abhijeet Deobhakta

Editorial Team Leader
Gagandeep Singh

Project Team Leader
Lata Basantani

Project Coordinator
Poorvi Nair

Proofreader
Andie Scothern

Production Coordinator
Aparna Bhagat

Cover Work
Aparna Bhagat

Graphics
Nilesh R. Mohite

Geetanjali Sawant

About the Authors

Ann L.R. McKinnell, a Colorado native, has been an OCP since Oracle 7.3.4. She has more than 16 years of IT experience; with over 8 years as a senior technical member of Oracle Global Support, specializing in Replication and Distributed system technologies. She was a recognized global technical expert for Oracle replication; earning the internal nickname "Replication Goddess". Ann has trained Oracle Support and Consulting personnel from many countries in Advanced Replication and Distributed System Internals and problem solving techniques. Ann has authored and co-authored many of the Oracle Advanced Replication notes found on Oracle Metalink, and was a technical reviewer for the Oracle University Pilot 9*i* Streams course material, as well as various Oracle Replication and Database Administration user manuals. Ann continues to specialize in practical implementation strategies and the development of distributed Oracle database systems, database architecture, and software and database design and integration, and is currently a Senior Principal Consultant with APG Technologies, LLC.

As we go through life, our paths are often greatly influenced by even the slightest of touches from others. Whether knowingly or not, near or far, well-known or acquaintances, you have all produced far reaching ripples in my life's stream.

Mike Pomphrey, for giving me my break into the IT business and introducing me to Oracle (not to mention providing tongue-in-cheek bragging rights that Lockheed-Martin waited at the door after hours for me!). Little did I know of the journey of opportunity that began that day at the Job Fair so long ago. Thank you, not only for recognizing a diamond in the rough, but for your friendship and support over these many years. Though we don't see each other often, I have come to believe that when our paths cross, it is God's way of telling me that great opportunities are right around the corner.

Andy Taylor, my greatest professional supporter. Friend, you never wavered in helping me attain what I myself never thought attainable. Your own talents and abilities have inspired me to reach far beyond my comfort zone and broaden my horizons. Whenever you saw the opportunity, you not only showed me the door, but opened it and pulled me through. Also, to Chip Brown, for so often handing Andy the "keys" to open those doors and "do it". It is these doors of opportunity that have led me here.

To my Replication mentors: Rhonda, David, and Janet.

Rhonda Cordonnier (the original Replication Goddess of Oracle Support). For taking advantage of my technical naivety so many years ago and convincing me that I DID want to learn Replication. David Russell "…of the UK" for inviting me to join the Replication PA team at Oracle and mentoring me in the best practices of technical writing for all those Metalink notes. Janet Stern, though it has been many years, the document and beta review invitations, and phone mentoring marathons are still fresh in my mind (it's been almost a decade since you sat on the phone with me for 5 hours explaining heterogeneous gateways, while 7 months pregnant and no break — I am STILL in awe!). Perhaps without even knowing it, you were my most instrumental technical mentor.

To the illustrious Mr. Yen for calling me up and asking "Have you ever thought of writing a book?" Wow! What a ride! Thank you for all your help and support, I never would have done this if it weren't for you. Can't wait for the next adventure!

To Rodger, and Tony of APG Technologies for your "Johnny on the spot" IT support and helping us with the test bed. Also to Eric Amberge, for giving us the thumbs-up to pursue this opportunity to push our personal boundaries and expand our horizons.

To the Oracle 11gR2 beta team for allowing us the opportunity to "play" with the latest and greatest incarnation. Thank you for your support and assistance.

To our publishing team at Packt Publishing for making this all possible. Also, to our editors and reviewers for all their hard work and dedication in bringing this book to intelligible print. Your support, patience, expertise, and assistance have been invaluable. And to Lavanya, for stepping in at the eleventh hour to help us with the final reviews.

To my friends and family who have been so supportive and understanding throughout the writing of this book. Thank you for not forgetting that I exist, and pulling me out of my "cave" every so often to remind me that the sun still shines in the sky and in the hearts of those close to me. To Renee, Patrick, and the helpful and handsome, blue-eyed cowboy (whose name is unknown) at the dude ranch at the end of the white fence; for helping me find my way back to one of my favorite places on earth to take the cover picture. And to God for giving me that incredible place all to myself that beautiful day.

To my parents, for life; and the brains, encouragement, and sense of humor to live it. I hope your life's choices have brought you the happiness and peace you sought with them, as mine have me.

To Rachel and Jacob, the greatest gifts and loves of my life. For the unwavering support, encouragement, and unconditional love. My strength and my joy. It is because of you that I am who I have become. You ARE the best of me.

Most of all, to Him and His; through whom all things are possible. For bringing each and every one of you into my life to help me come to this point.

Eric Yen began working with Oracle Databases at the time of version 7.3.4. Over the next 14 years, he obtained his Oracle DBA Certification starting with version 8 and maintaining it up to the current release and also earned the (ISC)2 CISSP certification. He began working with Oracle Streams with Oracle 9i Streams beta. As a Senior Principal Consultant with APG Technologies, LLC, Eric's work includes designing and implementing Streams solutions for Government clients using the more recent versions of Streams in Oracle 10 and Oracle 11. In his little spare time, you can find Eric exercising and tinkering around with Oracle products.

On occasion I have moments where I wonder "How did I get here?" Well, as we finish this book, now is the time to pause and reflect. I would like to thank the Professor who first taught me about Oracle, "Professor Hutch". "Professor Hutch" always challenged the students with the statement "go ahead and try that, see if it works", never giving us the easy way out and forcing us to learn through our actual experiences. To the friends and managers that were part of the Oracle SCHOLAR program where good memories were made being in the crucible. The Oracle SCHOLAR program was an unforgettable experience, for it set the foundations for what I am now with regards to Oracle.

Thanks to the "Replication Goddess" for saying "sure that sounds exciting" when I asked her to co-author this book. Ann, it's been one interesting and exciting journey and I could not have done it without you.

To the members of APG Technology, it's a pleasure to work with all of you. This is the best group of talent and personalities I have ever seen. To Mike Janeway and Eric Amberge, things have definitely changed since the meeting at the Proud Bird. Thanks to both of you for bringing me on board and providing support.

To the team at Packt Publishing, thanks for providing this platform for us. I never knew the amount of behind-the-scenes work and editing done to get a book published. This team rocks!

To Yvonne Yu for being part of my life in a way only you can be.

To B and Turtle, thanks for adding perspective outside of my work. Turtle thanks for more than you could ever know.

To my parents, thanks for always doing your best for my sister and I, even when I was not doing my best.

To Richard Rose, Connie Yen-Rose, Carlie Rose and Emma Rose love you all.

About the Reviewers

Shekar Kadur has over 23 years of experience in Information Systems specifically designing, developing, and managing complete system development lifecycle of projects involving Databases, Data warehousing, Business Intelligence, OLAP, SAP, and Enterprise Management Reporting applications in the automotive, finance, utility, retail, and healthcare industries.

He is a certified **PMP (Project Management Professional)**, a certified Hyperion instructor and a consultant proficient with all Oracle and Hyperion toolsets (Essbase, Planning, and so on). He is extremely proficient in project/program management of applications using Oracle, Hyperion, SAP, SAPBW, Business Objects, and web-based technologies. He has consulted, deployed, and managed IT projects at Ford Motor Company, Ford Motor Credit Corporation (Ford Credit), General Motors, Daimler Chrysler Financial Corporation, Daimler Chrysler, Consumers Energy, Guardian Industries, Oakwood Health Systems, General Dynamics, Management Technologies Inc, TRW, Constellation Brands Inc, Johnson Controls Inc, Deloitte Consulting, and Capgemini Inc.

He has delivered lectures on Data warehousing, Datamarts, Oracle, and Hyperion toolset in Michigan, USA and London, UK.

He has also been a technical reviewer of the *Oracle Essbase 9 Implementation Guide* book published by Packt in 2009.

Lavanya Kompella is an experienced Oracle DBA who started her Oracle career on V6. Her areas of expertise include Advanced Replication, Streams, and AQ. She is an Oracle Certified DBA (OCP) from V7 through to V11.

Her previous employers include Tata Consultancy Services and Oracle USA. She is currently part of the DBA team of WELLSFARGO in India.

I would like to thank my wonderful husband Chandra, who always wanted nothing but the best for me. Without his encouragement and cooperation I wouldn't be where I am today.

Table of Contents

Preface

This Preface and the entire book are a little bit different—and that is by design. Both authors wrote this book understanding that our target audience often does not have time to read a whole book, or the Oracle documentation, from cover to cover. As such, we wrote this book with the idea that the table of contents and headings should tell you *exactly* what is being covered. Bullet lists will be used to quickly highlight key points where appropriate. Where concepts need to be explained in more detail, a supporting narrative is supplied. Another difference is that we make multiple references to Oracle documentation rather than attempting to rewrite everything. This is also by design. Having seen Oracle documentation evolve over the years, both authors, and our publisher, recognize the intrinsic value of getting specific detailed information straight from the "horse's mouth". To promote the development of overall expertise, we focus on helping our readers effectively use all the tools available. The Oracle documentation is one of your most valuable tools. At times, Oracle documentation can be difficult to follow or find information within, but once you develop an expertise in using the documentation, the expertise in the functionality is not far behind. The focus of this book is not to replace the Oracle documentation, but rather to be a quick reference companion to the Oracle documentation.

Replication in general

The concept of replication is simply to duplicate. Birds do it, bees do it, and even cells do it. However, replication is not limited to the biological world. Accurately duplicating data from which information is derived is the foundation of human communication. Whether that data be the words or gestures used to convey a story that is handed down from generation to generation, or the numbers used to quantify the quantifiable, or the grouping of on/off bits stored in a computer file; humans have been replicating data since they discovered the need to communicate.

Now that we have evolved into the wonderful age of computerized technology, we recognize the limitless advantages of sharing data, and the need to accurately and efficiently duplicate and distribute that data.

Distributed database systems

We all know that a database is a collection of data objects that are typically accessed through a client/server architecture, and where the database is the **server**.

We also know that client/server architecture uses a network **communication channel** that allows the **client** to send or get data to/from the database. The client can be local (on the same computer as the database), or it can be remote (on a different computer than the database). Either way, the client uses some type of **network connection** to access the database.

The sharing of data between two or more databases constitutes a distributed database system (even if the databases reside on the same computer). Distributed database systems can be homogeneous (all on the same platform, such as Oracle) or heterogeneous (two or more platforms, such as Oracle, MS SQL Server, SYBASE, and so on.) These systems can utilize a number of data distribution methods (unidirectional, bidirectional, read-only, synchronous, and asynchronous). The glue that holds this all together is the network and database links between the various databases.

A **database link** is a one-way communication channel from one database (source) to another database (target) that allows the source database to access the objects in the target database.

Key terms that have been discussed and should be understood here are: database link, communication channel, and network connections. These all work to provide connectivity in a distributed system. It is very important to understand that network connectivity makes or breaks a distributed system. No network connection means no data distribution. An unstable network means unstable data distribution.

Now that you have a distributed database system, add client applications that access one or more databases in that distributed database system, and voila! You have a full-blown distributed system.

What is Data Replication?

Data Replication is literally the act of accomplishing data object changes throughout a distributed system. Period. Replication can be manual, or it can be automated. Automated is the preferred mode of 3 out of 4 DBA's surveyed (we do not really count the 4th, he's semi-retired and has nothing better to do).

How do "Replication" and "Distributed Systems" interact?

Replication makes data located in different databases available to all databases within the distributed system. So replication is the method behind a distributed system. It moves the data around to different sites.

Databases within a distributed system are often referred to as sites. As mentioned earlier, databases can be physically co-located on the same computer, but the databases themselves could still be referred to as separate sites. The term 'site' is more of a logical distinction, than a physical distinction.

Why would we want to replicate?

There are a number of reasons to replicate data, but it is a good bet that they all boil down to increased availability. This means that the same data is available at different sites, and the flow of data between those sites is automated. Replication supports increased availability by providing the following:

- **Change consistency**: Ensures that all sites get the same change.
- **Mass deployment/disconnected computing**: Data can be sent to secondary computers (laptops, desktops) so that it is available when these devices might be offline.
- **Faster access:** Load balancing is the art of distributing client connections over multiple databases. This comes in really handy when the system has a large number of users, and even more so if those users are geographically separated from the system databases. The user just connects the geographically closest database. Network load can also be reduced by directing traffic over different routers for different database sites.
- **Survivability**: Data is still accessible if one site fails.

When not to use replication for survivability purposes

If the need is to only support survivability and data changes made at a single site, there are better tools to use to support survivability that require a little less configuration, maintenance, and monitoring. For example: Data Guard!

Replication architecture

Replication architecture refers to the overall structure of the replicated environment. This includes what is replicated between the sites and the role of each site. The following terms are used to make these distinctions:

Master table/object: A table or object that is replicated to another database. A replicated table can be a master table for a snapshot/materialized view, or a table that is duplicated at a remote site. For tables, both the structure and the data are replicated. For non-table objects, the object definition is replicated.

Master/Source site: A database which hosts master tables/objects. The tables can be a master table for a snapshot/materialized view, or a table that is replicated to a remote master site.

Secondary/Target site: A database which hosts replicated objects to which changes are sent by a master site. This can be another master site, or a materialized view site. The expectation of a secondary site is that if a data conflict occurs when attempting to apply the change from the sending master site, the conflicting secondary site data is always replaced by the values from the sending master site.

Replication methods

A replication method describes how data is replicated between sites. This can be broken down into commit synchronization and directional flows.

Commit synchronization flow refers to when changes are committed at and between sites. There are two methods of commit synchronization; synchronous and asynchronous.

Synchronous replication requires that all sites be able to commit the change before it is committed at the originating site. If any site is not able to commit the change, the change is rolled back at all sites, including the originating site. This requires all database sites in the distributed system to be writable over network connections. The nature of synchronous replication keeps the data at all sites synchronized, thus (at least theoretically), eliminating the need for conflict resolution. Synchronous is used for real-time, mission-critical replication.

Asynchronous replication allows the transaction to be committed at the originating site regardless of whether it is successfully committed at the other target sites in the distributed system. In this method, if the commit is successful at the originating site, appropriate deferred transactions for each target site are created and stored to be propagated and applied at a later time (keep in mind "a later time" can be as little as a few seconds). This allows work to continue at the originating site even if the changes cannot be applied to the other sites within the distributed system immediately. This does, however, open up the possibility of data divergence, and requires some form of conflict resolution (manual or automated) to be implemented should divergence occur.

Replication from one site to another can only be synchronous or asynchronous. It cannot be both (in other words, it is mutually exclusive).

Directional flow refers to the direction in which changes are passed between two sites.

Unidirectional means that data changes only flow one way. In this case, changes are made at a primary master and are sent to a secondary site. Direct changes made at secondary sites are either not allowed, or not sent to the primary master site. If changes are made at a secondary site that causes data divergence from the primary master database, subsequent changes from the primary master will either fail due to the data differences, or overwrite that change if conflict resolution mechanisms are in place. Read-only snapshots are an example of unidirectional replication.

Bidirectional (N-Way) replication means that data changes can flow to and from sites within a distributed system. Changes can be made at any master or updateable snapshot site. These changes are then propagated to all other sites. If the bidirectional replication is asynchronous it can lead to data divergence, and requires some form of conflict resolution (manual or automated) to be implemented, should divergence occur. Master-to-Master and Updateable Snapshots are examples of bidirectional replication.

Replication of an object between two sites can only be unidirectional or bidirectional. It cannot be both (again, mutually exclusive).

A commit synchronization method can be applied to either directional flow method, and vice versa.

Replication configurations

Now that you understand replication architecture and methods, these can be combined to create a replication configuration. A replication configuration can also be referred to as a replication environment. The following define the different replication configurations that you can implement:

N-Way/Master-to-Master/Multi-Source: A distributed environment that has two or more change source sites. These source sites push changes to other change source sites and receive changes from other change source sites.

Uni-directional/Master-to-Secondary/Single-Source: A distributed environment where one site is the (change) source site (primary/master). It, in turn, pushes changes to other sites (secondary). If data changes directly at a secondary site, this could result in data divergence and must be addressed through conflict resolution methods.

Hybrid: A distributed environment that has a combination of multi and single source configurations.

Oracle Streams

As you can see, there are many components and methods that can be used to implement replication. Where do you start? What do you use, what don't you use, and when? And most importantly, how does Streams help?

The concept of Streams grew from pairing the distributed theory of Oracle's Advanced Replication with the redo change capture technology of Oracle's LogMiner. Rather than using triggers to capture database changes (as is done with Oracle's Advanced Replication), Streams uses LogMiner to capture the committed changes from the database on-line redo/archive logs. This allows for a more flexible replication architecture (like data capture, propagation, and apply rules that support site-to-site pass-through propagation and data transformations). However, by the nature of redo change capture, Streams replication is always, technically, asynchronous. The data change is committed at the source regardless if it can be committed at the destination. If you require a truly synchronous environment, you will want to explore Oracle Advanced Replication rather than Oracle Streams.

What this book is (and is NOT)

This book is intended to be a quick reference guide to Oracle 11*g* Streams. Along those lines we are going to quickly go over the basics and have you up and running with a simple Oracle 11*g* Streams environment in the first sections of this book. This is because we believe that hands-on is the only true and meaningful way of developing an expertise with a technology. Then we will evolve the simple Streams environment to cover areas of concern related to more advanced configurations and the administration of an Oracle 11*g* Streams configuration in a production environment. The authors do make an attempt to direct the reader to specific Oracle documentation, should the reader desire additional detailed information.

You should also be aware that this book is meant to be read chapter to chapter for the first three chapters. This provides you with the foundation that is needed for later chapters. If you have a background with Oracle Streams, consider jumping to specific configuration chapters (Chapter 4 through to Chapter 6).

Here is the high level layout of the chapters.

- Chapter 1: *All the pieces: The parts of an Oracle 11g Streams Environment* examines the different components of Oracle Streams and how they work together.

- Chapter 2: *Plot Your Course: Design Considerations* provides the reader with guidelines on what details to consider when designing a Streamed environment, as well as a design aid to help you to organize your environment requirements.

- Chapter 3: *Prepare the Rafts and Secure Your Gear: The pre-work before configuring Oracle 11g Streams* begins the implementation process by successfully configuring both Source and Target databases to support Streams Capture, Propagation, and Apply processes.

- Chapter 4: *Single-Source Configuration* looks at configuring single source streams replication using Enterprise Manager DB Console and review the PL/SQL API calls being issued behind the scenes.

- Chapter 5: *N-Way Replication* takes the concepts for setting up a single-source configuration and applies it to a multi-master, or N-Way Replication environment configuration.

- Chapter 6: *Get Fancy with Streams Advanced Configurations* covers the popular advanced features of Oracle Streams including Subsetting, Tags, Rules, Rule-based transformations, and 11gR2 new features such as Change tables, and XSTREAMS.

- Chapter 7: *Document What You Have and How It Is Working* addresses issues and concerns associated with losing a key member of a team responsible for a Streamed (or any) environment by creating and maintaining proper documentation.

- Chapter 8: *Dealing with the Ever Constant Tides of Change* consists of to sections. The first section of this chapter looks at the impacts of, and dealing with, expectedly changing your existing Streamed environment and what you can do to minimize the impact. The second section addresses troubleshooting techniques and what to look for when things "stop working" due to any unexpected changes.

- Chapter 9: *Appendix and Glossary* is the catch-all chapter dealing with subjects that did not quite fit into the previous chapters. It covers subjects that the authors wanted to mention but did not have the time/resources to fully develop into a standalone chapter.

Who this book is for

This book is *not* for the novice Oracle DBA. In order to gain the most out of this book, you should have a good background as a working Oracle DBA and have a good familiarity with the Oracle Streams Components mentioned in Chapter 1. However, Chapters 1 and 2 may prove helpful to the novice in gaining a high-level understanding of Streams architecture and components, and design considerations.

Conventions

In this book, you will find a number of styles of text that distinguish between different kinds of information. Here are some examples of these styles, and an explanation of their meaning.

Code words in text are shown as follows: "We can include other contexts through the use of the `include` directive."

A block of code is set as follows:

```
BEGIN
  DBMS_STREAMS_ADM.SET_UP_QUEUE(
    queue_table => '"STREAMS_CAPTURE_QT"',
    queue_name  => '"STREAMS_CAPTURE_Q"',
    queue_user  => '"STRM_ADMIN"');
END;
```

When we wish to draw your attention to a particular part of a code block, the relevant lines or items are set in bold:

```
BEGIN
  DBMS_STREAMS_ADM.SET_UP_QUEUE(
    queue_table => '"STREAMS_CAPTURE_QT"',
    queue_name  => '"STREAMS_CAPTURE_Q"',
    queue_user  => '"STRM_ADMIN"');
END;
```

Any command-line input or output is written as follows:

```
ALTER TABLE <table_name> ADD SUPPLEMENTAL LOG GOUP <log_group_name>
(col1, col2) ALWAYS;
```

New terms and **important words** are shown in bold. Words that you see on the screen, in menus or dialog boxes for example, appear in the text like this: "clicking the **Next** button moves you to the next screen".

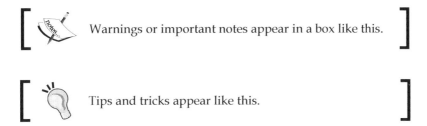

Warnings or important notes appear in a box like this.

Tips and tricks appear like this.

Reader feedback

Feedback from our readers is always welcome. Let us know what you think about this book — what you liked or may have disliked. Reader feedback is important for us to develop titles that you really get the most out of.

To send us general feedback, simply send an email to feedback@packtpub.com, and mention the book title via the subject of your message.

If there is a book that you need and would like to see us publish, please send us a note in the **SUGGEST A TITLE** form on www.packtpub.com or email suggest@packtpub.com.

If there is a topic that you have expertise in and you are interested in either writing or contributing to a book on, see our author guide on www.packtpub.com/authors.

Customer support

Now that you are the proud owner of a Packt book, we have a number of things to help you to get the most from your purchase.

Downloading the example code for the book

Visit http://www.packtpub.com/files/code/9706_Code.zip to directly download the example code.

The downloadable files contain instructions on how to use them.

Errata

Although we have taken every care to ensure the accuracy of our content, mistakes do happen. If you find a mistake in one of our books—maybe a mistake in the text or the code—we would be grateful if you would report this to us. By doing so, you can save other readers from frustration, and help us to improve subsequent versions of this book. If you find any errata, please report them by visiting http://www.packtpub.com/support, selecting your book, clicking on the **let us know** link, and entering the details of your errata. Once your errata are verified, your submission will be accepted and the errata added to any list of existing errata. Any existing errata can be viewed by selecting your title from http://www.packtpub.com/support.

Piracy

Piracy of copyright material on the Internet is an ongoing problem across all media. At Packt, we take the protection of our copyright and licenses very seriously. If you come across any illegal copies of our works, in any form, on the Internet, please provide us with the location address or web site name immediately so that we can pursue a remedy.

Please contact us at copyright@packtpub.com with a link to the suspected pirated material.

We appreciate your help in protecting our authors, and our ability to bring you valuable content.

Questions

You can contact us at questions@packtpub.com if you are having a problem with any aspect of the book, and we will do our best to address it.

So, grab your waterwings and let's jump into Streams...

1
All the Pieces: The Parts of an Oracle 11*g* Streams Environment

Oracle Streams provides a flexible data-distribution architecture, founded on Advanced Queuing. This architecture allows users to not only distribute data and changes between Oracle databases, but also non-Oracle databases. The architecture supports flexibility far beyond that of Oracle's Advanced Replication allowing users to direct, manipulate, and transform data changes as they flow through the distributed environment.

In the Preface of this book, we have discussed the concepts of replication and distributed systems and why they are used. Often, Streams is used to replicate data between different business units. One example of this is using Streams to replicate data from local offices to headquarters, or vice versa, allowing the local creation of reports at the destination or target database.

Streams is built into the database and is part of Oracle Enterprise Edition. As such, Streams has tighter integration to the database than any other third party product. Streams can be configured between single instance databases or used with Oracle Real Application Cluster.

This chapter provides a high-level review of:

- Streams architecture overview
- Capture process
- Instantiation
- Propagation process
- Apply process

- SCN co-ordination
- Logical Change Records (LCRs)
- Memory and storage architecture
- Data (DML) Change Auditing via Streams `Change_Tables`
- A brief word on XSTREAMS

The information presented in this chapter provides a quick overview of Oracle Streams components. Each component is introduced and some detail is provided. In subsequent chapters, we review Streams design considerations and database configuration, then move on to setting up our first Oracle Streams environment. For more detailed information on these components, please refer to the *Oracle 11g Streams Concepts and Administration Guide*. Throughout the chapter, we also provide references to other Oracle documentation that is beneficial in gaining a detailed understanding of the component discussed.

Streams architecture overview

Let's take a moment to briefly run through the replication topologies and process flow, and identify the Oracle functional components that are used by Streams.

Topology configurations

Distributed topology configurations are as limited as rocks in a river. However, many are not conducive to an efficient and maintainable system. The number one consideration when choosing a distributed topology is data ownership and conflict resolution requirements as discussed in Chapter 2, *Plot Your Course: Design Considerations*. To keep your Streams from becoming wild, untamed rivers, and drowning the DBA's, keep master sites to a minimum, if at all possible, and data flows in a tightly controlled and synchronized manner. Oracle recommends no more than four masters involved in full-on all-site N-way replication, and the authors second that recommendation with gusto.

In the Preface, we briefly described single-source, multiple-source, hybrid, and heterogeneous configurations.

The following images provide a synopsis of succinct, controlled single-source and multiple-source configuration examples. Of course these are not the *only* viable configurations, but they will help you to start developing a feel of how to control your Streams.

Keep in mind that the relationship between source and target (secondary) databases assumes they share the same data at some level. Two databases that handle totally different data would not be considered a source or secondary site to each other.

Single source

In a single-source configuration there is only one database that is the source of data changes that are being Streamed to other database site(s). At the other site(s)/target(s), the data can be applied and/or forwarded to another database. If data changes are forwarded from a destination database, the configuration is called a *directed network*. There are two types of directed network forwarding configurations; Queue forwarding and Apply forwarding. Queue forwarding involves propagating the change to a target database site but not applying the change at the database. Rather, the destination only forwards the change to a subsequent site to be applied down the line. Apply forwarding will apply the change, and forward it to subsequent destinations via local Capture and Propagation. Destination sites configured as Queue or Apply forwarding sites are often referred to as intermediate sites. Another single source configuration consists of a copy of the actual redo logs being forwarded from the source database, to a "downstream" target database. The actual Capture process and queue are configured on the downstream database rather than on the source database. This configuration is called *Downstream Capture* which is explained in more detail later on this chapter and in Chapter 6, *Get Fancy with Streams Advanced Configurations*.

In a single source environment, steps should be taken to avoid changes being made at the secondary destination databases to avoid data divergence and change conflicts.

Some illustrated examples of single-source configurations with a brief explanation of where the Streams processes are located are shown as follows.

Single database

A single database configuration hosts both the Capture and Apply processes on the same database. This can negate the need for a Propagation process as the Apply process can be created to dequeue from the same buffered queue into which the Capture process enqueues. However, there may be circumstances where you wish to configure separate buffered capture queue and persistent apply queues. In this case you would also configure a Propagation process between the two queues. The Apply process can be assigned an apply handler that processes the LCRs in a specific manner. This type of configuration can be used to support client application access to captured LCR data and heterogeneous configurations.

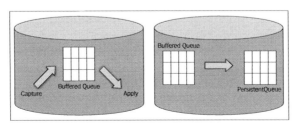

Uni-directional

In single-source to single-target configuration the Capture and Propagate processes and the Capture queue are located at the **Source** database. The Apply process and queue resides on the **Target**.

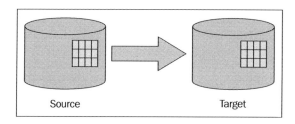

Cascaded/directed network

In a directed network configuration, Capture and Propagation processes and Capture queue reside on the Source. For Queue forwarding, the forwarding site has a queue, but no Apply process. For Apply forwarding, the forwarding site is configured with an Apply process and queue as well as a local Capture process and queue. Tags (discussed in Chapter 6) are used to coordinate the local "recapture" of the applied changes. Appropriate Propagation processes are configured from the forwarding site Capture queue to the destination sites. The final destination site is configured with a regular Apply process and queue.

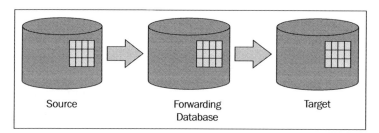

Hub-and-Spoke

In single-source Hub-and-Spoke configuration, data is Streamed from one source to multiple destinations (targets). This is often seen in "Headquarter to Branch (or Regional)" configuration. With this type of configuration, there is a Capture process and queue at the source as well as a Propagation process to each destination. An Apply process and queue are configured on each of the destinations.

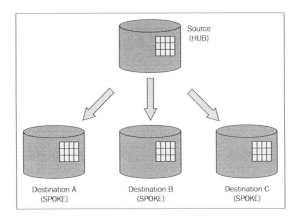

Multiple source

In a multiple source Streams configuration, shared data can be changed at two or more sites. A situation can arise where there is conflict caused by DML/DDL originating from one or more databases acting on the exact same data at nearly the same time. To overcome this conflict situation, conflict resolution must be implemented to determine which data changes should be kept and which should be discarded.

Below are some illustrated examples of multiple-source configurations.

Bi-directional/N-way/Master-to-Master

Bi-directional, N-way, Master-to-Master are all names for essentially the same thing. This configuration allows data changes to be made at all master sites and replicated to all other master sites. As such, Capture, Propagation, and Apply processes and queues must be configured at each master site. For the Capture processes at each site, you can choose to configure a single Capture process and queue for all Propagation processes, or a separate Capture process and queue for each Propagation process.

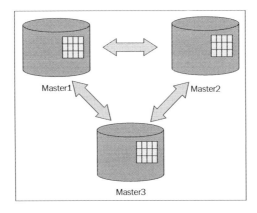

Uni-directional Spokes-to-Hub

In this configuration, the **SPOKES** are the origination point of the data change and the **HUB** is the destination. Capture and Propagation processes and Capture queue are configured on each of the SPOKE sights. An Apply process and queue for each SPOKE site is configured on the HUB. Conflict resolution should be configured at the HUB to accommodate potential data change conflicts from multiple sources.

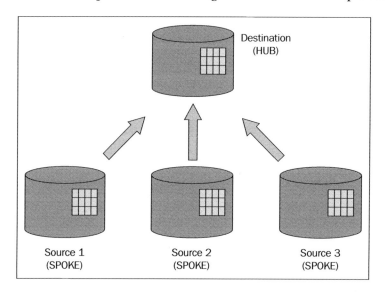

Bi-directional Spoke-to-Hub

This configuration is just an extension of uni-directional Spoke-to-Hub that allows the HUB to send its changes to each spoke. This means that at least one Capture process and queue must be configured on the HUB, and a Propagation process configured to each SPOKE. Note here that the HUB processes should be configured so that the HUB does not send the same change back to the SPOKE that originated it. This can be accomplished in a number of ways by using tags, and/or conditions (covered in Chapter 6). In addition, an Apply process and queue must be configured at each SPOKE to receive and process changes from the HUB, as well as the Capture process and queue and Propagation process to the HUB that we use in uni-directional Spoke-to-Hub.

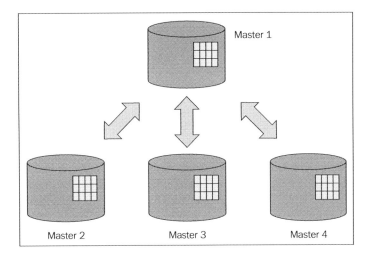

Hybrid

A Hybrid configuration is simply a combination of single and/or multiple- source configurations. For instance, one leg of your topology could be a directed network, while another leg could be a master-to-master. The trick is all in where you put your Capture, Propagate, and Apply processes.

Heterogeneous

Heterogeneous configurations include a source or target database that is not an Oracle database. Oracle Heterogeneous Gateways can be used to allow an Oracle database to send and receive changes to and from these non-Oracle sources. The gateways provide a "translation" level that converts Oracle SQL syntax to and from non-Oracle SQL syntax. This allows the users to transparently accomplish equivalent SQL operations from an Oracle database to a non-Oracle database. Oracle 11*g*R2 delivers the following Gateways to non-Oracle database platforms:

- Adabas
- APPC
- DRDA
- IMS
- Informix
- ODBC
- SQL Server
- Sybase
- Teradata
- VSAM

In a heterogeneous environment, the Apply process and queue must still exist in an Oracle database and be configured to use a database link to the non-Oracle database. The source database may or may not be an Oracle database. It could be such that the Oracle database is merely an intermediate database that is a directed network where a client application enqueues LCR constructed from data at a non-Oracle database into the Apply queue. Regardless of how the LCR is enqueued in the Apply queue, the Apply process on the Oracle database uses Heterogeneous Services and Transparent Gateway to apply LCR changes directly to database objects in a non-Oracle database through the database link to the non-Oracle database. In other words, the Apply process unpacks the LCR and constructs the necessary DML statement on the Oracle side. It then executes the statement through the gateway database link, using Heterogeneous services to translate the SQL to the proper non-Oracle SQL syntax. Capture and Propagation are configured at the source database. If the Apply process for the non-Oracle database is configured on the source database, Propagation between the Capture and Apply would not be required. A remote Oracle destination database can also be configured to apply the change to a non-Oracle database.

As mentioned above, data can also be sent to an Oracle database from a non-Oracle source. This can be done with Advanced queuing and XSTREAMS or JMS. Again the Apply queue and process are on the Oracle database. The non-Oracle database interface must be configured to enqueue a message to the apply queue on the Oracle database. That message is then dequeued and processed by an Oracle advanced queue process.

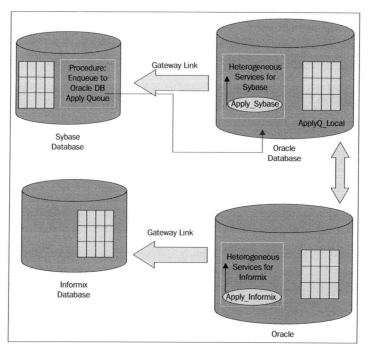

Important: Apply processes for a non-Oracle database can only apply DML, *not* DDL.

[💡 For more information on Streams Configurations, please reference the *Oracle Streams Extended Examples* manual.]

Simultaneous versus Synchronous replication

Synchronous replication in a distributed environment means that a change must be successfully committed at the source and *all* destination sites, or it is not committed at any site, including the source site.

As mentioned in the Preface, Streams is, by nature, an asynchronous replication. The pure fact that the change must be committed at the source site *before* it is even sent to other sites, means Streams is not a synchronous method of replication.

Even if you use Synchronous Capture, it is still not synchronous replication. The "synchronous" in Synchronous Capture refers to the enqueueing of the change to the Capture queue when it is committed to the source data, rather than having LogMiner mine the redo logs, find the change, and enqueue it. This does not mean that the change is successfully committed to the intended destination database data.

Can Streams be simultaneous (or near-simultaneous depending on data transfer and processing rates)? Yes, the Synchronous Capture, and the combined Capture and Apply (new in 11*g* and discussed later in this chapter) support simultaneous replication (though they cannot be used together). They reduce the mining, enqueueing, and dequeueing work required by normal implicit Streams. Just remember; we may be able to get the change to the other sites very quickly, but we cannot guarantee 100 percent that the change will be committed at the destination.

The moral of the story is: Streams replication, as it is today, can be "simultaneous", but it can never be "synchronous".

Oracle's Streams replication process flow

- A change is captured from a database redo stream via LogMiner, or simultaneous Capture mechanisms
- Any defined capture rules/transformations are applied to the change
- The Captured Change is molded into a **Logical Change Record (LCR)**
- The LCR is stored as a message in a specialized advanced queue to be sent to the target site

- The propagation job for the target site consumes the message, applies any defined propagation rules/transformations to the message, and sends it to a specialized advanced queue at the target site

- Oracle's advanced queuing guaranteed, fail-safe Propagation protocol ensures receipt of the message and coordinates the success/error result and handling of the advanced queue messaging

- The Apply process at the target site consumes the message from the advanced queue

- Any defined Apply rules/transformations are applied to the change

- The Apply process then attempts to apply the change to the target site

- All LCR transactions are validated at the target database by conflict detection to ensure the data is consistent between the source and target databases prior to applying the change

- When data inconsistencies are found by conflict detection:
  - If conflict resolution is defined, it is applied to the LCR data inconsistency
  - If conflict resolution is not defined, or fails to resolve the LCR data inconsistency, the LCR is not applied at the target but retained in the erred transaction queue for manual resolution

Streams components

The following Oracle components are used to support the Streams process flow:

- Log Miner: Captures the changes at the originating site.

- Advanced Queuing: Used to support transporting changes between sites.

- Capture, Propagate, Apply database processes: Persistent database processes that accomplish the Capture, Propagation, and Apply tasks.

- Capture, Propagate, Apply rules/transformation via PL/SQL: PL/SQL blocks that define how data should be manipulated by the various processes.

- Logical change record types: Specialized record types used by Streams to store and manage database change message payloads.

- Database links/Oracle Net: Provides an operating system independent connectivity between database sites.

- User authentication/authorization: Provides security access at the database connection and object levels.

- Guaranteed fail-safe propagation protocol: This ensures that a message is successfully delivered and enqueued at the destination site. If an error occurs, the propagation schedule is marked with an error at the originating site for manual resolution and the message is retained in the Capture queue until it can be propagated.

- Conflict detection: Internal protocol that determines if the record to which the change is to be applied matches the record at the originating site before the change was made. This supports data change synchronization.

- Conflict resolution via PL/SQL: Supplied or user defined PL/SQL blocks used to resolve data conflicts found via conflict detection.

About those Queues

Throughout our discussion on the Streams processes, we mention the Advanced Queues used by Streams to transport changes. These queues are either in-memory (buffered queues) or tables on disk (persistent queues). Oracle Streams uses both buffered queues and persistent queues. A buffered queue can only be an ANYDATA queue, while a persistent queue can be an ANYDATA or a TYPED queue.

ANYDATA and TYPED refer to the payload datatype of the message handled by the queue. An ANYDATA queue's payload is of the SYS.ANYDATA datatype. A TYPED queue has a specific datatype (such as Varchar2, CLOB, BLOB, Number). To determine the payload type of a queue, query the OBJECT_TYPE column of the DBA_QUEUE_TABLES view.

```
select owner, queue_table, object_type from dba_queue_tables;
```

The Oracle memory segment used by buffered queues is part of the STREAMS_POOL in the SGA. The type of queue used by Streams depends on the type of LCR that is being stored. Captured and buffered LCRs are stored in buffered queues. Persistent LCRs are stored in persistent queues.

For more information on Streams Queues, review the *Introduction to Message Staging and Propagation* section of the Oracle Streams Concepts and Administration user's manual.

It is always helpful to understand the whole picture and the pieces that make up the picture. As such, we start with the image as follows:

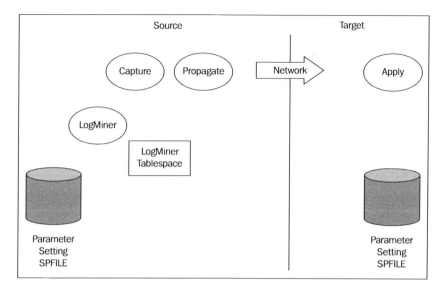

We use the image above as a reference in this chapter to explain the following processes:

- Capture
- Instantiation (Not in image above)
- Propagate
- Apply

So, let us start covering each of the main processes and components and it's role in the Streams environment.

Capture process—what are we supposed to stream?

The Capture process uses both LogMiner and Advanced Queuing to accomplish it's task (Note: Synchronous Capture uses internal triggers instead of LogMiner). The Capture process uses a LogMiner process to examine the database redo log for changes. A Capture process references a set of user-defined rules that determines exactly what needs to be captured for the Stream. These Capture rules identify specific changes to be captured from the redo logs.

These changes are then formatted into Logical Change Records (LCRs) and placed (enqueued) into an advanced queue. In most cases, the queue is a buffered queue (more about LCRs and buffered and persistent queues a little later). This method of capture enqueueing is called "Implicit Capture" and is most often used in a Streams environment. The following image shows the process:

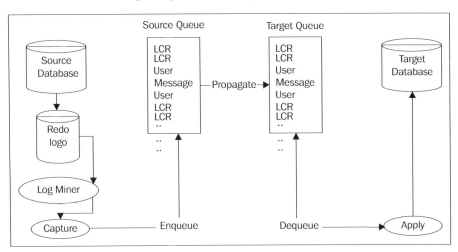

The other method of capturing involves user generation and enqueuing of a message directly into a buffered or persistent queue. This method is called "Explicit Capture" and is usually done by application software. These explicit messages can be either a user defined message or an LCR. For a more detailed explanation on Explicit Capture, refer to the *Oracle Streams Concepts and Administration Guide*.

A Capture process can capture a majority of database transactions. The Capture process specifically captures DML and DDL. The Streams Capture process can capture DML on columns of the following datatypes:

• VARCHAR2	• INTERVAL YEAR TO MONTH
• NVARCHAR2	• INTERVAL DAY TO SECOND
• FLOAT	• RAW
• NUMBER	• LONG RAW
• LONG	• CHAR
• DATE	• NCHAR
• BINARY_FLOAT	• UROWID
• BINARY_DOUBLE	• CLOB with BASICFILE storage
• TIMESTAMP	• NCLOB with BASICFILE storage
• TIMESTAMP WITH TIME ZONE	• BLOB with BASICFILE storage
• TIMESTAMP WITH LOCAL TIME ZONE	• XMLType stored as CLOB

In turn, Capture process can capture the following DDL.

• Tables	• Synonyms
• Indexes	• PL/SQL packages, procedures, and functions
• Views	• Triggers
• Sequences	• Changes to users or roles
	• GRANT or REVOKE on users or roles

There are limitations with the Capture process. The following DDL commands are not captured.

• ALTER SESSION	• LOCK TABLE
• ALTER SYSTEM	• SET ROLE
• CALL or EXECUTE for PL/SQL procedures	• NO LOGGING or UNRECOVERABLE operations
• EXPLAIN PLAN	• FLASHBACK DATABASE

If you take a careful look at the list above, you may notice that these commands are DDL that are instance specific. You want to avoid replicating them, so that you do not end up corrupting the target instance.

In addition, there are object specific DDLs that are not supported by Streams.

• CREATE CONTROL FILE	• CREATE, ALTER, or DROP SUMMARY
• CREATE or ALTER DATABASE	• CREATE SCHEMA
• CREATE, ALTER, or DROP MATERIALIZED VIEW LOG	• CREATE PFILE
	• CREATE SPFILE
• CREATE, ALTER, or DROP MATERIALIZED VIEW	• RENAME (Use ALTER TABLE instead.)

Looking at the lists above, one can start to think, "Is there a quick way to tell if my environment can be streamed?" Yes, Oracle Development did provide a quick way to find out. Simply query DBA_STREAMS_UNSUPPORTED view and you can find out the reason why a particular table could not be streamed. We suggest that you query this table as part of your planning a Streams environment.

```
SELECT * FROM DBA_STREAMS_UNSUPPORTED;
```

Pay particular attention to the REASON and AUTO_FILTERED column. The REASON column is self-explanatory. As for AUTO_FILTERED, if you see a YES value then Streams automatically filters out the object from being streamed.

Possible reasons include:

• **Index Organized Table (IOT)**	• Materialized view log
• Column with user-defined type	• Materialized view container table
• Unsupported column exists	• Streams unsupported object
• Object table	• Domain index
• AQ queue table	• IOT with overflow
• Temporary table	• IOT with LOB
• Sub object	• IOT with physical Rowid mapping
• External table	• Mapping table for physical row id of IOT
• Materialized view	• IOT with LOB
• FILE column exists	• IOT with row movement
	• Summary container table

The Capture process is the first Streams specific related process. However, if you look again at the diagram you will see LogMiner is also in the picture. The Capture does not do everything by itself. The Capture process uses LogMiner to do all the "heavy lifting". The Capture process takes advantage of LogMiner's ability to mine the database redo logs.

In 9*i*, the LogMiner tablespace defaulted to the SYSTEM tablespace. As of 10*g*, it defaults to the SYSAUX tablespace. As there will be additional usage of LogMiner with a Streams environment, we recommend that you isolate the tables related to LogMiner in its own tablespace. This can be accomplished with the following scripts.

```
CREATE TABLESPACE LOGMNRTS DATAFILE '/u05/oracle/data/logmnrtbs.dbf'
SIZE 100M AUTOEXTEND ON MAXSIZE UNLIMITED;

BEGIN
 DBMS_LOGMNR_D.SET_TABLESPACE('LOGMNRTS');
END;
```

This can help eliminate possible fragmentation in the SYSTEM or SYSAUX tablespace where the LogMiner tables are created by default. Depending on your tablespace file to disk distribution, it can also help with performance. If your database has been upgraded from an earlier version, the LogMiner tablespace may well be set to the SYSTEM tablespace. If it is, you are strongly cautioned to use the above method to reset the LogMiner tablespace to a non-system tablespace.

To actually identify the Capture and LogMiner processes that are running on the source database, look for the `background` process on the host of `CPnn` for Capture and `MSnn` for LogMiner where `nn` is a combination of letters and numbers. Both of these processes may not be constantly running, so they should be monitored over time. Also, there may be multiple Capture and/or LogMiner processes running.

Downstream Capture

The Capture process usually resides on the Source database. This configuration is called Local Capture (and sometimes Upstream Capture). The Source database is defined as containing both the Capture process and the tables being captured. There is another Capture configuration that can be used called Downstream Capture. For now, we will just give a quick example of when and why a Downstream Capture would be configured.

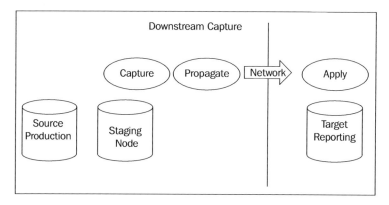

The Capture process consumes resources (memory and CPU) from the host. This may not be optimal in a high-volume production environment (this is but one case where Downstream Capture comes into play). Downstream Capture allows the Capture process and queue to be moved to another staging node. That staging node is the "worker" that can afford the additional overhead of Capture. Downstream Capture uses standby archived log destinations (just like those used by Data Guard) defined at the source database to direct a copy of the redo to the staging node. The Capture process at the staging node then mines those redo copies and enqueues the necessary LCRs. Propagation processes on the staging node then send the LCRs to the appropriate destination database sites. We will cover Downstream Capture and other advanced configurations in more detail in Chapter 6.

Synchronous Capture

Synchronous Capture is not Synchronous replication. We need to be clear on this.

Where regular Implicit Capture depends on LogMiner to extract data changes from the redo, Synchronous Capture actually enqueues the data change to its Capture queue directly when the change is committed at the source.

Synchronous Capture (SC) does have some limitations and differences from Implicit Capture. They are as follows:

- SC can only be created at the Table or Subset levels, not the Schema or Global

- SC cannot be created using the `DBMS_STREAM_ADM.MAINTAIN_*_SCRIPTS` procedures

- SC uses a persistent queue (queue data is stored on disk), so it requires a slightly different configuration than normal Implicit Capture

- SC only captures DML, no DDL

- SC does not capture changes for the following datatypes:
    - LONG
    - LONG RAW
    - CLOB
    - NCLOB
    - BLOB
    - BFILE
    - ROWID
    - User-defined types (including object types, REFs, varrays, and nested tables)
    - Oracle-supplied types (including ANY types, XML types, spatial types, and media types)

- SC can only capture changes for an **Index Organized Tables (IOT)** if it does not contain any of the above listed datatypes

- SC is not a valid configuration for Combined Capture and Apply (this requires a buffered (in memory) capture queue)

We will cover Synchronous Capture and other advanced configurations in more detail in Chapter 6.

Instantiation

We mention instantiation as part of this chapter to stress its importance. Instantiation refers to the creation of the replicated object at target databases, based on the source object. It also provides Streams with the information needed to determine what transactions to apply at the destination site(s). You can think of it as an agreement (starting point) that needs to be established between the source and destination before any Streaming can be accomplished. The main purpose of instantiation is to prepare the object structure and data at the destination site to receive changes from the source.

Instantiation is a process composed of three steps:

- Creating the object(s) at the destination Site
- Updating the Streams data dictionary with metadata
- Setting the Instantiation SCN for the object(s)

The database objects, which are either tables or other objects, need to exist on both the source and destination site. Table structures between a source and destination database can differ if there is a transformation or subsetting involved, though often the tables will have the same data and the same structure. If there is data that needs to be replicated in the table(s) then the data should be the same at the source and destination sites at the time of instantiation, unless there is some sort of transformation, subsetting, or other apply or error handler put in place to compensate for the data differences. This becomes apparent when an update or delete DML fails due to data NOT being at the destination site(s) or having different values in the replicated columns.

Once instantiation is complete, the instantiation SCN will be the same at both the source and destination site(s), indicating to Streams that it is from this SCN forward that changes should be captured, propagated, and applied for the destination. The following image demonstrates this concept as it shows the instantiated **Inventory Table** with the same instantiation SCN at both the **Source** and **Destination** site.

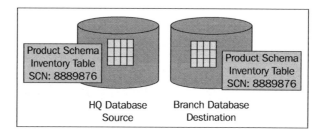

Instantiation Levels and Methods can be accomplished at different levels depending on your requirements. These instantiation levels include:

Instantiation Levels
Table Level
Schema Level
Database (Global) Level
Tablespace (this requires special steps)

Instantiation Methods
Data Pump
Transportable Tablespaces
RMAN for entire database
Manual method

The possible combinations of **Instantiation Levels** that can be used with **Instantiation Methods** can become confusing. So, with a handful of different methods to instantiate tables; How does one decide which method to use? In general, you can use Data Pump to instantiate all (or some) of the tables at Schema Level. You can also decide to move all tables to a particular tablespace and use transportable tablespaces. For now, we will focus on two methods that we use most often due to its ease of use and flexibility.

Using Data Pump to instantiate tables and schemas is fairly straightforward. The Data Pump export utility EXPDP will use Oracle Flashback to ensure that the export is consistent and at the same time capture the instantiation data. For greater control use the FLASHBACK_SCN or FLASHBACK_TIME parameters. On the import side, use the DataPump import utility IMPDP. If it is a full database import, use the parameter STREAMS_CONFIGURATION=y (the default value) to direct IMPDP to include any Streams related metadata that may be contained in the export.

STREAMS_CONFIGURATION is only relevant for FULL database imports via IMPDP. All the other functionality of Data Pump can also be used. So using Data Pump to export/import the entire database, schema, or specific tables can be accomplished with ease, and is the recommended method of export/import based instantiation as of Oracle 11*g*.

If the replicated structures and data are the same on both sites, we recommend that you use DataPump Export/Import to instantiate (this can be done via DBMS_STREAMS_ADM.MAINTAIN_* scripts).

If the replicated structures are the same, but the data different between sites, we recommend instantiating objects via DataPump with CONTENT=METADATA_ONLY, and manual calls to necessary DBMS_STREAMS_ADM.ADD_RULE and DBMS_CAPTURE_ADM subprograms.

> CONTENT=METADATA_ONLY is not supported with TRANSPORTABLE TABLESPACE mode. Make sure to include handling expected data differences between sites in your Capture and/or Apply processes as necessary (see Chapter 6 for more information on data transformation and conflict resolution techniques that can be useful).

If the replicated structures and data are different between sites, we recommend that you create and populate the objects at each site manually, then call the necessary DBMS_STREAMS_ADM.ADD_RULE and DBMS_CAPTURE_ADM subprograms manually. Make sure to configure transformation rules for the structural differences, and handlers for the data differences. One important thing to remember is that if Capture, Propagation and Apply processes and rules are added, or modified, you will need to re-instantiate the SCN between the source and destination. You can do this by following the manual method.

What sets the instantiation SCN and when?

Any of the DBMS_STREAMS_ADM.MAINTAIN_*_SCRIPTS subprograms will automatically set both the Source and Target instantiation SCNs.

The DataPump or Transportable Tablespace instantiation methods will automatically set the Source and Target instantiation SCNs.

Creating the Capture process via DBMS_STREAMS_ADM.ADD_RULE will automatically set the Source instantiation SCN only. You will need to manually set the Target instantiation SCN using the DBMS_APPLY_ADM.SET_*_INSTANTIATION_SCN (covered in the next section).

Creating the Capture process via DBMS_CAPTURE_ADM.CREATE_CAPTURE will not set any instantiation SCNs. You must manually set the instantiation at both the Source and Target sites.

Setting the instantiation SCN manually using the DBMS_CAPTURE_ADM.PREPARE_*_INSTANTIATION and DBMS_APPLY_ADM SET_*_INSTANTIATION_SCN for the proper instantiation level is simple.

The `DBMS_CAPTURE_ADM` contains the following packages used to prepare the objects for instantiation at the source:

- `PREPARE_TABLE_INSTANTIATION`
- `PREPARE_SCHEMA_INSTANTIATION`
- `PREPARE_GLOBAL_INSTANTIATION`

The `DBMS_APPLY_ADM` contains the following packages used to instantiate the object at the destination:

- `SET_TABLE_INSTANTIATION_SCN`
- `SET_SCHEMA_INSTANTIATION_SCN`
- `SET_GLOBAL_INSTANTIATION_SCN`

The steps for setting the instantiation SCN are as follows:

- Call the appropriate `DBMS_CAPTURE_ADM. PREPARE_*_INSTANTIATION` package at the source database
- Determine the current SCN at the source database using `DBMS_FLASHBACK.GET_SYSTEM_CHANGE_NUMBER`
- Call the appropriate `DBMS_APPLY_ADM SET_*_INSTANTIATION_SCN` at the destination database, specifying the SCN value returned in step 2

To state the obvious, you want to make sure that you use the same level for setting the instantiation at the destination that you used to prepare instantiation at the source. Code examples for setting the Instantiation SCN manually are provided in Chapter 3, *Prepare the Rafts and Secure Your Gear: The pre-work before configuring Oracle 11g Streams.*

The following views can help you determine what instantiation levels have been prepared at the source database:

- `DBA/ALL_CAPTURE_PREPARED_TABLES`
- `DBA/ALL_CAPTURE_PREPARED_SCHEMAS`
- `DBA/ALL_CAPTURE_PREPARED_DATABASE`

Propagate process

Now that we know about the Capture process, it is time to move to the Propagate process. The Propagate process does the actual Propagation between the source and target queues.

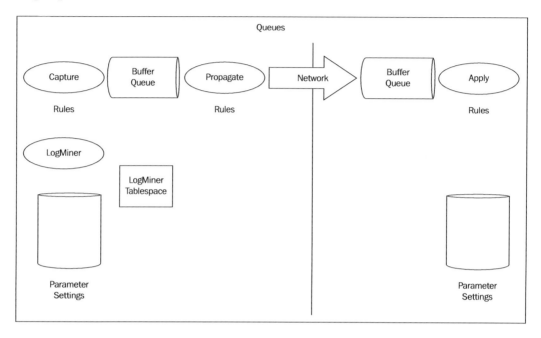

Propagation has two configuration options, queue-to-queue or queue-to-dblink. In the queue-to-queue configuration, each Propagation has its own propagation job. This allows multiple Propagations to be configured and scheduled to propagate at different times. It should be noted that queue-to-queue propagation is recommended for Streams in an RAC environment. The default configuration of queue-to-dblink has one shared propagation job. For queue-to-dblink configurations, having one shared propagation job may cause issues because making any propagation schedule change affects all the propagations that rely on the source queue and database link. This issue can be overcome by configuring different queues when using queue-to-dblink. For example, one queue would be set up QUEUE1 and be on its own SCHEDULE. Then a separate queue, QUEUE2 can be set up and have its own SCHEDULE. Propagation scheduler will be covered in a moment.

Propagation can be configured to propagate to different targets. With the use of RULES one can set up multiple Propagate processes, referencing one buffer queue on the Source. Each Propagation process will process from the same source queue. The source queue will only delete the LCR once it is consumed by each Propagation process registered as a consumer of the queue.

At this time, we need to mention Secure Queue. A secure queue can be used only by the owner of that secure queue. Think of it this way, the owner of the queue runs and controls it. No other users or processes may use a secure queue unless the owner allow it by granting explicit privileges to the user. For the purpose of this book, all queues will be secure queues. This is compared to an unsecure queue which any session or process is allowed to use.

So, how does Propagate know when to do its job? In Oracle 11*g*, Scheduler controls when the Propagation takes place (in previous versions, it was accomplished via regular database jobs). Later, when we work through our example Streams configurations, we will accept the default propagation schedule.

"What" gets propagated "Where" is controlled via Propagation rules is just like "What" is captured by the Capture process that is controlled via Capture rules. The creation of these rules is very similar to Capture process rules, so we won't go into the same level of detail again. Propagation process and rules can be created using either the DBMS_STREAMS_ADM.ADD_*_PROPAGATION_RULE for the replication level desired, or via the DBMS_PROPAGATION_ADM.CREATE_PROPAGATION procedure.

The main thing to understand is that Propagation needs to know what queue from which it must dequeue captured LCRs, what database link to use to send the changes and the destination database name, as well as the remote queue at the destination database in which to enqueue the LCR. As with Capture rules, you can control what the Propagation process sends based on the same type of parameters and rule conditions used in the Capture process.

It should be noted that even though you create a Propagation process using either the DBMS_STREAMS_ADM or DBMS_PROPAGATION_ADM procedures, you use the DBMS_AQADM Propagation Subprograms to schedule/unschedule, alter, enable, and disable propagation. You use the DBMS_PROPAGATION_ADM subprograms to create drop, start, and stop propagation jobs. This is because the Propagation process is separate from the propagation job. The Propagation process can remain running while the propagation job is disabled. This separation allows Streams to support queue-to-queue Propagation as well as queue-to-dblink propagation. Understanding the separation of the two, aids in understanding what procedure to use to control which piece of Propagation.

You can see this separation of duties by looking at the background processes for Propagation. The Propagation processes (similar to the Capture processes) are designated by Pnnn, where as the propagation jobs are separate job processes designated by Jnnn.

For more detailed information on creating and managing Propagation processes and schedules, please refer to the *Oracle Streams Concepts and Administration Guide* and the *Oracle PL/SQL Reference and Types* manual.

The Network: COMLINK

If you have a job title that ends in "Administrator", such as "DBA", you know one thing for sure and that is that the bottom line performance is dependent on the quality of hardware and network. To a certain point, Administrators hit the hardware or network performance wall and no amount of configuration tweaking will change the performance levels. As a DBA, we (hopefully) have some influence on the hardware selection for our databases. DBAs often have little (or no) input as to the network configuration or network hardware selected.

Why is this important? Streams depends on both hardware and network. If you have slow hardware and/or network, you can expect Streams to have low performance levels. The performance of Streams relates directly to your hardware and/or network limitations.

It is with this in mind that we address how to measure the network performance and its potential impact on Propagation before implementing Streams. In many cases Streams database links are configured to use the aliases in TNSNAMES.ORA. The TNSNAMES.ORA DESCRIPTION format can use different network protocols, though most often we see (PROTOCOL=tcp). Measuring, and knowing the network speed and protocol used between the SOURCE and TARGET nodes is important when diagnosing overall Streams' performance. We cover this in more detail in Chapter 3.

We are not saying "blame the network" when a performance problem occurs with Streams. What we wish to convey is that there are parts of the Streams environment that are in your direct control. There are also parts that are beyond your control that affect Streams' performance. Knowing how the network performs is crucial to your ability to diagnose all Streams' performance. Having a good working relationship with your Network Admin will also help when such problems arise. By working with the Network Admin closely, you may also be able to establish minimum service level agreements as well as set realistic client or user expectations where performance is concerned.

Propagation success/failure

How does a propagation job know that its payload has been successfully received and stored at the destination site? This is accomplished via Oracle's guaranteed fail-safe Propagation protocol that requires return notification of a successful commit of the LCR payload data at the destination before it allows the LCR to be removed from the Capture queue and the Capture `REQUIRED_CHECKPOINT_SCN` to be moved beyond that LCRs' SCN. If, after a number of tries (16 to be exact) destination enqueue fails, an error is logged in the `DBA_QUEUE_SCHEDULES` and `DBA_PROPAGATION` view, the propagation job will be disabled and will require manual restart.

> For more information on monitoring the Propagation process and jobs, please refer to the *Oracle Streams Concepts and Administration Guide*, and the *Oracle Streams Replication Administrators' Guide*.

Propagation Stream Split and Merge

Not all COMLINKs are created equal (unfortunately). It is quite possible to have a distributed environment where some network connections from a source database to the different destination databases may not move Streamed data at the same rate, or be equally stable. This inequality of transport to multiple destinations can cause the source queue to grow undesirably large as a result of enqueued LCRs that cannot be deleted until the destination site has confirmed receipt and successful enqueue of the LCR. This could result in Spilled transactions (the LCRs are written to disk from the buffered queue), and memory resource consumption. This also creates a negative performance impact as propagation jobs must scan all the entries in the queues to determine which they have and have not sent. In previous releases, the way to circumvent this was to create a separate capture queue that was used for slower moving or unstable destination connections. This allowed jobs using faster and more stable network connections to be assigned to less encumbered queues. 11*g* brings the ability to have the Propagation process create these types of queue segmentations on the fly, as needed, via Streams Split and Merge. A Propagation process can be configured to recognize when a destination site is exceeding expected transport times. If this happens, the Propagation process will (in a nutshell) clone the Capture process and queue, spawn a separate Propagation job from the cloned queue to the "slow" destination and remove the original Propagation job for the destination from the original queue. In essence, it "splits" the slow stream off to a separate queue allowing the original queue to service the faster destination Propagation processes without performance impact. If/when transport times for the "Split" destination Propagation return to normal, the cloned Capture process can be started to allow the rogue destination site to catch up. Once it does, the queues and processes are merged back to their original configuration automatically. We cover more on Stream Split and Merge in more detail in Chapter 6.

The following lists Propagation/Scheduler views that contain helpful information concerning your Propagation processes and job:

- DBA_PROPAGATION
- V$BUFFERED_SUBSCRIBERS
- V$BUFFERED_PUBLISHERS
- V$PROPAGATION_RECEIVER
- V$PROPAGATION_SENDER
- DBA_SCHEDULER_JOBS
  (filter on JOB_CLASS = 'AQ$_PROPAGATION_JOB_CLASS')

Apply process

We are over the hump and it's all downhill from here. From our previous image on Queues, we notice that we are now on the Target side of the Streams environment. On this side, we have a buffered queue and the **Apply** process. The queue on this side will be a secure queue that is the same kind as that on the Source. This secure queue (on the Target side) contains the LCRs sent over by the Propagation process.

At this point, the Apply process comes into the picture. The Apply process takes LCRs (or messages) from the secure queue and applies them to the Target database object, or hands it off to an Apply handler. An Apply handler is a user defined procedure that processes the LCR change. The user defined procedure takes a single LCR (or messages) as input. As with the Capture and Propagation, the Apply process uses rules to determine what LCR's to Apply.

The Apply process is made up of multiple parts. Those parts are as follows:

- **Reader server:** Takes the LCRs and converts it into transactions, preserving transactional order, and dependencies.
- **Coordinator process:** Takes the transactions from reader server and sends them to Apply server. This process also monitors the Apply server to ensure that the transactions are applied in the correct order.
- **Apply server:** Applies the LCR or message to the handler, either an Apply handler or message handler. Apply server also deals with placing the LCR or message into the appropriate error queue if it cannot be applied.

Keep in mind that there can be multiple Apply processes. The Apply reader and Apply server processes show up as background process on the host as ASnn. In addition, there can also be multiple Coordinator Processes (from above). The Apply coordinator background processes names appear as APnn. In both cases, nn is a number and letter combination (0–9 and a–z).

The Apply process itself is pretty straightforward; dequeue the LCR, evaluate the LCR against the Apply rules, if the overall evaluation is true, apply it (if it evaluates to FALSE ignore it), if the Apply fails, put the LCR in the Apply error queue. Where things can get complicated is at conflict detection, resolution, transformations, and user defined Apply handlers. To really get your head around conflict detection and resolution, you need to understand the LCR structure. Therefore, we save this discussion for the LCR section. Additional understanding of conflict resolution, transformations, and Apply handlers requires a strong understanding of Rule structures. Thus, we save these discussions for Chapter 5, *N-Way Replication*, for configuring conflict resolution and Chapter 6 for rule-based transformations.

Trigger firing and Apply

By default, Triggers do not fire when an Apply processes applies data to a table. This is intended behavior. This keeps changes to replicated tables that result from a trigger at the source site from being duplicated at destination sites. Case in point–if we did not take this precaution. Tables A and B are replicated from source to target. Table A has a trigger that updates table B on commit. These two table updates are replicated as both tables A and B are replicated. However, when the change to table A is applied at the destination, it would kick off the trigger to update table B. But, we also have the change to table B that was sent from the source. Either this change will be overwritten by the trigger, or it will fail because the original values of both records, do not match (see our discussion on conflict detection and LCRs later in this chapter). This yields a high potential for data divergence, which is highly undesirable in a replicated environment.

"Well" you say, "What if I need the trigger to fire because I don't replicate table B?". That can be accomplished by setting the trigger's firing property to allow the Apply process to fire the trigger. The trigger firing property default is set to "once", so that it fires once when a normal change is made. However, when the change is accomplished by an Apply process, the trigger will not fire if its firing property is set to "once". The trigger firing property is managed by the `DBMS_DDL.SET_TRIGGER_FIRING_PROPERTY` procedure. Be careful as the parameter to set the trigger firing to allow the Apply process to fire the trigger is a Boolean and can cause some initial confusion. If the value for `FIRE_ONCE` is set to `TRUE`, then Apply will not be able to fire the trigger. If `FIRE_ONCE` is set to `FALSE`, then the Apply will be able to fire the trigger.

So, if you want a trigger to fire for applied LCRs you will have a call to DBMS_DDL that looks like this:

```
sql>exec DBMS_DDL.SET_TRIGGER_FIRING_PROPERTY (
    trig_owner => '<schema>',
    trig_name  => '<trigger_name>',
    fire_once  => FALSE);
```

If you are not sure as to what the trigger firing property is set to, you can use the DBMS_DDL.IS_TRIGGER_FIRE_ONCE function. The function will return TRUE if the FIRE_ONCE property is set to TRUE (meaning the Apply process cannot fire the trigger), and FALSE if it is set to FALSE (meaning the Apply process can fire the trigger).

For more information on the Trigger firing property and the Apply process, please refer to the *Advanced Apply Process Concepts* chapter in the *Oracle Streams Concepts,* and the *Oracle PL/SQL Reference and Types* manual.

The following lists Apply views that contain helpful information concerning your Apply processes:

- DBA_APPLY
- DBA_APPLY_CONFLICT_COLUMNS
- DBA_APPLY_DML_HANDLERS
- DBA_APPLY_ENQUEUE
- DBA_APPLY_ERROR
- DBA_APPLY_EXECUTE
- DBA_APPLY_INSTANTIATED_GLOBAL
- DBA_APPLY_INSTANTIATED_OBJECTS
- DBA_APPLY_INSTANTIATED_SCHEMAS
- DBA_APPLY_KEY_COLUMNS
- DBA_APPLY_PARAMETERS
- DBA_APPLY_PROGRESS
- DBA_APPLY_SPILL_TXN
- DBA_APPLY_TABLE_COLUMNS
- DBA_HIST_STREAMS_APPLY_SUM
- V$STANDBY_APPLY_SNAPSHOT
- V$STREAMS_APPLY_COORDINATOR
- V$STREAMS_APPLY_READER
- V$STREAMS_APPLY_SERVER

Combined Capture and Apply

You've seen these movies and heard the famous songs where, when certain planets align in certain ways at certain times, special powerful things automatically happen. As of 11*g*, Streams has such a cosmic event potential. And when this cosmic event occurs, its called Combined Capture and Apply. Seriously, it really is like a cosmic event in the galaxy of optimization. When Oracle Streams is configured a particular way between two sites, the Capture process acts as the propagator, using its associated Propagation process rule set, and transmits the eligible LCR's directly to the Apply process at the destination via database link. This functionality automatically detects if the optimal configuration is in place and "flips the switch" to enable Combined Capture and Apply. The only way to control whether or not Combined Capture and Apply is enabled, is to change the configuration of your Streams so that one of the configuration "rules" is violated.

The configurations that cultivate this cosmic event are a little different depending on where the Apply process resides.

If the Apply process resides in a different database than the Capture process, the configuration is required:

- The Capture and Apply databases must be on release 11*g* Release 1 or higher
- The Capture process is the only publisher for the capture queue
- Propagation is configured directly between the capture and apply queues (no intermediate queues allowed)
- The Propagation is the only consumer for the Capture queue
- The Propagation is the only publisher for the Apply queue
- If a buffered Apply queue is used, the Apply process can be the only consumer for the queue
- If a persistent Apply queue is used, multiple Apply processes can be consumers for the queue

One behavior to point out here is that if the Apply process is unavailable at the destination database, the Capture process will hang in the INITIALIZING state at startup until the Apply process becomes available. Once the Apply process is enabled, the Capture process immediately transitions to CAPTURING CHANGES.

If the Apply process resides in the same database as the Capture process, the configuration is required:

- The database must be on release 11*g* Release 1 or higher
- The Capture and Apply process use the same queue
- The Capture process is the only publisher for the queue
- Propagation is configured directly between the capture and apply queues (no intermediate queues allowed)
- If a buffered queue is used, the Apply process can be the only consumer for the queue
- If a persistent queue is used, multiple Apply processes can be consumers for the queue

As the user has no control over the enablement of **Combined Capture and Apply (CCA)** beyond setting up the Streams configuration, it may not be immediately obvious when Combined Capture and Apply is enabled. You can determine if it is enabled by checking the V$STREAMS_CAPTURE and V$STREAMS_APPLY_READER views.

In V$STREAMS_CAPTURE, the APPLY_NAME will have the name of the Apply process and the OPTIMIZATION will be greater than 0 (zero, zed) if CCA is enabled.

```
select capture_name, apply_name, optimization from V$STREAMS_CAPTURE;
CAPTURE_NAME         APPLY_NAME                OPTIMIZATION
-----------------    ----------------------    ------------
HR_CAPTURE           HR_APPLY                             2
```

The PROXY_SID is not NULL in V$STREAMS_APPLY_READER.

```
select apply_name, proxy_sid from V$STREAMS_APPLY_READER;
APPLY_NAME                       PROXY_SID
-----------------------------    ----------
HR_APPLY                                132
```

You will also see a similar entry in the alert log:

Propagation Sender (CCA) HR_PROPAGATION for Streams Capture HR_CAPTURE and Apply HR_APPLY [on destination STRM2] with pid=28, OS id=6096 started.

When Streams is in Combined Capture and Apply mode, you will not see information concerning the Propagation in the DBA_QUEUE_SCHEDULES view. In this case, you will need to query the V$PROPAGATION_SENDER and V$PROPAGATION_RECEIVER views.

SCN Coordination—keeps it flowing smoothly

All of the Streams processes use SCNs to keep track of what change transactions they have processed and they share this information to coordinate who gets what, who still needs what, and what can be ignored (because it has already processed). This is why coordinating the Instigation SCN at the start is so important.

Capture and Apply object instantiation are not the only components of Streams that rely on SCN synchronization. The Capture process must also coordinate it's SCNs with the LogMiner process and available archived logs to ensure data integrity over time. This is done via FIRST_SCN, START_SCN and REQUIRED_CHECKPOINT_SCN.

The Capture process relies on a valid LogMiner Data Dictionary to access database object structure for redo capture to build LCRs. This LogMiner Data Dictionary is separate from the Database Data Dictionary, but is a "picture" of the Database Data Dictionary at the time the Capture process is created. Each Capture process either builds a new LogMiner Data Dictionary or accesses an existing one when it first starts. To build a LogMiner Data Dictionary, the Capture process must have access to the "picture" of the Database Data Dictionary from the redo logs at the time of the SCN from which it must first start capturing. This picture of the Database Data Dictionary is created in the redo logs by running the DBMS_CAPTURE_ADM.BUILD procedure. This procedure must be one at least once in the database before a Capture process can be created. The BUILD creates a picture of the Database Data Dictionary in the current redo log and records an entry in the V$ARCHVIED_LOG view indicating that the redo log contains a Data Dictionary information (DICTIONARY_BEGIN='YES') as of the SCN (FIRST_CHANGE#) at the time of the BUILD. The FIRST_SCN of the Capture process must correspond to a FIRST_CHANGE# for a BUILD. For the Capture process to start for the first time, the redo log for that FIRST_CHANGE# must be available to the database instance. The BUILD procedure can be run multiple times, and different Capture processes can use any one of these builds when it is created by specifying one of the FIRST_CHANGE# values for a build for the Capture process FIRST_SCN parameter (as long as the necessary redo logs are available to the instance). The Capture process will access the redo log containing the Dictionary information, and build its LogMiner Data Dictionary if needed. You can find eligible FIRST_SCN values by querying V$ARCHIVED_LOGS for FIRST_CHANGE# values generated by a build.

```
select distinct NAME, FIRST_CHANGE# from V$ARCHIVED_LOG where
DICTIONARY_BEGIN = 'YES';
```

The NAME column has the name of the redo log(s) in which the BUILD resides. All redo logs from this redo log forward, must be available for the Capture process to first start.

If you specify a FIRST_SCN for a new Capture process from a BUILD for which another Capture process has already built a LogMiner Data Dictionary, the new Capture process will use the existing LogMiner Data Dictionary.

If you do not specify a FIRST_SCN (default is NULL) when creating a Capture process, the creation will call DBMS_CAPTURE_ADM.BUILD procedure, and set the FIRST_SCN for the Capture process to the FIRST_CHANGE# generated by the build. If you create a Capture process using one of the procedures in the DBMS_STREAMS_ADM package, the FIRST_SCN parameter is automatically set to NULL, forcing the capture creation to do a BUILD.

The SCNs of Capture

The following synopsizes the SCNs of a Capture process; how they are used, and rules of usage.

FIRST_SCN

- The lowest SCN at which the Capture process can begin capturing
- Must correspond to a FIRST_CHANGE# value in V$ARCHVIED_LOG for a Data Dictionary BUILD in the redo logs
- Points the Capture process to the redo log(s) that hold the Data Dictionary information from which to build its LogMiner Data Dictionary if necessary, and begin scanning redo for changes on the Capture process first startup
- If REQUIRED_CHECKPOINT_SCN is 0, the Capture process will begin scanning at FIRST_SCN on subsequent capture startups
- It can be changed by the following:
  - Manually using DBMS_CAPTURE_ADM.ALTER_CAPTURE
  - Automatically by CHECKPOINT_RETENTION_TIME purge process
- Change can only be to a value greater than the current FIRST_SCN value
- FIRST_SCN cannot be greater than REQUIRED_CHECKPOINT_SCN when REQUIRED_CHECKPIONT_SCN is greater than 0

START_SCN

- The SCN at which the Capture process will actually begin capturing changes on startup

- `START_SCN` must be greater than or equal to `FIRST_SCN`

- If a Capture process's `FIRST_SCN` is changed (either manually or via `CHECKPOINT_RETENTION_TIME` purge process) to a value greater than its `START_SCN`, the `START_SCN` is automatically increased to the new `FIRST_SCN` value

- `START_SCN` can be changed manually using `DBMS_CAPTURE_ADM.ALTER_CAPTURE`

- `START_SCN` can be set to a value lower than its current value, as long as the new value is not less than the `FIRST_SCN` value for the Capture process

- `START_SCN` is usually only manually changed if a point-in-time recovery has been performed at a destination site, and the point-in-time recovered to requires changes to be resent to the destination site

> If the point-in-time recovery requires an SCN before the Capture process `FIRST_SCN`, that process cannot be used to send changes to the recovered site. If a Data Dictionary `BUILD` is available in the archived logs with a `FIRST_CHANGE#` less than or equal to the SCN required for the point-in-time recovery, a new Capture process can be created specifying the appropriate `FIRST_CHANGE#` for the `FIRST_SCN`. Otherwise, the Streamed objects must be re-instantiated from the source at the destination.

REQUIRED_CHECKPOINT_SCN

- Set to 0 (zero, zed) when the Capture process is created

- Incremented by the Capture process LogMiner checkpoint process

- Value determined by the lowest `APPLIED_SCN` for all destination sites for the Capture process queue

- The lowest SCN that the Capture process must be able to access from the redo logs to be able to restart

- The redo log that includes this SCN and all subsequent redo logs must be available to the Capture process database instance, for the Capture process to successfully start

- If value > 0 (zero, zed), the Capture process starts scanning from this SCN when restarted

- The REQUIRED_CHECKPOINT_SCN is only changed when a checkpoint is completed. This happens either by:
  - ° Automated by LogMiner Checkpoint process
  - ° Manually via command

    DBMS_CAPTURE_ADM.SET_PARAMETER('<capture_name>', '_checkpoint_force','Y')

CAPTURED_SCN

The most recent SCN scanned by the Capture process.

APPLIED_SCN

- The most recent SCN dequeued and processed by any Apply process that receives changes from the Capture processes queue
- Corresponds with the low-watermark SCN for an Apply process

MAXIMUM_SCN

- The SCN at which a Capture process must stop capturing changes and disable
- The Capture process will disable when it reaches this upper limit SCN
- Changes with and SCN greater than or equal to the MAXIMUM_SCN are not captured by the Capture process
- If the value is infinite (default), the Capture process captures changes without upper limit

LAST_ENQUEUED_SCN

- This is the last SCN enqueued by the Capture process
- This value is dynamic and will increase as the Capture process captures and enqueues LCR
- Can be used to gauge latency of Propagation and Apply

SOURCE_RESETLOGS_SCN

The SCN at the last RESETLOGS action.

MAX_CHECKPOINT_SCN

The SCN at which the latest checkpoint was taken.

 For more detailed information on how FIRST_SCN, START_SCN and REQUIRED_CHECKPOINT_SCN are used by the Capture process, please refer to the *The LogMiner Data Dictionary for a Capture Process, Capture Process Checkpoints,* and *Multiple Capture Processes for the Same Source Database* sections in *Chapter 2: Oracle Streams Information Capture* of the Oracle Streams Concepts and Administration guide 11g.

The SCNs of Propagation

A Propagation process really only tracks one SCN value. This is the ACKED_SCN which is the SCN sent to the Propagation process from the destination for which the Apply process has *acknowledged* by all Apply queue subscribers as successful dequeued and processed. This means the dequeued LCR was either successfully applied or successfully committed to the Apply error queue. This value is used by the Capture checkpoint to help determine its REQUIRED_CHECKPOINT_SCN.

The SCNs of Apply

The following synopsizes the SCN's of an Apply process; how they are used, and rules of usage.

IGNORE_SCN

- The SCN below which changes received should not be applied
- Only set when instantiation is accomplished via Export/Import
- Corresponds with the SCN set at the source database when the object was prepared for instantiation
- The instantiation SCN must be equal to or greater than this SCN

MAXIMUM_SCN

- The SCN at which an Apply process must stop applying changes and disable
- The Apply process will disable when it reaches this upper limit SCN

- Changes with and SNC greater than or equal to the MAXIMUM_SCN are not applied by the Apply process
- If the value is infinite (default), the Apply process applies changes without upper limit

OLDEST_SCN_NUM

- This is the latest SCN of a received LCR that was successfully dequeued and applied
- In the case where a point-in-time recovery is performed on the destination, this value should be used to reset the START_SCN for the associated Capture process at the source site to recapture changes
- Does not pertain to synchronously captured changes received

Low-watermark SCN

- The lowest SCN that can be guaranteed dequeued and applied by an Apply process
- Corresponds to the APPLIED_SCN of the Capture process

There are a myriad other SCNs that have used the Apply process internally. The SCNs listed above are the ones you gain the most for understanding. You can find detailed information on Apply SCN and transaction tracking in the Oracle Streams Replication Administrators' Guide.

SCN SYNC-hronization

As you can see, if your SCNs are out of sync between the LogMiner Dictionary, Capture, and Apply processes your Streams may not work as expected; or even not at all. Obeying the following formula when implementing your Streams environment will keep you out of SCN SYNC-hole.

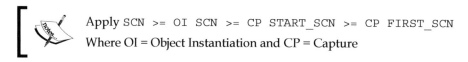

Apply SCN >= OI SCN >= CP START_SCN >= CP FIRST_SCN
Where OI = Object Instantiation and CP = Capture

Once you have implemented Streams, avoid changes to SCNs unless it is necessary to compensate for a destination site point-in-time recovery or an unrecoverable archive log.

Capture checkpointing

The Capture process keeps track of the lowest SCN that has been recorded by its Propagation processes as greatest SCN that has been acknowledged by its Apply destination as being applied. The Capture process cannot set its REQUIRED_CHECKPIONT_SCN great than this SCN or there is a potential for data loss. This is controlled by checkpointing.

The Capture process will conduct checkpoints in which it coordinates its SCNs. By default these checkpoints happen with the capture of 10 MB of redo and the checkpoint metadata is retained in the database for 60 days. You can also force a checkpoint if the need arises. These checkpointing options are all controlled by the following capture parameters:

- _CHECKPOINT_FREQUENCY: The number of megabytes captured which will trigger a checkpoint. Default value is 10 but can be changed with DBMS_CAPTURE_ADM.SET_PARAMETER().

- CHECKPOINT_RETENTION_TIME: Number of days to retain checkpoint metadata. Default 60 but can be changed with DBMS_CAPTURE_ADM.ALTER_CAPTURE() procedure.

- _CHECKPOINT_FORCE: This will force a Capture checkpoint. Accomplished via DBMS_CAPTURE_ADM.SET_PARAMETER, pass in Y for the value. It will set itself back to N when the checkpoint is complete.

You can determine the current values for these parameters by querying the DBA_CAPTURE_PARAMETERS view.

The following lists captures views that contain helpful information concerning your Capture processes:

- DBA/ALL_CAPTURE
- DBA/ALL_CAPTURE_PARAMETERS
- DBA/ALL_CAPTURE_EXTRA_ATTRIBUTES
- V$STREAMS_CAPTURE
- V$STREAMS_TRANSACTION
- DBA/ALL_STREAMS_RULES

Archive Log availability

When a Capture process starts up, it will check its `REQUIRED_CHECKPOINT_SCN` (if it's 0, it will use the `FIRST_SCN`) and look for the redo log that contains that SCN and begin scanning at the redo log forward. If the SCN is in an archived log that is no longer available; or if any subsequent redo logs (archived or online) from that SCN forward are no longer available, the Capture process will not start. You can overcome this by either of the following:

- Restoring the required archive logs
- Dropping and recreating the Capture process

This leads to the obvious question of "what happens when my archive logs are in my `flash_recovery_area` and are aged out?" The obvious answer here is, "It will break your Capture process if/when the archive log containing your Capture `FIRST_SCN`/`REQUIRED_CHECKPOINT_SCN` is aged out". This would be why Oracle documentation specifically and highly recommends that you do not use the `flash_recovery_area` as your only archive log repository if you are using Streams. If you use the `flash_recovery_area`, configure a separate archive log destination to accommodate the archive redo logs needed by Streams. Now, if you really want to only have archive logs in the `flash_recovery_area`, take pity on the on-call DBA and make sure that your Capture process `checkpoint_retention_time` intervals are set within the archive log retention period of the `flash_recovery_area`.

- The following views can be used to help determine what archived redo logs are required by the Capture process and which can be purged:
  `V$ARCHVIED_LOG`
- `DBA_REGISTERED_ARCHIVED_LOG`
- `DBA_LOGMNR_PURGED_LOG`

 For more detailed information on `flash_recovery_area` and Streams, please refer to *Are Required Redo Log Files Missing?* section of Chapter 20 of the Oracle Streams Concepts and Administration guide.

LCRs—what they are and how they work

Knowing how LCR moves from source to target is only part of the story. What an LCR contains is also important. Let's start by going over what we know about database transactions. Every transaction in a database is assigned a unique transaction ID. The transaction itself can be composed of one or more DML or DDL instructions.

Most implicit DDL LCRs will have a single DDL instruction, due to the implicit commit nature of Oracle's handling of DDL.

Each one of these instructions is associated to its parent transaction via this ID. When we attempt to commit a transaction, all the instructions in the transaction must be successfully completed or the whole transaction fails/rolls back. This means that all the DML/DDL instructions within that transaction do not get applied to the database. Remember this. It will be important when you have to troubleshoot situations where a user demands "Where did my data go?"

As mentioned above, an LCR is a logical change record that is created by the Capture process. The content of the LCR is the actual steps the database took to accomplish the change instruction(s) of a transaction. These steps are stored in a special, ordered format that is then parsed by the Apply process to rebuild the SQL to duplicate the original transaction. We know that a transaction can have multiple instructions, thus, an LCR can include multiple steps. Each one of these steps is a message. When you look at the LCR metadata (where available; usually in error queues), you will see that each LCR has a message count, and that each message has a sequential ID.

The message itself is composed of metadata from which the Apply process builds the SQL to accomplish the instruction. This information includes (but is not limited to) the following:

- Message ID/Sequence
- Message type name: LCR or User Enqueued Message
- Source database: where the LCR originated
- Owner: Schema owner for the object/table which the message is changing
- Object: Name of the object/table
- Is Tag Null: Indicates if there are any tag values. (Y means no tag values)
- `command_type`:
    ○ If a DML message, this will be
      `INSERT/UPDATE/DELETE/LOB_UPDATE`
    ○ If a DDL message, this will be `CREATE/ALTER/DROP/` and
      so on

- Change Values:
  - ° If a DML message: You will see the old, new, and data type values for each field in the row
    - The values included depend on the command type:
      - ° Command type: INSERT, you will only see new values
      - ° Command type: DELETE, you will only see old values
      - ° Command type: UPDATE, you will see both old and new values
    - For special field data types, you may also see a typename value as well (such as timestamp). If a DDL message: you will see the actual command text.

There is additional information stored in LCRs. If you wish to familiarize yourself with the content of LCRs you can review the *Types of Information Captured with Oracle Streams* section in the Oracle Streams Concepts and Administration user's manual, and SYS.LCR$_ROW_RECORD and LCR$_DDL_RECORD type definitions found in the Oracle PL/SQL Packages and Types Reference manual. These types are visible to the user for use in explicit capture and are used by implicit capture as well.

Extracting data from an LCR

For regular, implicit Streams, you will most likely only need to extract data from an LCR in the event of an apply error. You would extract and review this data to determine what was in the LCR to help determine what caused the error. You can drill down to the LCRs in the Apply Error Queue using Enterprise Manager or you can create your own procedures that use Oracle APIs to extract the LCR data (we will go over this in more detail in Chapter 8, *Dealing with the Ever Constant Tides of Change*, dealing with how to administer and monitor Oracle 11g Streams).

Conflict detection and the LCR

In an Oracle replicated environment (Streams or Advanced), Conflict detection is always turned on. Conflict detection acts as a guard-dog to the LCR. When the Apply process attempts to apply the changes in an LCR, it first calls Conflict detection to verify that the change can be applied without the unexpected loss of data at the Apply site. Conflict detection identifies the row to be changed by the LCR. It then compares values in the LCR with the actual values in the existing row (if they exist). Depending on the change type, if certain values don't match (also known as data divergence), Conflict detection will attempt to find any conflict resolution rules assigned to the Apply process.

If none are found, or the conflict resolution rules do not resolve the conflict, the Conflict detection will not allow the change to be applied by raising an error to the Apply process. If this happens, the Apply process will place the LCR, along with the error raised by Conflict detection, in the Apply Error queue.

> If an LCR is placed in the Apply Error queue, the DML/DDL messages in that LCR have not been applied to the database object. This means all messages (DML/DDL instructions) in the LCR, not just the one(s) that failed. If you have multiple messages in the LCR, there may only be one message that fails, but the entire LCR transaction fails because of that one message failure. Keep this in mind when developing your transactions. The more messages you have in an LCR, the more difficult it is to determine which message(s) caused the failure.
>
> If an LCR fails, all subsequent LCRs dependent on that failed LCR will also fail. This makes it very important to have as much understanding about how data changes will flow through your distributed environment before you implement production. If not carefully planned, all your changes could easily end up in your target error queue. It also makes it very important to faithfully monitor the Apply Error queues and address errors as quickly as possible.

The key to conflict detection and LCR playing nicely together is planning and conflict resolution. These activities are discussed in more detail in the following chapters.

Controlling conflict detection

As discussed earlier, conflict detection will compare all the values of all the columns by default. You do have some control on whether or not a non-key column value should be compared or can be ignored and when. This is accomplished with the DBMS_APPLY_ADM.COMPARE_OLD_VALUES procedure.

This procedure allows you specify a list of non-key columns in a table that are either included or excluded from conflict detection value comparison. Use this power with caution! Make sure you have identified all the ramifications to data convergence if you choose to exclude column values from conflict detection to avoid unexpected data loss.

The key term is is "non-key columns". The DBMS_APPLY_ADM.COMPARE_OLD_VALUES procedure will not let you exclude key columns. It will raise an error. If you absolutely, positively, without question, must exclude a key column from conflict detection, you will need to redefine the table's key column list using the DBMS_APPLY_ADM.SET_KEY_COLUMNS. Again, use this with reserve.

For more detailed information on Conflict Detection control, please reference the *Streams Conflict Resolution* chapter in the Oracle Streams Concepts and Administration Guide, and the Oracle PL/SQL Reference and Types manual and Administrators' Guide.

Types of LCRs and how they get created

The method used to create an LCR determines the LCR type.

- If an LCR is created by an asynchronous Capture process (implicitly) it is a *captured* LCR

- If the LCR is created by a user application (explicitly), by a synchronous Capture process, or enqueued by an Apply process, it is a *persistent* LCR

- If an LCR is explicitly created by an application and enqueued with `delivery_mode` set to `BUFFERED`, it is a *buffered* LCR

Oracle 11g memory and storage architecture (basic) relating to Streams

At this point, we want to remind you that Streams interacts with the Oracle database architecture in many different ways. Interaction and changes to the SGA and SPFILE should be done prior to configuration of Streams. If subsequent changes are needed, make sure to review those changes. The isolation of tables related to LogMiner (already mentioned above) is also part of the pre-work that should be done as part of the Streams configurations. The location of the redo logs and archive logs and the retrieval speed from disk or disk cache should also be considered. The retention time of archived logs must be coordinated with Capture process SCN requirements.

The use of **Automatic Memory Management (AMM)** or Dynamic SGA is suggested when configuring Streams to ease administration. One of the parameters that will need to be configured is STREAMS_POOL_SIZE. STREAMS_POOL_SIZE controls the size of the Streams Pool in the SGA memory. A properly sized STREAMS_POOL_SIZE allows for proper performance of the Capture and Apply processes. Streams Pool also stores LCRs (or messages) in buffered queues. If the Streams Pool is undersized, you can see issues with "Spilled transactions" for the Apply. This means that the Apply process ran out of Streams Pool and had to write the LCRs to disk until they could be loaded back to memory. This is where an undersized Streams Pool can have a significant impact on Streams performance. If this happens, you will see error messages in the alert log, as well as entries in the V$BUFFERED_QUEUES.

If you see entries in the DBA_APPLY_SPILL_TXN view, this is a result of transaction size or age exceeding the Apply process txn_lcr_spill_threshold and txn_age_spill_threshold parameter values respectively.

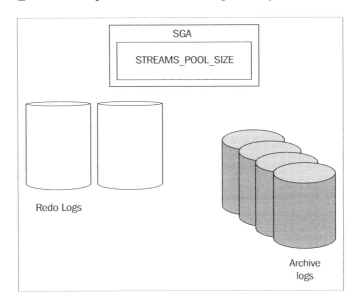

We will go into details about configuration of the database in Chapter 3. For now just be aware that the database needs to be configured specifically for a Streams environment.

A word on performance

We have briefly mentioned some performance-related concerns when setting up a Streams environment. Having robust hardware and a fast, stable network greatly affects overall Streams performance. Configuration of the database will also have an impact on performance. This chapter was more about understanding the key components of Streams. In Chapter 7, *Document What You Have and How it is Working*, we will go into detail about Streams performance.

Streams Change tables

The current ethical climate of computing unfortunately mandates the need to identify who made what changes to what data, when and from where. Corporations must now comply with stringent data change auditing mandates associated with such regulations as SOX (Sarbanes–Oxley Act), FISMA (Federal Information Security Management Act); to name a couple. Prior to Oracle 11gR2, the Capture and Propagation of data change audit information had to be manually included in Streamed environments. Oracle 11gR2 introduces the DBMS_STREAMS_ADM.MAINTAIN_CHANGE_TABLE procedure that allows the DBA to quickly configure a separate change audit table for a Streamed table, as well as to propagate the change audit data from the source site to all target destination sites. This procedure can also be used to create one-way replication of a table along with the change capture from a source to a destination database. Change tables can be implemented for local or downstream capture, and local or remote apply configurations.

The DBMS_STREAMS_ADM.MAINTAIN_CHANGE_TABLE procedure creates all the components necessary to capture, send, and record data change information to the change table.

The DBMS_STREAMS_ADM.MAINTAIN_CHANGE_TABLE procedure is run at the capture site and accomplishes the following:

- Creates a separate change table for the change audit data
    - The change table can be located in the same database or a remote database
    - The change table columns tracked for its source table are based on the column_type_list
    - Additional audit data columns that can be added to the change table include:
        - value_type
        - source_database_name
        - command_type
        - object_owner
        - object_name
        - tag
        - transaction_id
        - scn
        - commit_scn
        - compatible
        - instance_number
        - message_number

- ○ row_text
- ○ row_id
- ○ serial#
- ○ session#
- ○ source_time
- ○ thread#
- ○ tx_name
- ○ username

- Creates a Capture process to capture source table changes
- Creates a Propagation process for remote apply
- Creates an Apply process at the destination site
- Creates and adds DML handlers to the specified Apply process that record change information in the change table based on row LCR information
- Configures the Apply process to execute the row LCR on the remote source table if EXECUTE_LCR is TRUE

    This supports the optional one-way replication.

The following figure shows configuration with local capture, remote Apply with Source table replication.

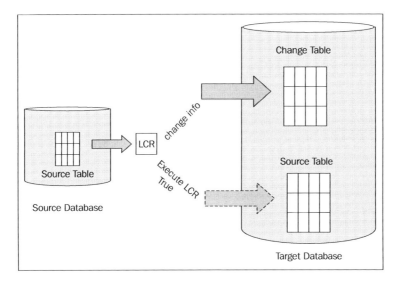

Before configuring change tables, you want to make decisions as to:

- The type of environment to configure
- The source table columns to track
- If/what metadata to record
- The values to Track for Update Operations (old, new)
- Whether to configure a KEEP_COLUMNS transformation
- Whether to specify CREATE TABLE options for the Change Table
- Whether to perform the Configuration Actions Directly or with a Script
- Whether to replicate the Source Table as well

> For more information on Streams Change Tables, please refer to Chapter 20, *Using Oracle Streams to Record Table Changes* in the Oracle Streams Concepts and Administration 11g Release 2 Guide.
>
> For more information on the MAINTAIN_CHANGE_TABLE procedure, please reference the Oracle PL/SQL Packages and Types Reference—DBMS_STREAMS_ADM: subprogram MAINTAIN_CHANGE_TABLE.

Oracle GoldenGate XSTREAMS

With the acquisition of GoldenGate, Oracle 11gR2 incorporates GoldenGate XSTREAMS technology providing client applications with the ability to insert and extract LCR datatypes directly into an implicit or explicit Stream.

> To use the XSTREAMS API's, you must purchase an Oracle GoldenGate product license. See the Oracle GoldenGate documentation at http://download.oracle.com/docs/cd/E15881_01/index.htm.

The following lists views that supply helpful information for XSTREAMS:

- ALL_APPLY
- ALL_APPLY_ERROR
- ALL_XSTREAM_INBOUND
- ALL_XSTREAM_INBOUND_PROGRESS
- ALL_XSTREAM_OUTBOUND
- ALL_XSTREAM_OUTBOUND_PROGRESS

- ALL_XSTREAM_RULES
- DBA_APPLY
- DBA_APPLY_ERROR
- DBA_APPLY_SPILL_TXN
- DBA_XSTREAM_INBOUND
- DBA_XSTREAM_INBOUND_PROGRESS
- DBA_XSTREAM_OUTBOUND
- DBA_XSTREAM_OUTBOUND_PROGRESS
- DBA_XSTREAM_RULES

XTREAMS is built on Oracle Streams infrastructure and thus can take advantage of Oracle Streams' functionality and flexibility.

The Oracle database is configured to support XSTREAMS using the DBMS_XSTREAMS_ADM package subprograms. Specialized *server* processes are configured to handle inbound and outbound traffic to standard Oracle Streams queues. Outbound server processes can be created to dequeue from an existing Streams queue, or its own queue. Inbound server processes are created with their own Streams queue which can then be configured for use via normal Streams apply rule creation. These server processes are accessed via the OCI or Java API function interfaces.

XSTREAMS provides the ability to share information across a heterogeneous environment with excellent flexibility, usability, and performance. This functionality can be used as an alternative to replicating with Oracle Heterogeneous Gateways, and **Java Messaging Service (JMS)** clients.

> For more information on XSTREAMS, please reference the Oracle Database XSTREAMS Guide.
>
> Special Documentation Notes:
>
> The DBMS_XSTREAM_ADM package is documented in the Oracle Database XSTREAMS Guide rather than the Oracle PL/SQL Packages and Types Reference.
>
> XSTREAM OCI interfaces are found in the Oracle Database XSTREAMS Guide.
>
> XSTREAM Java API's are found in the XSTREAM Java API Reference.

Summary

This is the foundation chapter for the rest of this book. We went over the basics of what Streams can do and the background processes that make up a Streams environment. Those background processes being Capture, Propagate, and Apply. Knowing each of these processes well is crucial to implementing a robust production level Streams environment. Not knowing these background processes can cause you difficulties when setting up Streams and future problems. Instantiation was covered in this chapter to point out not only what it is but to also stress its importance in the Streams environment and its role in SCN synchronization.

Streams is also dependent on the hardware and network that it runs on. Having properly sized hardware is within a DBA's influence. The network is often beyond the DBA's control. As the network is so crucial to Streams, we included discussion on the impacts of network speed and stability on Streams performance.

We also went into what an LCR is and its function. An LCR contains the DMLs and/or DDLs that are sent from Source to Target. Not all DMLs and DDLs are supported by Streams and we showed how to quickly identify what objects are supported and those that are not (query DBA_STREAMS_UNSUPPORTED).

We began to go into the Oracle Architecture (and components needed to support Streams) and Streams Performance. Chapter 7 will cover capturing Streams performance statics because it deserves its own special place. We will go into detail about how to configure the database in Chapter 3 to support optimal performance. Finally, we focus on two new Oracle 11gR2 features: Streams Change tables and XSTREAMS.

Now that we have reviewed the components of Oracle Streams Replication, let us move on to Chapter 2 where we will explore the many, many things to consider and options available when designing your Streamed environment.

2

Plot Your Course: Design Considerations

Successful implementation starts with a well thought-out plan.

The information presented in this chapter provides guidelines on details to be considered while designing your streamed environment. The design of an environment is highly dependent on your business's particular data requirements. Every business is different. While businesses may share common architectures, the details of their data requirements can be as different, and as numerous, as snowflakes in a snow storm (or so says Confucius, or maybe would have, if he were alive today). The authors' goal is to point out what to look for in the details as this will be the "meat" of your design.

In a perfect world, every Database architect and System Engineer would have the luxury of the 80/10/10 methodology. 80% design, 10% implementation, and 10% maintenance (preferably proactive). Unfortunately, in the real world, the methodology ends up being more like 10/40/50, with maintenance being reactive rather than proactive. However, by taking into consideration the following design components of your system, you can get a better idea of how much implementation and maintenance you will have ahead of you.

In this chapter, we will cover a number of design considerations to be taken into account before implementing your Streamed environment, including (but not limited to):

- Data ownership and movement: Who, What, When, Where, Why, and How
- Resource availability and limitations
- Application and business rules
- Best practices
- The Streams Site Matrix Design Aid

In journalism, the recipe for a good article includes "who, what, when, where, why, and how." This same recipe can be applied to your distributed environment design.

Why?

First, look at why you want to replicate data.

- Is it only to provide an alternative identical database if the primary database fails or becomes unreachable?
- Do you need to support DML and/or query load balancing?
- Must you distribute different data subsets to different locations?

Your reason could be any one, or a combination of, the above; as well as other reasons not mentioned. Understanding why you want to replicate will actually help you determine why you would use one tool or functionality over another. You will need to differentiate between the efficiencies of similar tools and functionalities available to you. The key word here is efficiencies. You may be able to effectively accomplish your goal using one or the other, but the reason why you would want to use one tool or functionality instead of another is determined by how efficiently the tool or functionality allows you to accomplish your goal.

What?

Next, look at what needs to be replicated.

- Do you need to replicate the whole database or just certain schemas?
- Do only certain tables need to be replicated?
- Of those tables are there only specific rows or columns that should be replicated?
- What changes should be replicated?
- Just DML?
- Which DML; inserts, updates, and/or deletes?
- Do you need to replicate object structure changes, aka DDL, as well?
- And again, what DDL changes need to be distributed?
- Do you need to replicate dependant application objects; like packages, indexes, views, privileges, triggers, and so on?
- What are the dependencies between these objects?
- Many of these objects require special handling (privileges, procedures, views, sequences, and triggers) which means additional configuration.

Also look at what role each site will play. Will the site be:

- A master: Changes are made at the site and sent to other sites. These sites usually contain the full copy of the distributed data and communicate continuously with the other master sites. Any interval between Propagation should be relatively short to avoid data divergence.

- A secondary or slave: The site contains all, or a subset of, the distributed data and receives changes from one (ideally) or more masters. Direct changes are rarely made at this site. If changes are made at this site, any conflicts with master site data will result in the change being overwritten by the master site data at the next Propagation interval.

- A directed network site: A master or secondary site that receives changes from another site, may or may not apply the change to itself, then passes the change to another database.

A word of caution on how many sites you choose to be master sites. For each site that you allow to be a master site, you increase your risk of data divergence exponentially. The more master sites you allow, the more conflict resolution definitions you will need to put into place. As the number of master sites increases, conflict resolution becomes statistically impossible, and over all maintenance and administration becomes unfeasible.

Understanding what you want to replicate will help you determine how much configuration work you will have ahead of you. It will also help you identify potential problem areas that may require special handling.

Where?

Now you want to look at where the data changes will originate and where these changes need to be sent to allow users to access.

- Will the changes only be made at one site?

- At what sites will data changes be made?

- Are these sites where changes are not allowed at the site, but will receive changes from other sites?

- Will a site have to pass changes that it receives from an originating site to other sites?

- Are there any special handling rules at each individual site depending on what data is received and from where?

Part of this step is also to determine if the change flow is unidirectional or bidirectional. A unidirectional change flow means that between two sites, changes are only made at one site and sent to the other site. A bidirectional change flow means that changes can be made at either of the two sites and are sent to the other site.

Network pathing is also essential to your design. In many systems, there may not be a direct network connection between the source and target database. The network topology may require routing the Propagation through an intermediate database. This is known as a directed network environment. While the intermediate database may be used to route the change, you may or may not need or want to apply the change at that database. If the change is not applied but "passed" to another database; this is known as a "pass-through" transaction.

- Is there a direct network path between the source and target database or does Propagation have to flow through an intermediate database?
- Do changes need to be applied to intermediate databases?

Again, understanding where changes are being made, sent, and applied will help you determine how much configuration work you will have ahead of you. You will identify any special handling rules that will need to be defined at each site. This step dictates which sites must be configured for capture, which sites to configure propagation, and which sites must be configured for apply. You also take it down a level by determining any special tagging and/or transformation and handling rules that need to be defined and coded for each of the capture/propagate/Apply processes and directed networks.

Who and How?

The next step is to look at who will use the data and how they will use it. When you design your Streamed environment, take into account considerations such as.

- Will some users only need to query (read) the data?
- Which sites will create the data?
- Which sites will be allowed to change or delete the data?
- If data diverges, which version of the data is kept and which is overwritten?

In short, who owns the data? Let's talk about what this means.

Data ownership refers to the right to create, change, or delete data. Data ownership can be described by a level and model.

Data ownership can be enforced at the site, user, and table levels. Table level ownership can be further subsetted at the row (horizontal) and column (vertical) levels. For instance, regional databases may have access to personnel data, however, only headquarters can make changes to the data (Site level). A further limitation could be that only HR employees are allowed to change the data (user level). However, these HR employees are only allowed to change HR data (table level). Of these HR employees, only those HR employees responsible for a division can change the records for the employees in that division (row level/horizontal). And one last limitation, only the division lead can change the salary and bonus fields for those employees (column level/vertical).

Data ownership models are more specific to the site level of ownership. Single-Site ownership means that only one site in the distributed environment is allowed to make changes to a piece of data. A standalone Oracle database provides single-site ownership enforcement by default. Dynamic ownership is a single-site ownership model, but the ownership moves to the transaction site that is changing the data at a point in time. A master-slave distributed configuration is indicative of the dynamic ownership models. These models avoid data conflict by limiting data changes to a single "owner". If data changes are made at the slave sites, they are overwritten when the master site sends its data down to the slave site. This ensures that all users will have the same picture of the data when the master change is committed and distributed. Shared ownership means that anyone can update the same piece of data at any time, at any site. A multi-master environment with asynchronous distribution is indicative of a shared ownership model. This model can lead to data divergence and conflicts, as multiple owners could be making different changes to the same data at different sites. Once these changes have been committed, the data diverges between the sites. For distributed environments using a shared ownership model with asynchronous propagation, you must implement some method of conflict resolution to reconcile the data conflicts. The conflict resolution will dictate what changes are kept, or discarded in the event of data change conflicts. Oracle's Replication provides support for the dynamic and shared ownership models.

Put the where, who, and how together and you get Single-Site ownership with unidirectional change flow or Dynamic and Shared ownership with bidirectional change flow. Amazing how it all comes together!

Distinguishing between who owns the data, and who will just use the data, will drive how changes flow through your distributed system and where capture and Apply processes must be configured. It will help you determine what conflict resolution rules are required. Each site Apply process must be configured to enforce these rules. It will also influence your table design in that you must make sure you have the necessary columns in the table to support the conflict resolution method implemented.

When and How?

Once you have determined why and what you are replicating and to which sites, you want to look at when the data needs to be delivered to each site and how to keep the data synchronized between all the distributed sites. This will help you determine your propagation schedule and method. We have already explained what Propagation means in Chapter 1, *All the Pieces: The Parts of an Oracle 11g Streams Environment*. Now, let's dig a bit deeper and look at how Propagation and data synchronization interrelate.

Data Propagation is one aspect of data synchronization; conflict detection and resolution are the other two aspects.

The two methods of data Propagation are Synchronous and Asynchronous.

Synchronous propagation is a distributed transaction in its truest form. All sites have to "agree" to commit the change before it can be committed anywhere; including the originating site. This means that all sites take out a lock on the piece of data until the transaction is committed at all sites. While the distributed transaction has a lock on the data, no other processes can modify that data. Thus, synchronous propagation, enforces the dynamic ownership model, and ensures immediate data synchronization.

Due to the "all or nothing" commit of synchronous propagation, it is not recommended for use between any two sites that have intermittent or unstable connectivity. If any site involved in the transaction is not reachable, the transaction cannot be committed anywhere, even at the origination site. This can have a significant negative impact on work flow and business productivity. Synchronous propagation should only be used for business data requiring immediate transactional consistency (for instance, banking, tickets/reservations, financial, and so on). In these cases, network connectivity, and stability must be of paramount design focus.

With this said, remember that Streams replication is, by nature, asynchronous.

Asynchronous propagation allows autonomy between the replicated sites, but still supports eventual data synchronization via the autonomous distribution of a copy of the transaction to each site. Asynchronous propagation also allows data divergence. Asynchronous propagation allows a change to be committed at the originating site without "agreement to commit" from the other sites where the change will be sent. This means that over some amount of time, the data between the sites will temporarily diverge. If a user changes the same piece of data at a target site before the previous change is received, it will cause a permanent divergence of data that will require conflict resolution when the initial change is received and applied at the site.

This means that special attention needs to be paid to when you schedule your asynchronous propagation between sites to avoid permanent data divergence. If your change flow is unidirectional, your propagation schedules may be more relaxed in Single-Site ownership models. However, if your change flow is bidirectional , you will want to reduce Propagation lag as much as possible.

To help determine when and how you will distribute data changes throughout your distributed system, take into account the following:

- Does your business require synchronous propagation?
- Which sites require synchronous propagation?
- What will the business impact of the temporary data divergence in an asynchronous distribution environment be and is it acceptable?

Other factors to consider

Now that you have looked at the core factors of your design, you need to turn your attention to extraneous factors that will have an impact on your environment. Some of these factors will play a major role in determining your design while others a minor role. Either way, include these factors in your design consideration, and you will be glad you did.

Network capabilities

You always want to know what your network capabilities will be from the start. Network bandwidth and stability—we just can't say it enough—is the key. If you have a low network bandwidth, the connection may bog down or collapse with the push of a large number of changes. Unstable networks mean unstable propagation and higher risks of data loss. Also, look at network traffic high and low peaks. Can you relieve network workload by propagating at low peak hours?

Another factor is the site or data location and availability. Once again, network limitations come into play. Look at the geographic location and associated WAN/LAN performance. Are there any "Window" limits; when and how long connections can be made. If the Propagation cannot complete within the scheduled amount of time, repeated failures will disable the Propagation all together.

Avoid scheduling Propagation to sites that have limited or intermittent connectivity (laptops, mobile users). This can cause queue back up and slow propagation to other sites scheduled to propagate from the same queue. Consider creating separate capture queue(s) for sites with limited or intermittent connectivity. Or, consider materialized views as part of your distributed environment. Materialized views are alive and well in 11*g* and can greatly enhance the flexibility of your streamed environment by accommodating those "hard to reach places".

Transaction sizes

Be cognizant of transaction sizes (the LCR message count). Remember that basic Streams replication is at the row level and generates a message for each row changed. If the transactions are large bulk updates, consider user enqueued procedure calls as an alternative to large row level LCR's. This may require more application coding, but will alleviate issues encountered by LCR with a large number of messages. You will need to include conflict detection and resolution in the procedure code as well as tags to avoid change cycling.

Potential queue growth

Be aware of the rate at which LCR's are enqueued and dequeued. Queue growth is the biggest factor here. If the Propagation and Apply process dequeue cannot keep up with the enquiring, the queues will keep growing. This can cause buffered queues to spill on to the disk, and persistent queues to require additional extents. Network speed and stability plays a large role in allowing the queue operations and size to remain consistent.

Additional hardware resource requirements

You also want to understand your hardware system requirements when planning your streamed environment. Streams replication requires additional resources such as:

- System O/S resources: More memory (shared pool) and O/S processes/threads
- Disk space: You will need more storage for structures (queues, streams metadata, additional rollback, and so on)
- CPU time: Streams generates additional background processes that require CPU. Those processes are listed next:
  - Propagation is CPU intensive
  - Near-Real time constantly uses CPU
  - If you plan to use parallelism—this means multiple processes are using CPU as well as the associated dependency tracking
  - Heavy DML means larger data transfers are using more CPU
- Things to watch out for that cause CPU and other resource contention:
  - Avoid conflicts with other CPU intensive operations
  - Avoid propagation during hot backups
- Every system is different; testing is the best way to determine the impact of Streams on CPU resources

Administration and maintenance costs

Don't underestimate your administration costs. Enterprise Manager offers a number of features to help reduce the time and effort in the actual implementation and maintenance of a Streamed environment. However, it is only a tool. The blue-print comes from the design and planning stage. This will, and should be, where the bulk of your time is spent.

The activities to include in your plan are:

- **Implementation**:

  Design: Global and single site designs must be developed to meet the goals of the Streamed environment.

  Setup: Each site must be configured for its role in the environment; master, secondary, pass-through, and so on.

- **Backup** and **recovery**:

  Design: The backup plans need to be designed to allow for the most efficient and effective recovery for foreseeable failure scenarios.

Test: The backup and recovery procedures should be tested to ensure restorable backups and successful resynchronization.

- **Schema/application changes**:

  Design: The schema and application changes will have global and single site impacts. These impacts must be studied and incorporated in the design.

  Test: All changes should be tested globally and singularly to avoid implementation problems.

  Setup: Changes must be implemented at all required sites in such a way that structure and data divergence are kept to a minimum.

- **Resynchronization of Diverged Data**: Propagation failures can cause data divergence and manual review, recovery, and resynchronization may be required. Additional administration is required for continual monitoring of the apply error queues. The erred LCRs will need to be reviewed to determine the cause of the error, the cause corrected, and the LCR reapplied. This can be very time consuming; especially if the conflict resolution has not been adequately defined.

- **Database Tuning**: Streams introduces additional processes and resource consumption. Tuning may need to be revisited after instantiating Streams and as the environment matures.

The administration of a streamed environment requires extra hours from the DBAs to monitor the system and streamed sites. These DBAs will require specialized training to understand how to keep the system and Streams healthy.

Third party application requirements

In the event that your distributed environment is configured as part of an implementation of a third party technology stack, make sure you understand the full scope and design of that implementation. Review your third party application documentation to identify how Streams replication is implemented, and used by the application, what database user accounts and schemas are created and what privileges are granted to what accounts.

Security

Database security requirements should be reviewed. Certain database users must be created to administer the streamed environment, and capture, send, receive, and execute the LCR's. These users require a higher level of database privileges than the normal application end user. This must be taken into consideration along with the environment's security requirements. The basic security models that can be implemented are **Trusted** and **Untrusted**:

- **Trusted**: This model implements lower security measures. One user is usually configured to administer the environment as well as capture, propagate, and apply the LCR's. This user has access to all stream queues at all sites, as well as being able execute any procedure. This results in decreased security, but allows for increased flexibility.

- **Untrusted**: This model separates the administration, capture, send, receive, and execute roles and privileges between different users. This allows each user to be only granted those privileges needed to accomplish their particular role. This results in higher security, but less flexibility in the overall Stream flow. It also requires additional implementation and design coordination.

Keep in mind that the replication of data within a Streams distributed environment is at the database level. It is highly recommended that the user accounts configured to support Streams replication be specifically and exclusively assigned for the task and separate from all other database and third party application database user accounts. This is due to the level of access to database objects that must be granted to the Streams users. This access level, if granted to application user accounts, could result in unexpected and unknown security loopholes that can be exploited.

Change auditing

When using Oracle Streams, regular Oracle auditing will not capture the same change audit information from the originating site at the apply site. You can expect that change audit information will be specific to the Apply process that is applying the change at the destination site. In cases where you need to track change audit information throughout a Streamed environment, it can be done by including the change audit information as fields in the replicated tables that are associated with the changed data. This can be accomplished in a number of ways. The main focus is that, if the change audit data needs to be persisted throughout the distributed environment, the structure of the change audit data should be included in the replicated data model and the collection of the required data values supported at the application level and persisted with the associated changed data. In Oracle 11gR2, you can use the DBMS_STREAMS_ADM.MAINTAIN_CHANGE_TABLE feature as discussed in Chapter 1.

Platform and version compatibility

Database platform compatibility and interoperability will have an impact on your design. If your system is homogeneous (All Oracle), it is preferable, and highly recommended, to have all Oracle databases on the same release and patch level. Overall capability of the Streamed environment is limited to the capabilities of the lowest Oracle version.

If your system is heterogeneous (Oracle and Non-Oracle), you will need to accommodate special configuration. Streaming between Oracle and non-Oracle platforms is supported via Oracle Gateway and user enqueued messages. Capture and apply queues and processes will always be on the Oracle database. Be cognizant of data type conversions and special handling that may be required when using Oracle Gateway connectivity.

KISS

Keep it simple and sweet. The greatest advantage that Streams has over Oracle's Advanced Replication is its flexibility. The golden rule of functionality is that with flexibility comes complexity. Flexibility is not a bad thing; you just need to plan for the additional complexity that implementation and maintenance will incur. One way to reduce complexity is to use the most efficient tool for the job. Do your research and choose your foundation and tools wisely (no doubt, the tower builders in Pisa, Italy would tell you the same).

A special note on Streams versus Data Guard.

In the *Why?* section, we discussed understanding why you would choose one tool over another tool to accomplish your goal. The key word we used in that discussion was 'efficiencies'. While you may be able to use either tool to accomplish your goal, one tool may be more efficient than the other.

A note about using Streams versus Data Guard to support a redundant failover system. A redundant failover system is by design, single-site ownership with unidirectional change flow.

If your main purpose is to provide a redundant failover system, do yourself a favor and avoid making mortal enemies of the production DBAs; use Data Guard's physical standby database. If you wish or need to access the standby for queries as well, use Data Guard's logical standby database—it is built on the same Streams apply technology (sent via remote procedure calls rather than advanced queues). However, Data Guard enforces single-site ownership without you having to define conflict resolution and error handling rules as you must do with Streams. This recommendation is not made lightly. Oracle highly recommends Data Guard over Streams for the purpose of a redundant failover site, and has done so since the inception of both technologies. Data Guard physical and logical standby functionality is included in the Enterprise License just as Streams, so there is no extra cost. Enterprise Manager Grid Control provides setup and maintenance support for Data Guard just as for Streams. Since Logical Standby and Streams use the same underlying technology, your data type and DDL limitations are about the same, as well as your network dependencies. The main difference is that there is less work in setting up and maintaining, and DBA's will have less work in monitoring the system. And maybe, they even thank you for the available automated switchover/failover, and database recovery capabilities that Data Guard provides (I know I would). Data Guard is designed to focus on zero or minimal data loss in the case of switchover/ failover, this is not the main focus of Streams.

If you use Streams, you will need to incorporate the development and implementation of conflict resolution rules for each piece of data that is replicated. In some cases, one rule may be sufficient for all data. In other cases, you will need to differentiate how change conflicts are resolved based on data ownership requirements.

Streams is not a "set and forget" environment. It must be continually monitored to ensure transactions are successfully captured, propagated, and applied at all sites.

Recovery and resynchronization of a failed or lost site may require a full re-instantiation of the site was well as data. Remember, Streams does not guarantee zero or minimal data loss in the case of failure. Depending on the number of objects replicated, capture, propagation, and apply rules defined, and amount of data, this could take anywhere from minutes to days. Special consideration and procedures must be followed if a point-in-time recovery is necessary.

Think of Streams versus Data Guard this way: yes, you can use Streams to provide a redundant failover system. But would you use a butter knife to cut a steak? Yes, you could do it, but you'd have to work a lot harder than if you used the steak knife that is in the same drawer (over to the left, next to the dinner forks).

Never say never: Now, the above recommendation does not intend to imply that you cannot or should not use a streamed database that has been configured to support shared ownership as a fail-to instance should a primary site fail. If it is there, and maintains data consistency at the required level, go ahead and use it. Every business circumstance is different. In some circumstances you may decide you want to use Streams to support a redundant failover system. Just think twice about implementing Streams specifically to support a redundant failover system rather than Data Guard.

Design aid: Streams site matrix

If a picture is worth a thousand words, then a matrix should be worth at least 500. This section discusses the use of a handy-dandy little tool that we like to call the Streams Site Matrix. This matrix provides a visual summary of who sends what where, and who's changes get applied to where and how. Overall, this matrix, when combined with the design considerations, helps you more accurately predict the level of effort to implement Streams and identify, early on, potential data and design conflicts, as well as identify resource requirements and potential limitations. For instance, from this matrix, you can accurately provide information concerning necessary hardware, Oracle licensing, network connections needs to your system architects; necessary user application data values to support the distributed data model, and optimal DML transaction behavior to your software architects; and, additional data fields necessary to support conflict resolution, and change audit throughout the distributed environment to your data architects. The Matrix also provides a succinct, organized list of the Capture, Propagation, and Apply processes and queues, advanced functionality such as conflict resolution, transformations, and so on, needed for each site.

The Matrix template

First, let's talk about the matrix template. The template shown here provides a starting point. It highlights the main components of our intended Streamed environment. As you work through your own designs, feel free to modify and expand the template to reflect information that makes the most sense to you and your business. Add more detail as you develop your design. You will find that doing so produces an excellent overview to include with your environment documentation.

Streams Site Matrix for:	Replication Level:	Schema		Color Key:	Existing
	Name:	HR			*Add/Remove*
	Add/Remove:	Add	Comment:	Single Source	
				STRM1 master to STRM2 secondary	
		Remote Site			
Local Sites		STRM1	STRM2		
STRM1					
Capture	Process Name:				
	Queue Name:				
	DDL (Y/N):				
	Transformations:				
Propagate	Process Name:				
	From Queue Name:				
	To Queue Name:				
	DDL (Y/N):				
	Transformations:				
Apply	Process Name:				
	Queue Name:				
	DDL (Y/N):				
	Transformations:				
	Conflict Resolution				
STRM2					
Capture	Process Name:				
	Queue Name:				
	DDL (Y/N):				
	Transformations:				
Propagate	Process Name:				
	From Queue Name:				
	To Queue Name:				
	DDL (Y/N):				
	Transformations:				
Apply	Process Name:				
	Queue Name:				
	DDL (Y/N):				
	Transformations:				
	Conflict Resolution				

Our template begins with listing information in the first couple of rows that help us understand the type of replication environment we are designing: Adding Single-Source schema level replication for the HR schema where STRM1 is the master site and STRM2 is the secondary site. Artistic license is allowed, modify this section as needed to show information that is helpful to you and your business; but DO show it.

Streams Site Matrix for:	Replication Level:	Schema		Color Key:	Existing
	Name:	HR			Add/Remove
	Add/Remove:	Add	Comment:	Single Source	
				STRM1 master to STRM2 secondary	

Then we begin our matrix.

In column A, we list out each site that needs to be configured for Streams, listing the three streams processes under each site section. Column B lists specific information that we want to identify for each Streams process at that local site. For instance, process and queue names, whether or not the process includes DDL, has associated advanced components like transformations rules, tags, and so on (covered in Chapter 6, *Get Fancy with Streams Advanced Configurations*), and conflict resolution (for Apply processes only—covered in Chapter 5, *N-Way Replication*). If you are replicating tables rather than schemas, you may want to include a link to a list of tables associated with each process. Again, show information that is helpful to you and your business.

Local Sites	
STRM1	
Capture	Process Name:
	Queue Name:
	DDL (Y/N):
	Transformations:
	Table list
Propagate	Process Name:
	From Queue Name:
	To Queue Name:
	DDL (Y/N):
	Transformations:

Apply   Process Name:

       Queue Name:

       DDL (Y/N):

       Transformations:

       Conflict Resolution

STRM2

Capture   Process Name:

       Queue Name:

       DDL (Y/N):

       Transformations:

Propagate Process Name:

       From Queue Name:

       To Queue Name:

       DDL (Y/N):

       Transformations:

Apply   Process Name:

       Queue Name:

       DDL (Y/N):

       Transformations:

       Conflict Resolution

One variation here would be that you have multiple Capture processes. To show this, add a sub-section for each Capture process, like so:

STRM1

Capture   Process Name:

       Queue Name:

       DDL (Y/N):

       Transformations:

       Process Name:

       Queue Name:

       DDL (Y/N):

       Transformations:

Propagate	Process Name:
	From Queue Name:
	To Queue Name:
	DDL (Y/N):
	Transformations:
Apply	Process Name:
	Queue Name:
	DDL (Y/N):
	Transformations:
	Conflict Resolution

In the subsequent columns, list each database site that is a member of the distributed system.

Remote Site	
STRM1	STRM2

As we move across the columns, we record what needs to be created at this local site for each of the processes in the appropriate column for the remote site. If the local site does not interact with a remote site, leave the remote site column blank (showing which sites do not interact is just as important as showing what sites do interact). If the "local" Site is the same as the "remote" site, don't worry that it is not technically "remote" (if you are that detail—oriented—a.k.a "anal"; might we recommend taking up a right-brained hobby such as Yoga?). This is a great section to record the Capture information for the Local Site. Think of it as "we are setting up capture AT this site, FOR this site".

Let's define our Single-Source design (See Chapter 4, *Single-Source Configuration,* for actual implementation). As mentioned, this design is just a simple 2-site, Single-Source environment. STRM1 is the site where changes are made. STRM2 is the secondary site to which we will replicate these changes. This means we need a Capture process and queue at STRM1 for the HR schema, and a Propagation process at STRM1 (to STRM2) that will be from queue-to-queue. We also need an Apply process and queue at STRM2. Since this is a Single-Source configuration, we do not need to create any capture or Propagation processes on STRM2, or an Apply process on STRM1. This not only reduces the internal operations for replication, it protects the data at STRM1 from potential changes made at STRM2. We will call our Capture process SCHEMA_HR_CAPTURE and assign it to the SCHEMA_HR_CAPTURE_Q queue. We will call our Apply process SCHEMA_HR_APPLY and assign it to the SCHEMA_HR_APPLY_Q queue. Our Propagation process name will be SCHEMA_HR_PROPAGATION, and will propagate from the SCHEMA_HR_CAPTURE_Q queue at STRM1 to the SCHEMA_HR_APPLY_Q queue at STRM2. We want to include DDL changes in this stream, so we will show this for all processes as well.

Based on this, let's fill in our Site Matrix:

First, the Capture at STRM1:

Local Sites		Remote Sites STRM1	STRM2
STRM1			
Capture	Process Name:	SCHEMA_HR_CAPTURE	
	Queue Name:	SCHEMA_HR_CAPTURE_Q	
	DDL (Y/N):	Y	
	Transformations:		

Next, the Propagation at STRM1 to STRM2:

Local Sites		Remote Sites STRM1	STRM2
STRM1			
...			
Propagate	Process Name:		SCHEMA_HR_ PROPAGATION
	From Queue Name:		SCHEMA_HR_CAPTURE_Q
	To Queue Name:		SCHEMA_HR_APPLY_Q
	DDL (Y/N):		Y
	Transformations:		

And finally, the Apply at STRM2:

Local Sites		Remote Sites STRM1	STRM2
STRM2			
...			
Apply	Process Name:	SCHEMA_HR_APPLY	
	Queue Name:	SCHEMA_HR_APPLY_Q	
	DDL (Y/N):	Y	
	Transformations:		
	Conflict Resolution		

The completed Streams Site Matrix appears as follows:

Streams Site Matrix for:	Replication Level:	Schema		Color Key:	Existing
	Name:	HR			Add/Remove
	Add/Remove:	Add	Comment:	Single Source	
				STRM1 master to STRM2 secondary	
		Remote Sites			
Local Sites		STRM1	STRM2		
STRM1					
Capture	Process Name:	SCHEMA_HR_CAPTURE			
	Queue Name:	SCHEMA_HR_CAPTURE_Q			
	DDL (Y/N):	Y			
	Transformations:				
Propagate	Process Name:		SCHEMA_HR_PROPAGATION		
	From Queue Name:		SCHEMA_HR_CAPTURE_Q		
	To Queue Name:		SCHEMA_HR_APPLY_Q		
	DDL (Y/N):		Y		
	Transformations:				
Apply	Process Name:				
	Queue Name:				
	DDL (Y/N):				
	Transformations:				
	Conflict Resolution				
STRM2					
Capture	Process Name:				
	Queue Name:				
	DDL (Y/N):				
	Transformations:				
Propagate	Process Name:				
	From Queue Name:				
	To Queue Name:				
	DDL (Y/N):				
	Transformations:				
Apply	Process Name:	SCHEMA_HR_APPLY			
	Queue Name:	SCHEMA_HR_APPLY_Q			
	DDL (Y/N):	Y			
	Transformations:				
	Conflict Resolution				

Even though we will not be sending changes from STRM2 to STRM1, we still need to consider that changes can be made (whether intended or not) directly at STRM2 that can result in data conflicts and apply errors for changes from STRM1. While we don't address it in this example, you would want to implement some form of conflict resolution to avoid having to continually monitor for these conflicts (the OVERWRITE method would be recommended here). See Chapter 5 for discussion on conflict resolution.

Let's now expand this concept to show an N-Way Replication configuration (See chapter 5 for actual implementation). In this configuration, we are going to replicate a single table EMPLOYEE in the LEARNING schema. DML and DDL changes to the table can be made at either STRM1 or STRM2 and replicated to the other master site. Since data changes can be made at either site, as good DBAs we know we need conflict resolution defined for our Apply processes. Our business rules tell us that the latest change should "win" in the case of a data conflict so we will implement maximum—time resolution (a.k.a. latest timestamp resolution for all you Advanced Replication buffs).

Our Streams Site Matrix appears as follows:

Streams Site Matrix for:	Replication Level:	Table		Color Key:	Existing
	Name:	Learning.employee			Add/Remove
	Add/Remove:	Add	Comment:	N-Way Replication	
				STRM1 and STRM2 Masters	
		Destinations			
Source Sites		STRM1	STRM2		
STRM1					
Capture	Process Name:	STREAMS_CAPTURE			
	Queue Name:	STREAMS_CAPTURE_Q			
	DDL (Y/N):	Y			
	Transformations:				
Propagate	Process Name:		STREAMS_PROPAGATION		
	From Queue Name:		STREAMS_CAPTURE_Q		
	To Queue Name:		STREAMS_APPLY_Q		
	DDL (Y/N):		Y		
	Transformations:				
Apply	Process Name:		STREAMS_APPLY		
	Queue Name:		STREAMS_APPLY_Q		
	DDL (Y/N):		Y		
	Transformations:				
	Conflict Resolution		Type: Maximum resolution column: time conflict columns: all		
STRM2					
Capture	Process Name:		STREAMS_CAPTURE		
	Queue Name:		STREAMS_CAPTURE_Q		
	DDL (Y/N):				
	Transformations:				
Propagate	Process Name:	STREAMS_PROPAGATION			
	From Queue Name:	STREAMS_CAPTURE_Q			
	To Queue Name:	STREAMS_APPLY_Q			
	DDL (Y/N):	Y			
	Transformations:				
Apply	Process Name:	STREAMS_APPLY			
	Queue Name:	STREAMS_APPLY_Q			
	DDL (Y/N):	Y			
	Transformations:				
	Conflict Resolution	Type: Maximum resolution column: time conflict columns: all			

The Streams Site Matrix provides a simple yet elegant visual aid. From here you can develop your level of effort and resources requirements, detail level blueprints, and understand what you need to implement your Streamed environment.

Summary

While Chapter 1, is the foundation chapter for the rest of this book, Chapter 2 is the blue print chapter. In this chapter, we went over the major design considerations to take into account when designing your distributed environment.

We discussed the who, what, when, where, why, and how factors to consider for your replicated system. Why are you replicating? What are you replicating? Who will use the data and how? Where are you replicating to and from? How will you propagate the data between sites and when? How will you handle the data divergence between sites? Taken on-board together, this all helps you to determine the most efficient tools and functionality to employ in your design. It also helps you predict the time and effort needed to implement the environment, and subsequently maintain the environment.

The number one goal of a successful Streamed environment is to avoid data divergence. Data divergence leads to data conflicts, and data conflicts lead to unsynchronized data mayhem in a distributed environment. Establishing overall business rules for data ownership and change flow is the precursor to understanding what your conflict resolution design will require.

We also looked at additional considerations that you will want to take into account. These included network connectivity, propagation volume (transaction size and queue growth), database security and user privileges, database platform and version compatibility, additional hardware resource requirements, administration and maintenance costs, and the flexibility-to-complexity factor (using the best tool for the job).

The Streams Site Matrix was introduced and demonstrated to show us how to succinctly organize and visualize the sites and components needed to build your distributed environment using Oracle Streams technology.

Now that we have plotted our course, we next turn our attention to the vehicles we will use to get there. In Chapter 3, *Prepare the Rafts and Secure Your Gear: The pre-work before configuring Oracle 11g Streams*, we will properly set up the database and make the necessary configuration changes to support a Streams environment. We will go over the changes and provide the reasons for those changes. We won't go into all the minute details and bore you with too much analysis of mundane configurations. If you wish additional information, please refer to the *Oracle Streams Concepts and Administration Manual* and the *Oracle Streams Replication Administrator's Guide*.

We now know what we need to build and the tools we have available to us for building it, so let's start configuring the database! (Ok, maybe take a quick bio-break first.)

3

Prepare the Rafts and Secure Your Gear: The pre-work before configuring Oracle 11*g* Streams

Chapter 2 provided the insight needed to design and plan a Streams environment and "chart" the course of our distributed environment. This chapter takes the next step of preparing your "vessels", also known as databases and servers. The basic source and target server and database configurations for Streams are the same. In this chapter, we address the verification and configuration of the following:

- Network connectivity
- Database parameters and logging settings
- Stream Administrator user and privileges
- Data Pump and Instantiation preparation
- Optional creation of the Oracle Example schemas

At this point, the assumption is that you have already created your databases at each site involved in the Distributed Environment. This could have been accomplished with the Oracle software installation, or later using the Database Creation Assistant, or your own custom scripts. It is also assumed that you are able to connect to each database as SYSDBA.

 For more information on creating an Oracle Database, please reference the *Creating and Configuring an Oracle Database* chapter in the Oracle Database Administrator's Guide.

Network connectivity

We mentioned earlier in Chapter 1 and Chapter 2, how important having a stable and reliable network is to the Streams environment. Without this comlink you just have a Source and Target with no ability to "stream" the data over the wire. Knowing this, having a good working relationship with the Network Administrator is vital. Network Administrators have additional tools and methods that can influence the performance of Streams. The Streams Administrator or DBA does not know the network path taken by the data from Source to Target unless a situation causes the question to come up. Be proactive, work with the Network Administrators, and ask the following questions:

- How does this data packet move from Source to Target?
- What is the typical network speed along that path?
- Is this a dedicated path?
- Is the network shared?
- What are the usage patterns of the network?
- Are there times when we can expect the network to be slower?

These questions are not the fun ones that most Network Administrators like to hear. However, by being proactive and knowing about your network performance, you will avoid headaches in the future. Just think of it this way: you can have a perfect Streams setup, but the data still has to cross the network and it is difficult to move a mountain of data through a straw-size network. Believe us; we have tried it too many times!

Streams uses the network in the Propagation process. When we define Propagation we will reference a dblink. That dblink uses the destination database global_name, and either an entry in the tnsnames.ora file or a tns descriptor. We will provide full examples of this configuration in Chapter 4, *Single-Source Configuration,*. For now, it should suffice to say, that the performance of Streams is dependent on the performance of the network. As Streams Administrators or DBAs, we do not usually get to tune the network, so work with your Network Administrators. We take ours out to lunch to stay on his good side!

Check the waterways

The use of basic network tools such as ping and tracert can be used to determine network capabilities. Here are some examples of ping and tracert that should be run from the Source host (to the destination):

```
ping <IP ADDRESS>
tracert <IP ADDRESS>
```

where <IP ADDRESS> is the IP address of the Target host. You may also want to run the same test going from Target host to Source host. Please also check with your Network Administrator as he/she may have additional tools and techniques to measure network performance that are already being used.

The following is a ping from IP 129.193.117.13 to 129.193.117.14 on Linux/Unix:

```
[oracle@dev-db01 ~]$ ping 129.193.117.14
PING 129.193.117.14 (129.193.117.14) 56(84) bytes of data.
64 bytes from 129.193.117.14: icmp_seq=1 ttl=64 time=0.103 ms
64 bytes from 129.193.117.14: icmp_seq=2 ttl=64 time=0.091 ms
64 bytes from 129.193.117.14: icmp_seq=3 ttl=64 time=0.089 ms
64 bytes from 129.193.117.14: icmp_seq=4 ttl=64 time=0.088 ms
64 bytes from 129.193.117.14: icmp_seq=5 ttl=64 time=0.089 ms
64 bytes from 129.193.117.14: icmp_seq=6 ttl=64 time=0.091 ms
64 bytes from 129.193.117.14: icmp_seq=7 ttl=64 time=0.088 ms
64 bytes from 129.193.117.14: icmp_seq=8 ttl=64 time=0.089 ms
64 bytes from 129.193.117.14: icmp_seq=9 ttl=64 time=0.090 ms
64 bytes from 129.193.117.14: icmp_seq=10 ttl=64 time=0.090 ms
64 bytes from 129.193.117.14: icmp_seq=11 ttl=64 time=0.088 ms
64 bytes from 129.193.117.14: icmp_seq=12 ttl=64 time=0.088 ms
64 bytes from 129.193.117.14: icmp_seq=13 ttl=64 time=0.087 ms
64 bytes from 129.193.117.14: icmp_seq=14 ttl=64 time=0.089 ms
64 bytes from 129.193.117.14: icmp_seq=15 ttl=64 time=0.089 ms
64 bytes from 129.193.117.14: icmp_seq=16 ttl=64 time=0.088 ms
64 bytes from 129.193.117.14: icmp_seq=17 ttl=64 time=0.088 ms
64 bytes from 129.193.117.14: icmp_seq=18 ttl=64 time=0.088 ms
64 bytes from 129.193.117.14: icmp_seq=19 ttl=64 time=0.089 ms
64 bytes from 129.193.117.14: icmp_seq=20 ttl=64 time=0.090 ms
64 bytes from 129.193.117.14: icmp_seq=21 ttl=64 time=0.088 ms
64 bytes from 129.193.117.14: icmp_seq=22 ttl=64 time=0.089 ms

--- 129.193.117.14 ping statistics ---
22 packets transmitted, 22 received, 0% packet loss, time 21000ms
rtt min/avg/max/mdev = 0.087/0.089/0.103/0.009 ms
```

Pay particular attention to the summary results at the end.

The result of running `tracert` from 172.26.12.12 to 172.26.13.23 shows two "hops " in the network between two servers.

```
[root@db01 ~]# tracert 172.26.13.23
traceroute to 172.26.13.23 (172.26.13.23), 30 hops max, 40 byte packets
1 172.26.12.1 (172.26.12.1) 0.948 ms 1.220 ms 1.462 ms
2 db02.apgtech.com (172.26.13.23) 0.157 ms 0.171 ms 0.171 ms
```

The following shows examples of the `ping` and `tracert` commands on Windows:

```
C:\>ping 209.191.92.52


Pinging 209.191.92.52 with 32 bytes of data:
Reply from 209.191.92.52: bytes=32 time=53ms TTL=52
Reply from 209.191.92.52: bytes=32 time=54ms TTL=52
Reply from 209.191.92.52: bytes=32 time=52ms TTL=52
Reply from 209.191.92.52: bytes=32 time=54ms TTL=52


Ping statistics for 209.191.92.52:
    Packets: Sent = 4, Received = 4, Lost = 0 (0% loss),
Approximate round trip times in milli-seconds:
    Minimum = 52ms, Maximum = 54ms, Average = 53ms


C:\>tracert 209.191.92.52
Tracing route to f20.www.mud.yahoo.com [209.191.92.52]
over a maximum of 30 hops:
```

(Notice this IP takes over 30 hops! What gets output is the starting IP, and then the last 13 hops. The Request timed out on hop 2, and this is the one-liner catch-all for all the other hops)

```
1    <1 ms    <1 ms    <1 ms   <ip>
2    *        *        *        Request timed out.
3    9 ms     11 ms    9 ms    ge-2-3-ur01.....net [<ip>]
4    12 ms    11 ms    11 ms   te-0-2-0-1-ar02.....net [<ip>]
5    10 ms    11 ms    11 ms   <ip>
```

6	25 ms	26 ms	26 ms	pos-0-3-0-0-cr01...net [<ip>]
7	46 ms	43 ms	51 ms	pos-1-7-0-0-cr01...net [<ip>]
8	53 ms	53 ms	53 ms	<ip>
9	44 ms	42 ms	44 ms	<ip>
10	52 ms	54 ms	52 ms	<ip>
11	51 ms	52 ms	52 ms	<ip>
12	52 ms	53 ms	52 ms	ae2-p111.msr2.mud.yahoo.com [<ip>]
13	58 ms	53 ms	52 ms	te-9-2....yahoo.com [<ip>`1]
14	54 ms	52 ms	52 ms	UNKNOWN...yahoo.com [<ip>]
15	53 ms	52 ms	52 ms	f20.www.mud.yahoo.com [<ip>]

```
Trace complete.
```

Here are some suggestions on how to establish a baseline on the network that you have.

- Use `ping` command to see how long it takes to reach the TARGET from the SOURCE node

- Use `tracert` to determine which route packets cross the network

- Work with the Network Administrator to determine if there are different times when network performance changes

Configure the Oracle Net "Current"

Next, make sure that your Oracle Net files are configured to allow connectivity to and between the databases.

- `TNSNAMES.ORA`: This file provides aliases that can be used for client connections. The aliases can be for local and remote databases.

  Special considerations: In many cases, the aliases contained in the `tnsnames.ora` files are configured with multiple addresses in the address list to accommodate high availability client failover. In the case of a Streams connection, we do not want to redirect our connection to a different database. So, if needed, add a single address `tnsnames` alias to the `tnsnames.ora` to be used by Streams connections.

  Example of basic `tnsalias` entries:

```
STRM2 =
  (DESCRIPTION =
    (ADDRESS = (PROTOCOL=TCP)(HOST=DB_SRV2)(PORT=1521))
    (CONNECT_DATA =
```

```
        (SERVER = DEDICATED)
        (SERVICE_NAME = STRM2)
    )
  )

STRM1 =
  (DESCRIPTION =
    (ADDRESS = (PROTOCOL=TCP)(HOST=DB_SRV1)(PORT=1521))
    (CONNECT_DATA =
      (SERVER = DEDICATED)
      (SERVICE_NAME = STRM1)
    )
  )
```

- SQLNET.ORA: This file provides client/server connection parameters that control client access and database connectivity.

  Special considerations: If your server side SQLNET.ora is set up with INVITED_NODES, make sure to add the server IP or DNS name of all servers that host databases that will be connecting to the local database(s), to the invited nodes list. Otherwise, SQLNET will not allow the database links to connect to the database.

  Example of sqlnet.ora entries:

  ```
  SQLNET.AUTHENTICATION_SERVICES = (NTS) --Windows only

  AUTOMATIC_IPC = OFF
  TRACE_LEVEL_CLIENT = OFF
  NAMES.DEFAULT_DOMAIN = mydomain.com
  #SQLNET.CRYPTO_SEED = "12101751101259991325"
  NAMES.DIRECTORY_PATH = (TNSNAMES)

  TCP.VALIDNODE_CHECKING = YES
  TCP.EXCLUDED_NODES= (138.3.33.33, NODB.mydomain.com)
  TCP.INVITED_NODES=(localhost, DB_SRV2.mydomain.com)
  ```

- LISTENER.ORA: This file provides connection information to the local databases on the server. All client connections to a database come in through a listener process (with the exception of bequeath connections, but we don't use those here).

  Special considerations: Make sure listener processes are configured to start automatically if the server is rebooted. Otherwise, Streams (and other client) connections cannot be established with the database, even though the database may be up and running after reboot.

Example of Basic `Listener.ora` entries:

```
SID_LIST_LISTENER =
  (SID_LIST =
    (SID_DESC =
      (GLOBAL_DBNAME = strm1)
      (SID_NAME = strm1)
    )
  )

LISTENER =
  (DESCRIPTION =
    (ADDRESS = (PROTOCOL=TCP)(HOST=DB_SRV1)(PORT=1521))
  )
```

For more information on configuring Oracle Net Services, please reference the Oracle Database Net Services Administrator's Guide.

Configure the database

The Streams environment requires proper configuration of the database initialization parameters that support the underlying functionality prior to the configuration of Capture, Propagate, and Apply process. It also requires that we "turn on" additional redo logging functionality. With all this added activity being turned on, we can expect a larger amount of metadata to be accumulated to keep track of all this. As much of this metadata is dynamic, it can cause fragmentation in the SYSTEM and SYSAUX tablespaces where it would be created by default. Due to this, we also recommend (as does Oracle) to move Logging and Streams schemas to their own tablespaces. This also feeds into the ease of "separation of duties" between tablespaces and database schemas and objects that enhance transportability.

Initialization parameters

These database parameters govern database naming, redo activity, connectivity, and SGA and PGA memory structures.

Beginning with Oracle 11*g*, the management of memory structures can be automated. We suggest the use of Oracle 11*g*'s Automatic Memory Management which can be enabled by setting the MEMORY_MAX_TARGET and MEMORY_TARGET parameters. Then, by setting specific values for the remainder of the memory-related parameters, configures that parameter value as the minimum value.

The following is a list of parameters that should be set for Streams along with a quick description and notes.

Parameter Name	Description	Notes
COMPATIBLE	Specifies the version at which the Oracle server must maintain compatibility.	If set lower than the current version, certain functionality introduced in the current version will not be available.
GLOBAL_NAMES	Forces dblink to have the same name as the database.	Set to true.
LOG_ARCHIVE_DEST_n LOG_ARCHIVE_DEST_STATE_n	Specifies location for archived redo logs and the ability of the database to copy a version of the archived log to the destination.	Especially important if you are using the flash recovery area. To avoid having required archived logs "aged" out of the flash recovery area, set, and enable a separate archive log location.
LOG_BUFFER	Buffer used by redo entries prior to writing redo logs.	Increasing this allows the Capture process to read from buffer rather than log
MEMORY_MAX_TARGET	Maximum memory allocated to Oracle system wide.	Set this as high as possible based on the available memory on the host.
MEMORY_TARGET	Oracle uses this parameter to dynamically control the SGA and PGA.	Use a percentage of MEMORY_MAX_TARGET leave room to adjust upward to MEMORY_MAX_TARGET.
OPEN_LINKS	Specifies the maximum number of concurrent open connections to remote databases in one session.	This number needs to be increased to support additional connections used by Streams. Relates to the amount of dblink opened by one session.
PROCESSES	Specifies the maximum number of operating system user processes that can simultaneously connect to Oracle.	Increase to account for Capture, Propagate, and Apply process and all slaves of those processes.

Parameter Name	Description	Notes
SESSIONS	Specifies the maximum number of sessions that can be created in the system.	Derived from the PROCESESS parameter value by default. Increasing PROCESSES will automatically increase SESSIONS if left to default. Otherwise, increase this by 1 for every Capture, Propagation, or Apply process to be created.
SHARED_POOL_SIZE	Contains shared cursors, stored procedures, control structures, and other structures.	Larger values can improve performance in a multi-user system. Consider increasing the shared pool by 10% of the amount of the STREAMS_POOL_SIZE. If STREAMS_POOL_SIZE is 0 and AMM is used, then AMM will allocate 10% of this memory to the streams memory pool.
STREAMS_POOL_SIZE	This is the segment of memory allocated to handle buffered queues and allocate Capture, Propagation, and Apply process memory.	If set too low, Streams processes may not run, or buffered queues may "spill" to disk. Rule of thumb, set to a minimum value of the sum of:

10 MB for each Capture process parallelism.

10 MB or more for each buffered queue.

1 MB for each Apply process parallelism. |
| TIMED_STATISTICS | Set STATISTICS_LEVEL to TYPICAL or ALL. | Allows gather of performance metrics. |
| UNDO_RETENTION | Specifies (in seconds) the amount of committed undo information to retain in the database. | Adjust higher to avoid snapshot to old. |

Logging features

Oracle Streams requires that enhanced logging features be enabled to support the mining and capture of data changes in the redo logs.

Archive logging

When configuring your database for Streams, additional logging information is required. Most Production DBAs normally configure their database in ARCHIVELOG Mode to support the use of online database backups and point-in-time recovery. Being in ARCHIVELOG is also a requirement of Streams. If your database is not in ARCHIVELOG mode, you can enable it through the SQLPLUS as a SYSDBA:

Log in to SQLPLUS as SYSDBA.

```
SHUTDOWN    --you can take an offline (cold) backup
            --at this point if you wish
STARTUP MOUNT
ALTER DATABASE ARCHIVELOG;
ALTER DATABASE OPEN;
```

At this point, any previous backups taken in NOARCHIVELOG mode are no longer usable with the current control file. You may wish to take a full backup of the database and control file.

```
SHUTDOWN IMMEDIATE;    --backup up from here.
```

 For more information on putting a database into ARCHIVELOG mode, please refer to the *Controlling Archiving* chapter in the Oracle Database Administrators Guide.

Supplemental logging

Supplemental logging instructs the database to record additional data at the column level to the redo logs. This means that supplemental logging instructs Oracle to include the old and unchanged values of certain columns in the redo. LCRs are created using the additional data by the Capture process. When the Apply process applies the LCR, these supplemental values can be used by conflict detection and resolution, and other apply handlers.

Activation of supplemental logging can be accomplished at the database or table level. It can also be accomplished for key (primary, unique, and foreign) and non-key columns. Table level supplemental columns can be grouped together in a Supplemental Log Group.

Some examples of `Table` level key column supplemental logging:

```
ALTER TABLE hr.employees ADD SUPPLEMENTAL LOG DATA (PRIMARY KEY)
COLUMNS;

ALTER TABLE hr.departments ADD SUPPLEMENTAL LOG DATA
  (UNIQUE, FOREIGN KEY) COLUMNS;
```

Example of `Table` level key column supplemental logging:

```
ALTER TABLE hr.employee ADD SUPPLEMENTAL LOG GROUP log_group_emp_pk
  (department_id, manager_id) ALWAYS;
```

Example of `Database` level key column supplemental logging:

```
ALTER DATABASE ADD SUPPLEMENTAL LOG DATA
  (PRIMARY KEY, UNIQUE, FOREIGN KEY) COLUMNS;
```

If your system storage can accommodate the additional redo generated by including supplemental logging on all columns, you can activate supplemental logging once at the database level. This alleviates the need to add logging for any new tables created. To accomplish this, use the following example:

```
ALTER DATABASE ADD SUPPLEMENTAL LOG DATA (ALL) COLUMNS;
```

Keep in mind that this level of supplemental logging can generate a significant amount of additional redo. Setting it can quickly max out your archive log destinations and stop the database cold. While we would recommend setting supplemental logging at this level in databases with a small number of tables, columns, and rows or data changes, use it with caution, and monitor your archive log destinations.

Forced logging

For a Capture process to capture changes from the redo logs, the changes must be recorded in the redo logs. It is possible for a user session to "turn-off" redo logging (ex: using NO LOGGING option) or to bypass redo generation through direct loads. This ability could cause unexpected data divergence. To avoid this, you place the database in "Forced Logging" mode. In this mode, the database will log all changes regardless of the session level logging settings. To turn on forced logging mode, log in as SYSDBA.

```
ALTER DATABASE FORCE LOGGING;
```

Forced logging is persistent. Once it is set, it stays set through subsequent database restarts.

Separate tablespaces

Another highly recommended best practice is to create separate tablespaces for specialized users, such as the LogMiner and Streams administrators. A number of justifications can be made for creating these separate tablespaces; the main thing to understand is that it is a good idea. You will find that the separation of objects will by far outweigh the addition of a couple of data files.

LogMiner tablespace

If the LogMiner tablespace is the SYSTEM tablespace, set it to a different tablespace. Not doing so jeopardizes the integrity of the SYSTEM tablespace and the operation of the database.

You may also determine that the LogMiner should be moved out of the SYSAUX tablespace and into a different tablespace for performance reasons.

Use the DBMS_LOGMNR_D.SET_TABLESPACE procedure to set a different tablespace for LogMiner.

First, create the desired tablespace if it does not exist:

 Set the SIZE and MAXSIZE to something that will fit on your disk. If you have AUTOEXTEND on and limited disk space, avoid setting MAXSIZE to unlimited, as this could lead to a full disk and a hung database if not properly monitored.

```
CREATE TABLESPACE ts_lgmnr
DATAFILE '/u05/oracle/oradata/tslgmnr1.dbf'
SIZE 100M
REUSE AUTOEXTEND ON MAXSIZE 5G;
```

Second, set the LogMiner tablespace to the new tablespace using DBMS_LOGMNR_D.SET_TABLESPACE.

```
EXECUTE dbms_logmnr_d.set_tablespace('ts_lgmnr');
```

Streams Administration tablespace

Create a separate tablespace for the Streams Administrator user(s). This will separate out Streams-specific database objects from the mainstream database objects. This also helps segment Streams objects for exclusion from tablespace level exports; allowing Data Pump transportable tablespaces to be leveraged for production schemas. Create a separate tablespace for Streams on each Streamed database.

```
CREATE TABLESPACE streams_ts
DATAFILE '/u05/oracle/oradata/streams_01.dbf'
```

```
SIZE 100M
REUSE AUTOEXTEND ON MAXSIZE 5G;
```

When you create your Streams Admin user(s), assign this tablespace as the user's default tablespace. Do *not* assign the SYSTEM tablespace as the Streams Admin user default tablespace.

Streams users and privileges

Repeat the following: Never use the SYS or SYSTEM users as Streams administrators. These users are assigned the SYSTEM and SYSAUX tablespaces as default tablespaces, as well as very powerful database privileges.

As mentioned in Chapter 2, *Plot Your Course: Design Considerations*, the Stream user(s) can be configured for a trusted or untrusted security environment. In a trusted environment, a single Streams Administrator user is configured at each database site. All capture, propagation, and apply duties and supporting object ownership are in the security context of this user. In an untrusted environment, the duties of capture, propagation, and apply can be separated and assigned to different users with different privilege levels sufficient to perform the duties.

Trusted Streams Administrator user configuration

In this book, we use the STRMADMIN user as our Streams Administrator. The user ID can be whatever makes the most sense to you. The expectation is that this user is only used exclusively for Streams purposes and is not referenced directly by user applications. This user has a high level of privileges, so we recommend that the login information be limited to the DBAs that are responsible for maintaining the Streamed environment.

Make sure that the Streams Administration user is not assigned the SYSTEM tablespace as a default or temporary tablespace. Here, we create our STRMADMIN user with the STREAMS_TS tablespace as the default tablespace.

```
Create the strmadmin account with the appropriate role and privileges:
CREATE USER strmadmin IDENTIFIED BY <password>
DEFAULT TABLESPACE streams_ts
TEMPORARY TABLESPACE TEMP
QUOTA UNLIMITED ON streams_ts;

GRANT DBA TO strmadmin;

BEGIN
```

```
DBMS_STREAMS_AUTH.GRANT_ADMIN_PRIVILEGE(
   grantee           => 'strmadmin',
   grant_privileges => TRUE
);
END;
/
```

As mentioned above, this should be performed on each database in the streamed environment.

 The configuration of the Streams Administration user can be accomplished as a part of the setup through the Enterprise Manager Streams Setup Wizard if desired. We address it here, as well as in Chapter 4, for clarity of usage.

Untrusted Streams capture, propagation, and apply user configuration

The following describes how to go about configuring "separation of duties" for an untrusted Streams configuration.

Streams Administration user

Even though you may intend to have separate capture, propagation, and/or apply users, it is recommended that you have a Streams Administration user to manage the overall Streams environment. You can either create a Streams Administration user using the same method above for a trusted environment, or use an existing DBA user.

If you wish to configure an existing DBA user as a Streams Administrator, ensure that the SYSTEM tablespace is not assigned as the DBA users' default and temporary tablespaces (this is why it is strongly recommended not to use SYS or SYSTEM for your Streams Administrator). If the DBA users' default and/or tablespace is SYSTEM, either ALTER the user to reassign these, or create a new DBA user.

To configure an existing DBA user as a Stream Administrator, run the following command:

```
BEGIN
DBMS_STREAMS_AUTH.GRANT_ADMIN_PRIVILEGE(
   grantee           => '<dba_user>',
   grant_privileges => TRUE
);
END;
/
```

Capture user

The Capture user must have DBA privileges.

It is recommended that you use the DBMS_CAPTURE_ADM.CREATE_CAPTURE package to create the Capture process. The DBMS_STREAMS_ADM package makes assumptive associations between the execution user and queue and rule ownership, and captures user assignments that can get a little tricky.

When using DBMS_CAPTURE_ADM.CREATE_CAPTURE, the CAPTURE_USER can be specified at the creation of a Capture process. This user is configured as a secure queue user and is granted enqueue privileges on the capture queue.

However, you must also make sure that the user is explicitly granted the following privileges:

- EXECUTE on all rule sets used by the Capture process.

  This can be done by either:

```
DBMS_RULE_ADM.GRANT_OBJECT_PRIVILEGE (
    privilege      IN   BINARY_INTEGER,
    object_name    IN   VARCHAR2,
    grantee        IN   VARCHAR2,
    grant_option   IN   BOOLEAN    DEFAULT FALSE);
where privilege =>  'SYS.DBMS_RULE_ADM.EXECUTE_ON_RULE_SET'
and object_name =>   <schema>.<rule_set_name>
```

  OR

```
DBMS_RULE_ADM.GRANT_SYSTEM_PRIVILEGE (
    privilege      IN   BINARY_INTEGER,
    grantee        IN   VARCHAR2,
    grant_option   IN   BOOLEAN    DEFAULT FALSE);

where privilege =>  'SYS.DBMS_RULE_ADM.EXECUTE_ANY_RULE_SET'
```

> For more information on granting privileges on rules and rule sets, please refer to the *Oracle PL/SQL Packages and Types Reference* manual.

- EXECUTE on all rule-based transformation functions used in the positive rule set.
- EXECUTE on all packages (Oracle-supplied and user created) invoked by rule-based transformations run by the Capture process.

These privileges must be granted explicitly, they cannot be granted through roles.

Propagation user

Messages are propagated by the user who owns the source queue. The owner of the source queue is not necessarily a capture user. The source queue owner must have the following privileges to propagate messages:

- EXECUTE on the rule sets used by the propagation (see capture user for specifics).

- EXECUTE on all custom rule-based transformation functions used in the rule sets.

- Enqueue privilege on the destination queue if the destination (apply) queue is in the same database.

- Own the database link used by the propagation if destination (apply) queue is on a remote database. The user to which the database link connects at the remote database must have enqueue privileges on the destination (apply) queue.

Security note: It is possible for the database link to be a public database link. However, this opens up many security issues by having a database link in an untrusted system that any user can use to potentially exploit access to the remote database. Due to the high security risks of public database links, it is adamantly recommended that public database links not be used in either a trusted or untrusted Streams configuration.

Apply user

The apply user must have DBA privileges.

It is recommended that you use the DBMS_APPLY_ADM.CREATE_APPLY package to create the APPLY process for the same reason mentioned in the "Capture user" section.

When using DBMS_APPLY_ADM.CREATE_APPLY, the apply_user can be specified at the creation of an Apply process. This user is configured as a secure queue user and granted dequeue privileges on the apply queue. However, you must also make sure that the user is explicitly granted the following privileges:

- DML and DDL privileges on the apply objects

- EXECUTE on the rule sets used by the Apply process (see capture user for specifics)

- EXECUTE on all rule-based transformation functions used in the rule set

- EXECUTE on all apply handler procedures

- EXECUTE on all packages, including Oracle-supplied packages, that are invoked in subprograms run by the Apply process

Again, these privileges must be granted explicitly, they cannot be granted through roles.

Database links

When creating the database links, we again stress—use private database links, not public, in order to avoid security breaches through the links. Create the database link when connected as the user that will use the database link. This should be the only user that uses this database link. The overheads for maintaining private database links is well worth the security breach potential that a shared database link opens up.

We also recommend using the TNS Description parameter in the database link connection clause rather than a TNS Alias to avoid unintended or malicious misdirection of a database link if the local TNSNAMES.ora is ever changed, moved, or replaced. However, we have provided examples of TNSNAMES.ora files above, should you choose to go down that route.

Database link creation with TNS Description:

```
Create database link STRM2
connect to strm_admin identified by strm_admin
using '(DESCRIPTION =
    (ADDRESS = (PROTOCOL = TCP)(HOST = STRM2_HOST)
      (PORT = 1521)
    )
    (CONNECT_DATA =
      (SERVER = DEDICATED)
      (SERVICE_NAME = STRM2)
    )
  );
```

Database Link creation with TNS Alias:

```
Create database link STRM2
connect to strm_admin identified by strm_admin
using 'STRM2';
```

Trusted versus untrusted configurations

After running through the privileges needed for an untrusted configuration, it becomes obvious that the "separation of duties" does not really save us anything from a security perspective. The capture and apply users must have DBA privileges which our trusted STRMADMIN user has. The source queue owner is the propagator, so if you create the queue as STRMADMIN, this makes STRMADMIN the propagator anyway. Then, you add in the best practices of keeping the number of users with DBA or higher privileges to a minimum, the trusted model becomes a better option even in an untrusted environment. The only time untrusted buys you any advantage is if you are in an environment where you are not allowed to create a DBA user specific to Streams, but you do have a non-SYS and non-SYSTEM DBA user that you can work with. By using private database links and secure queues, you can lock down many of the security loopholes with distributed systems.

Understanding your Instantiation tools

In Chapter 1, *All the Pieces: The Parts of an Oracle 11g Streams Environment*, we discussed Instantiation and Instantiation SCN theoretically. In our examples in this book, we use Data Pump for Instantiation. We provide a quick review of Data Pump commands and configuration here to prepare for its use when we begin building Streams. We also provide practical examples of how to go about setting the Instantiation SCN manually, should you need to do so.

Using Data Pump to Instantiate

If you plan to use Data Pump to instantiate your target sites, you will need to create work directories in which Data Pump will create and access the resulting dump file for export and import. The naming convention you use is up to you. If you used the Database Creation Assistant to create your database, you may already have a DATA_PUMP_DIR (destination C:\Oracle\11gR2\product\11.2.0\db_1\rdbms\log\). You can determine this by querying the DBA_DIRECTORIES view.

At the Source site, create a work directory for the Data Pump export, setting the destination to what suits your needs best (it doesn't have to be the default {oracle_home}/rdbms/log/). Best practice; specify the full path explicitly.

Windows:

```
CREATE DIRECTORY 'DATA_PUMP_DIR' AS 'c:\oracle\dpump\export\';
```

Unix:

```
CREATE DIRECTORY 'DATA_PUMP_DIR' AS '/u01/oracle/dpump/export/';
```

Note: This can also be done through the EM Console: **Schema | Database Objects | Directory Objects**.

Setting Instantiation SCN manually

As mentioned in Chapter 1, you can use the `DBMS_CAPTURE_ADM.PREPARE_*_INSTANTIATION`, `DBMS_FLASHBACK.GET_SYSTEM_CHANGE_NUMBER` and `DBMS_APPLY_ADM SET_*_INSTANTIATION_SCN` packages to manually set the Instantiation SCN between a capture and an Apply process.

The steps for setting the instantiation SCN are as follows:

1. Call the appropriate `DBMS_CAPTURE_ADM.PREPARE_*_INSTANTIATION` package at the source database.

2. Determine the current SCN at the source database using `DBMS_FLASHBACK.GET_SYSTEM_CHANGE_NUMBER`.

3. Call the appropriate `DBMS_APPLY_ADM SET_*_INSTANTIATION_SCN` at the destination database, specifying the SCN value returned in step 2.

The following provides examples using all three packages from the Source side and Destination side. The procedures below must be run as the Streams Administrator and uses a database link owned by the Streams Administrator user and connects to the Streams Administrator at the remote database.

The database links used for examples are as follows:

Database Links		
From /Source	**To/Destination**	**Database Link Name**
HQ	**Branch**	`BRANCH.US.APGTECH.COM`
Branch	**HQ**	`HQ.US.APGTECH.COM`

The example below is run on the Source side (`HQ.US.APGTECH.COM`). The object(s) are prepared for instantiation at the source. The SCN is captured on the source side once the table is instantiated. That SCN is then set for the same table at the Destination (`BRANCH.US.APGTECH.COM`) across a database link.

```
DECLARE
iscn NUMBER; -- Variable to hold instantiation SCN value

BEGIN
DBMS_CAPTURE_ADM.PREPARE_TABLE_INSTANTIATION(
table_name =>   'product.inventory',
```

```
supplemental_logging => 'keys'  --default
);
iscn := DBMS_FLASHBACK.GET_SYSTEM_CHANGE_NUMBER();

DBMS_APPLY_ADM.SET_TABLE_INSTANTIATION_SCN@BRANCH.US.APGTECH.COM(
source_object_name => 'product.inventory',
source_database_name => 'HQ.US.APGTECH.COM',
instantiation_scn => iscn);
END;
/
```

This pattern of capturing the Instantiation SCN on Source side and applying it to the Destination side continues in the examples below for SCHEMA and GLOBAL level.

For SCHEMA level:

```
DECLARE
iscn NUMBER; -- Variable to hold instantiation SCN value

BEGIN
DBMS_CAPTURE_ADM.PREPARE_SCHEMA_INSTANTIATION(
table_name =>   'product.inventory',
supplemental_logging => 'keys'  --default
);

iscn := DBMS_FLASHBACK.GET_SYSTEM_CHANGE_NUMBER();

DBMS_APPLY_ADM.SET_SCHEMA_INSTANTIATION_SCN@BRANCH.US.APGTECH.COM(
source_schema_name => 'product',
source_database_name => 'HQ.US.APGTECH.COM',
instantiation_scn => iscn
recursive => TRUE);
END;
/
```

The recursive parameter provides instructions to apply the proper Instantiation SCN to each table in the schema.

For GLOBAL level:

```
BEGIN
DBMS_CAPTURE_ADM.PREPARE_GLOBAL_INSTANTIATION(
supplemental_logging => 'keys'  --default
);

iscn := DBMS_FLASHBACK.GET_SYSTEM_CHANGE_NUMBER();
```

```
DBMS_APPLY_ADM.SET_GLOBAL_INSTANTIATION_SCN@BRANCH.US.APGTECH.COM(
source_database_name => 'HQ.US.APGTECH.COM',
instantiation_scn => iscn
recursive => TRUE);
END;
/
```

The recursive parameter provides instructions to apply the proper Instantiation SCN to each of the tables in all schemas.

In most situations we find the use of either DBMS_APPLY_ADM.SET_TABLE_INSTANTIATION_SCN or DBMS_APPLY_ADM.SET_SCHEMA_INSTANTIATION_SCN to be the most appropriate.

The examples above have shown the "pushing" of the instantiation SCN from the Source side to the Destination side. The reverse can also be accomplished essentially "pulling" the instantiation SCN to the Destination from the Source side. This can be accomplished by simply running the same code above and changing the location and entry of the database link mentioned above from BRANCH.US.APGTECH.COM to HQ.US.APGTECH.COM. The example at the table level for clarity is shown as follows. This is run on the Destination side (BRANCH.US.APGTECH.COM).

```
DECLARE
iscn NUMBER; -- Variable to hold instantiation SCN value

BEGIN
DBMS_CAPTURE_ADM.PREPARE_TABLE_INSTANTIATION@HQ.US.APGTECH.COM(
table_name =>   'product.inventory',
supplemental_logging => 'keys'  --default
);

iscn := DBMS_FLASHBACK.GET_SYSTEM_CHANGE_NUMBER@HQ.US.APGTECH.COM();

DBMS_APPLY_ADM.SET_TABLE_INSTANTIATION_SCN(
source_object_name => 'product.inventory',
source_database_name => 'HQ.US.APGTECH.COM',
instantiation_scn => iscn);
END;
/
```

The code above "pulls" the instantiation SCN from the Source Side (HQ.US.APGTECH.COM) and applies it the Destination Side (BRANCH.US.APGTECH.COM).

One important point that needs to be mentioned is that we include preparing objects for instantiation manually. If you used the DBMS_STREAMS_ADM package to build the Capture process, the call to DBMS_CAPTURE_ADM.PREPARE_*_INSTANTIATION is done automatically.

To check that instantiation was done properly use the following queries:

```
-- Run on the Source Side
COLUMN TABLE_OWNER HEADING 'Table Owner' FORMAT A15
COLUMN TABLE_NAME HEADING 'Table Name' FORMAT A15
COLUMN SCN HEADING 'Prepare SCN' FORMAT 99999999999
COLUMN TIMESTAMP HEADING 'Time Ready for|Instantiation'

SELECT TABLE_OWNER,
       TABLE_NAME,
       SCN,
       TO_CHAR(TIMESTAMP, 'HH24:MI:SS MM/DD/YY') TIMESTAMP
FROM DBA_CAPTURE_PREPARED_TABLES;

-- Run on the Destination Side
COLUMN SOURCE_DATABASE HEADING 'Source Database' FORMAT A20
COLUMN SOURCE_OBJECT_OWNER HEADING 'Object Owner' FORMAT A15
COLUMN SOURCE_OBJECT_NAME HEADING 'Object Name' FORMAT A15
COLUMN INSTANTIATION_SCN HEADING 'Instantiation SCN' FORMAT
99999999999

SELECT SOURCE_DATABASE,
       SOURCE_OBJECT_OWNER,
       SOURCE_OBJECT_NAME,
       INSTANTIATION_SCN
 FROM DBA_APPLY_INSTANTIATED_OBJECTS
WHERE APPLY_DATABASE_LINK IS NULL;
```

There are occasions where you may need to remove an instantiation SCN. This is usually only done when an attempt at instantiation has failed or gone wrong. This being the case, you can clear the apply Instantiation SCN with DBMS_APPLY_ADM.SET_*_INSTANTIATION_SCN procedure and setting the Instantiation SCN to NULL. This removes the entry from the associated dictionary view. Where * is one of the following levels: TABLE, SCHEMA, or GLOBAL. You would then prepare the object for instantiation at the source and use that SCN to retry setting the Instantiation SCN at the apply site.

Oracle Demo Schemas

In this book, we use the ever-familiar Oracle Demo Schemas in our Streams examples. If you wish to practice with the scripts provided in this book and your database does not have the Demo Schemas, you can use the Load_Demo_Schemas.sql that can be downloaded from the Packt website.

The demo schemas use the EXAMPLES tablespace and include the following schemas—HR, OE, PM, IX, BI, and SH. Please be aware and forewarned, that if you use the Load_Demo_Schemas.sql, the EXAMPLES tablespace (and datafiles), and the HR, OE, PM, IX, BI, and SH schemas will be dropped and recreated. If needed, back up your database or export your existing demo schemas before running the script.

Summary

In this chapter, we have seen the steps necessary to prepare our databases to support Streams, and our tools to instantiate our Streamed objects.

We have looked at a way to verify our network connectivity and throughput with the ping and tracert commands.

We configured our database initialization parameters to support Streams processes and memory structures. We enabled archive logging and supplemental logging to support Streams capture and apply.

We discussed configuring our Streams user(s) for trusted and untrusted security environments as well as best practices for database links.

We then addressed creating directories objects to be used during instantiation with Data Pump and how to manually set Instantiation SCNs for corresponding capture and Apply processes.

And last but not least, we covered how you can create the Oracle Demo Schemas in your database so that you can practice along with us, as we go through examples of setting up the different Stream configurations.

So, hop aboard, grab your paddles (or keyboards in this case) and let's float onto Chapter 4 where we will bring this all together with a uni-directional scenario and start Streaming!

4

Single-Source Configuration

The stream flows one way: Downhill

In this chapter, we will look at configuring single-source streams replication using **Enterprise Manager** (**EM**) DB Console (this can also be applied if you are using Enterprise Manager Grid Control). We will also provide the PL/SQL API calls being issued behind the scenes. The PL/SQL for these calls can be copied to a script and used to configure Streams from the command line as well. This chapter is organized as follows:

- **The Enterprise Manager**: This takes you step-by-step through the EM Streams setup wizard, using a schema-level replication example

- **The code behind the curtain**: A step-by-step walk-through the PL/SQL code that configures the Stream

- **Sequences, and triggers, and apply**: Points out expected behavior of sequence and triggers in our example, as well as special case considerations

- **Other levels at which to replicate**: Provides a brief description of other replication levels that can be used and the beauty of the `DBMS_STREAMS_ADM.MAINTENANCE_*` scripts

The pre-requisite for the examples in this chapter is to include the demo schemas in your source database. Please see Chapter 3, *Prepare the Rafts and Secure Your Gear: The pre-work before configuring Oracle 11g Streams*, for instructions on including the demo schemas in your database if you wish to "practice along" with our example.

For our example, we are going to set up Streams for the HR Schema between two instances. STRM1 will be our source master database and STRM2 will be our destination target database.

The single-source model is uni-directional replication. This means that it changes the flow only one way; from the source master to the destination target. Thus, we will create a capture queue and process at the source master, and a propagation job and process at the source master to the destination target (queue to queue). We then create an Apply queue and process at the destination target.

The Enterprise Manager

Log into EM DBConsole to the source master database.

At the homepage, click on the **Data Movement** sub-tab.

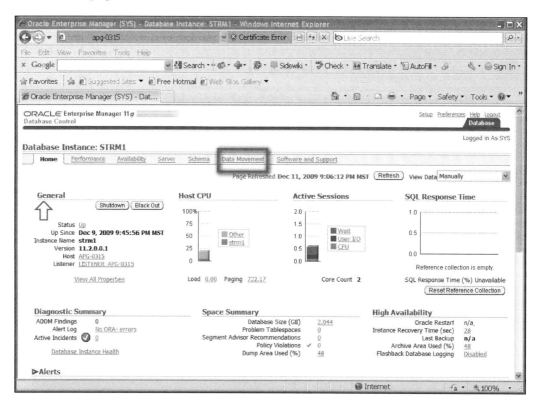

Click on the **Setup** link under Streams.

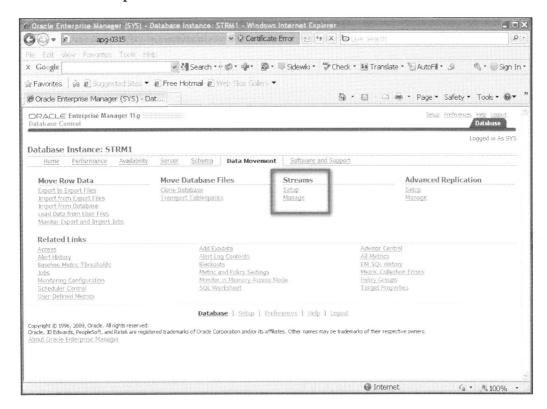

The EM has a 15 minute idle time-out by default. If you are not able to complete the configuration pages within that time period, you will need to start over. So, it doesn't hurt to read through this first, determine what you will need to enter where, and then start the setup.

Setup options

Select **Streams Global, Schema, Table and Subset Replication Wizard** and
click **Continue**.

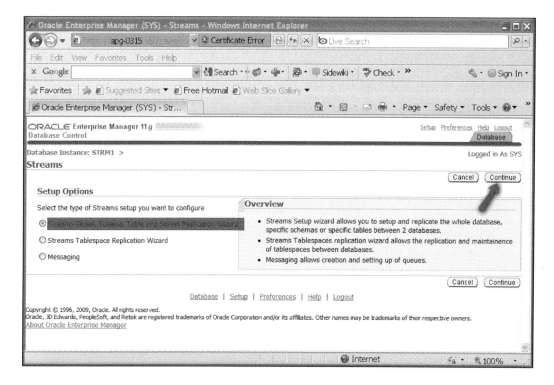

Specify the Streams Administration username and password.

OR

If your designated Streams Administration user does not already exist in the source
master database, click **Create Streams Administrator** button.

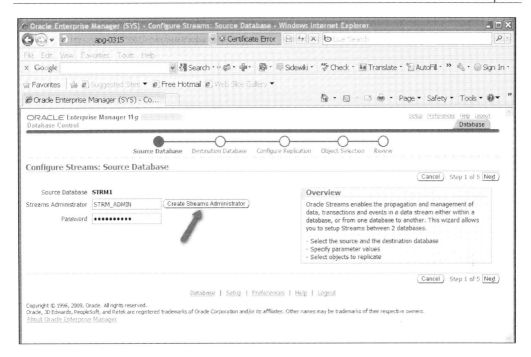

Enter a SYSDBA username and password, and the username and password for the Streams Administration user. Take note of the privileges that will be granted to the new user.

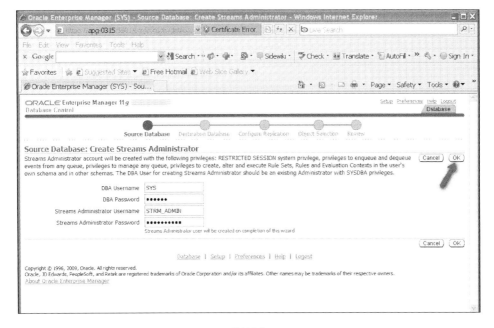

Click **OK**.

This will return you to the specify Streams Administrator screen, click **NEXT**.

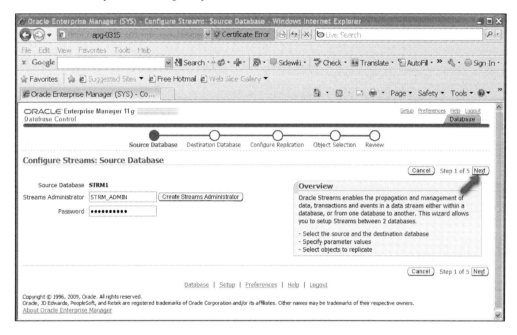

Next, you will specify information for the destination or target database.

Again, if the Streams Administrator user does not exist on the target database, click **Create Streams Administrator** button.

Specify the appropriate information and click **OK**.

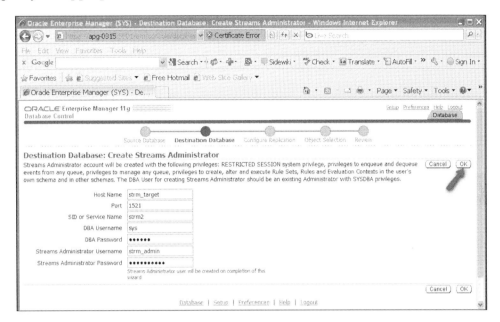

This will take you back to the configure destination database page. Click **Next**.

Configure replication

This page allows us to specify our replication options. First, we specify what level of replication we want to configure. The levels are as follows:

1. **Global Rule** means we want to replicate all the schemas and their objects in the database (of course this does not include schema's proprietary to the database like sys, system, and so on). We will have the option of excluding specific schemas and/or tables in a later step.

2. **Schema Rule** means we want to replicate all objects in one or more specific schemas. We will have the option of excluding specific tables in the schemas specified in a later step.

3. **Table Rule** means we want to replicate only specific tables. This can be all the data in the table or a subset of data in the table through a where clause specified in a later step. The tables do not need to belong to the same schema.

In this example, we want to replicate the full HR schema. So, we will select **Schema Rule**.

Processes

Here we specify the names for each of the processes that we will want to use/create.

 Specify a name that is specific to the process configuration. Why? You can have multiple capture, propagate, and Apply processes in an instance. Different rules can be associated to these different processes. Using meaningful names provides a quick visual aid to differentiate between the processes.

In our example, we are going to use the following naming to help us identify which processes work together to support this configuration. We will use SCHEMA_HR and forego using STREAMS since we already know it is Streams. Keep in mind that you do have a length limitation of 30 characters here. Keep it short. Feel free to abbreviate. KISS it.

Directory objects

The Streams setup wizard will use Data Pump to instantiate the destination/target database. This is where you specify where the resulting dump and log files will be written/read. You can use an existing directory (click on the flashlight to select from a list), or create one. To make life easy, let's use one that already exists for Data Pump purposes. It's the **DATA_PUMP_DIR** (convenient isn't it?)

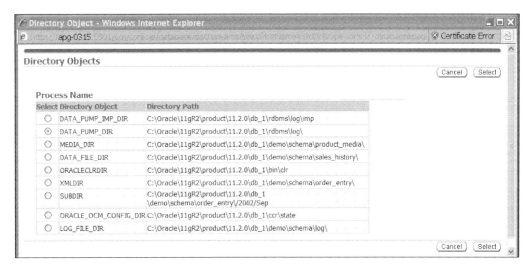

Options

This is where we specify what changes get sent (DML and/or DDL) and the direction in which they are sent. By default, the page selects only DML and bi-directional (master-to-master). In our example, we want a single-source master. So, we will uncheck **Setup Bi-directional replication**. We want to replicate DDL changes to any of our HR schema objects as well as DML (data) changes, so we will check **Capture, Propagate, and Apply data definition language (DDL) changes**.

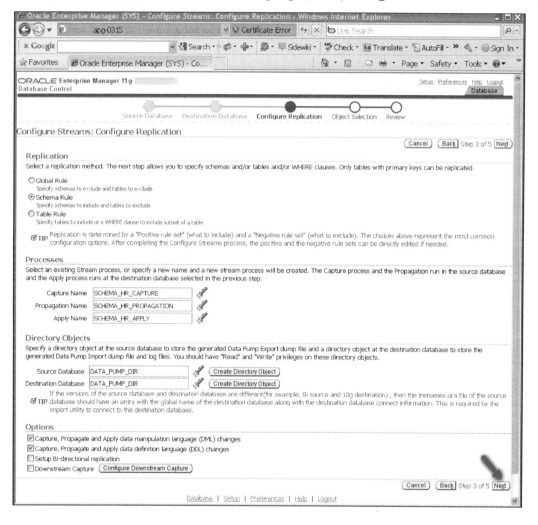

Click **Next**.

Object selection

This is where we specify any or all objects in the database schema that we do or do not want to replicate. What you see presented to you on this page will depend on what replication rule you selected on the previous page (global, schema, table). You can select any or all of the schemas listed to replicate. Please note that the table shows only 10 at a time, so if you don't see the schema you want to at first, use the table navigation button to traverse the list. If you wish to exclude any tables that belong to your selected schemas, you can do so by adding them to the **Exclude Tables** list in the next section (click **Add**).

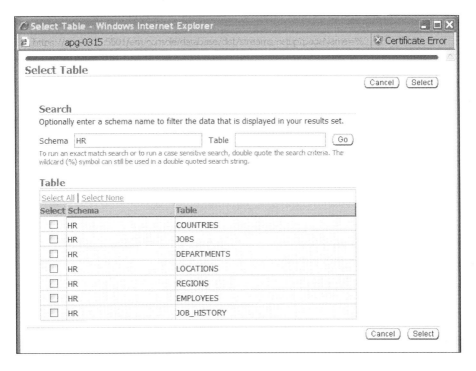

In our case, we want just the HR schema with all its tables.

Click **NEXT**.

This brings us to our **Review** summary sheet.

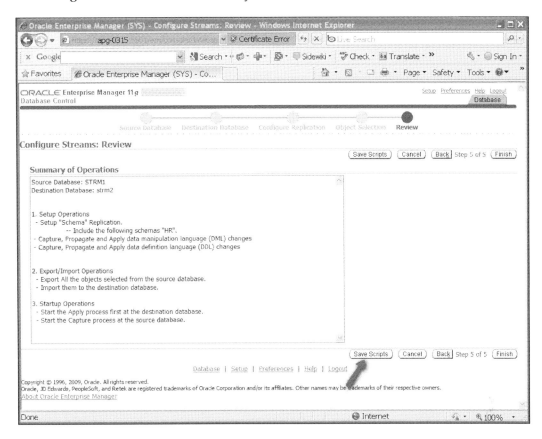

Review

The **Summary of Operations** lists the tasks in the order that the Setup wizard will accomplish them, based on the configuration parameters you have specified. A nice feature here is the **Save Scripts** button. This will allow you to save a copy of the generated SQL code to a file (default name is setup.sql).

In this example, the saved script will contain the PL/SQL to create the STRM_ADMIN user on both STRM1 and STRM2 instances and grant the necessary privileges, create the necessary database links, and then call the DBMS_STREAMS_ADM.MAINTAIN_SCHEMAS procedure passing in the parameters you defined in the wizard. It is this DBMS_STREAMS_ADM.MAINTAIN_SCHEMAS procedure that actually generates and executes the PL/SQL to build streams. We will see more on this in our "The code behind the curtain" section.

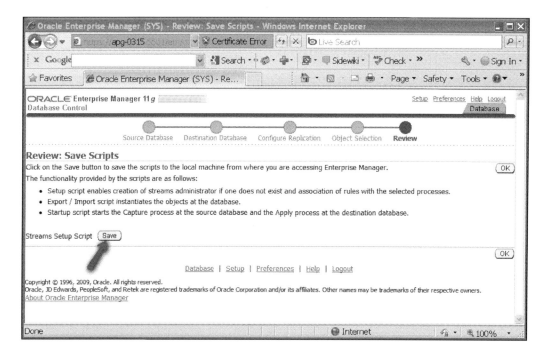

The **Save** operation will prompt you for the save confirmation and location. It then returns you to the **Review** page.

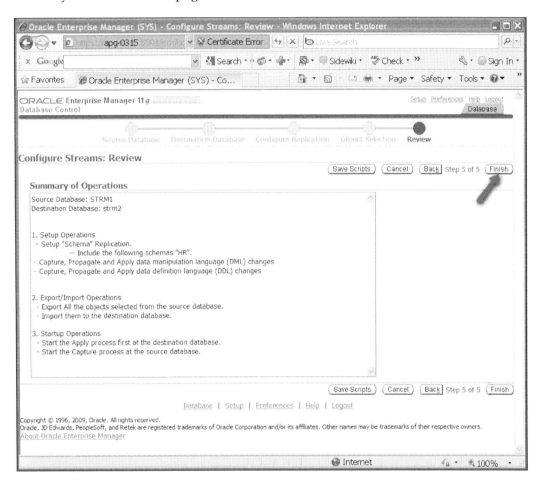

Click **Finish**.

Schedule Streams setup job

You can choose to either set up streams immediately or schedule the setup for a later time (perhaps at night when users are not using the system).

In our case, we will run the setup **Immediately**. Note that you will also need to specify **Host Credentials**. This would be an O/S user and password. Please note that the user must have appropriate privileges to run jobs through the EM. For more information on the required privileges, please refer to your O/S specific Oracle maintenance manual. Click **Submit**.

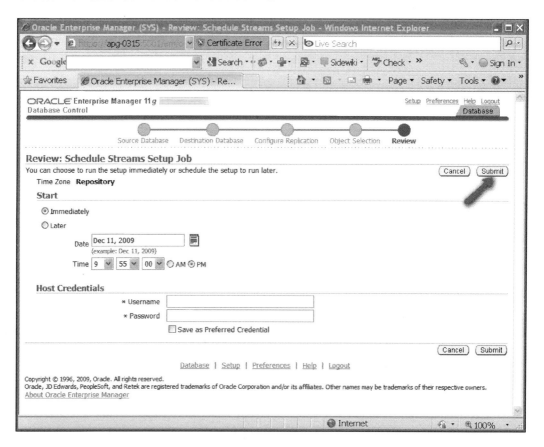

This will bring you to the job confirmation page. It provides a link to the job monitoring page if you wish to monitor the progress of the job.

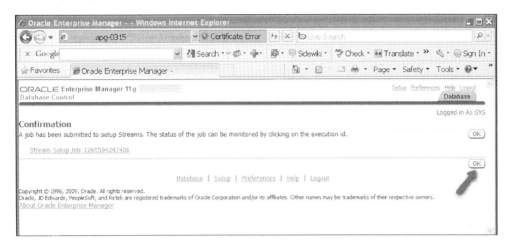

Click **OK**, and you will return to the initial Streams setup page.

Verify

When the job is complete, you can verify your Streams environment from the **Streams Management** page. Navigate to the **Data Movement** page and select **Manage** under **Streams**.

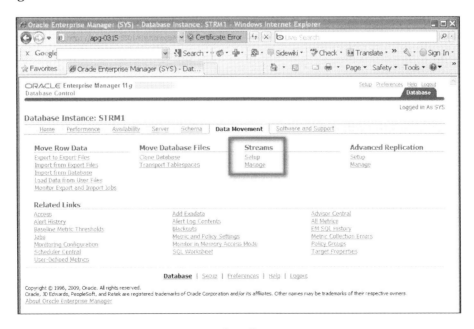

This will take you to the **Overview** page. Click on **Capture**.

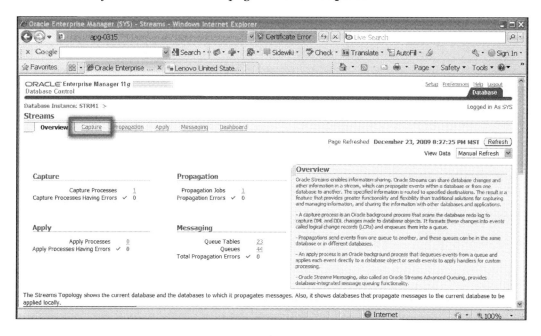

Notice that the **Capture** process is enabled. This means your process is currently capturing changes. To stop/start (disable/enable) the process, click the radio button under the select column for the Capture process, and then click **Start** or **Stop**.

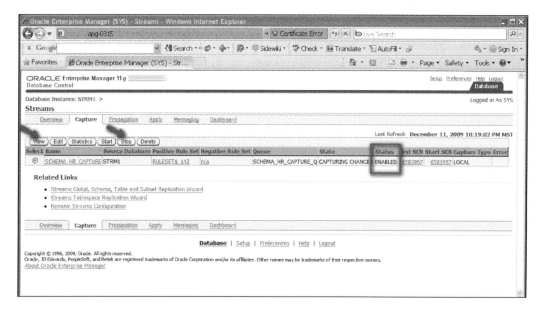

You can view process statistics by clicking on **Statistics**.

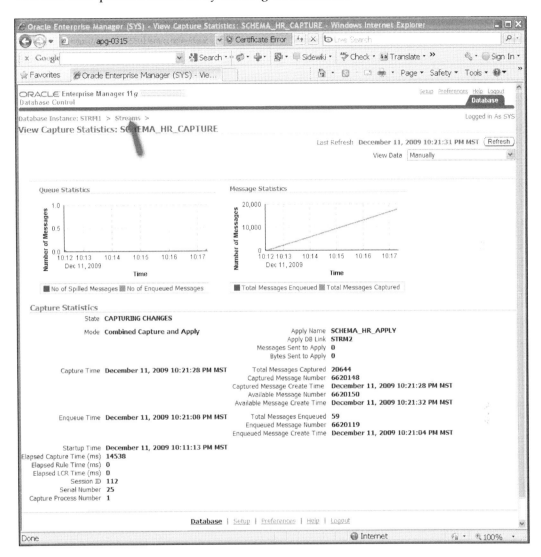

Click on the **Streams** breadcrumb link to return to the **Capture** page.

Click on the **Propagation** link. Verify the status is **Enabled**.

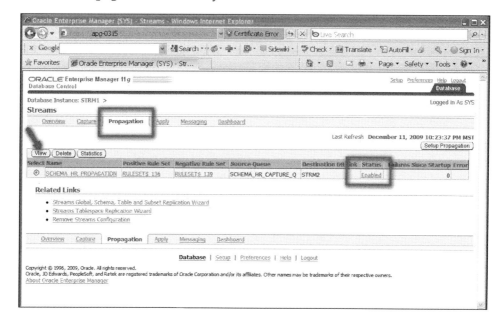

You can view the information and propagation rule sets by clicking on **View**.

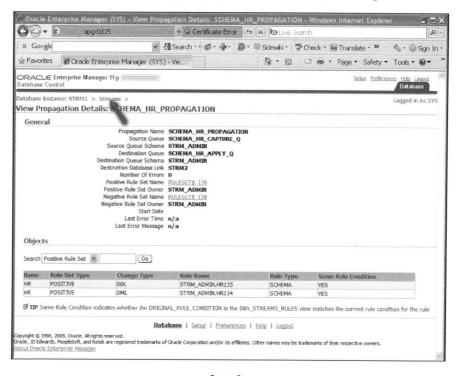

Click on the **Streams** breadcrumb link to return to the **Propagation** page.

We then go to our destination site EM DBConsole and we see our **Apply** process and verify that it is enabled.

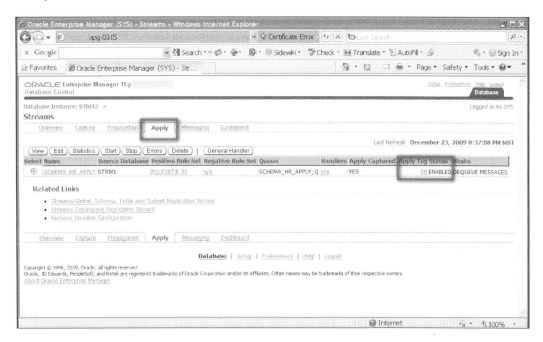

At our destination site (STRM2), the absence of a Capture process for the schema and a Propagation process back to STRM1 ensures uni-directional single-source master replication. However, it does not keep changes from being made directly to the destination site. So, it is still possible for data to diverge, and lead to data conflicts. To avoid this, we recommend implementing site priority conflict resolution error handling at the destination site (see Chapter 5, *N-Way Replication*, for conflict resolution).

The code behind the curtain

This section addresses the PL/SQL package procedures and functions that are executed behind the scenes by EM to actually create the Streams replication. We have included these procedures in PL/SQL block code that can be used individually to accomplish each step of the process at a time, or combined in a "master" script (with some minor modifications). Please note that you may need to make minor modifications to accommodate your specific environment setups (like machine names, connections, db links name and so on).

Checking the waters

When you use the EM Streams setup wizard to generate the code to configure your single source, EM generates and runs PL/SQL that does the following:

- Creates the Streams Administrator user account (if not already done) on both the source and destination instances

- Grants the necessary privileges to the Streams Administrator account (if not already done) on both the source and destination instances

- Creates database links for the Streams Administrator user (first, dropping the link if it already exists)

- Calls the appropriate DBMS_STREAMS_ADM.MAINTAIN_* procedure to configure Streams between the two databases

The call to a DBMS_STREAMS_ADM.MAINTAIN_* procedure sets parameters that tell the procedure what to capture, propagation, and to apply queues and processes to create and where to create them, as well as script naming and location specification. You can also direct the procedure to only generate the the necessary scripts and not run them. For specific details on the DBMS_STREAMS_ADM.MAINTAIN_* procedures, please refer to your *Oracle PL/SQL Packages and Types Reference Manual*.

In our example, it is the DBMS_STREAMS_ADM.MAINTAIN_SCHEMAS procedure.

At the time of publishing, the EM Streams setup wizard has an undocumented feature in that even though you uncheck "Setup bi-direction replication" on your configuration it may still pass a "TRUE" value to the DBMS_STREAMS_ADM.MAINTAIN_* procedure bi_directional parameter. A "FALSE" value for the bi_directional parameter tells the procedure to set up single-source replication, A "TRUE" value for the bi_directional parameter tells the procedure to set up master-to-master replication. Check the script before running it by doing a "Save Scripts" on the Review page. If the script has the bi_directional parameter set to "TRUE", you can cancel out of the setup wizard, edit the saved script to set the value to "FALSE", and run the script from SQLPLUS.

The DBMS_STREAMS_ADM.MAINTAIN_* procedure in turn will generate and run scripts that set up single-source replication by doing the following:

- Add supplemental logging to the necessary tables on the source database

- Create the capture queue at the source database

- Create the Propagation process at the source database

- Create the schema Capture process at the source database
- Configure and execute Data Pump schema export/import to/from the source/destination database
- Instantiate the capture SCN
- Create the apply queue and process on the destination database
- Instantiate the apply SCN
- Start the capture, apply, and Propagation processes

It is possible to run the `DBMS_STREAMS_ADM.MAINTAIN_*` procedure to generate the PL/SQL to build the Streams, but not actually run it. This is done by setting the `perform_actions` parameter to "FALSE".

To generate a full set of scripts, you can begin by running through the EM Streams setup wizard, save the script at the review page, and then cancel out the wizard without finishing. You can edit the saved script, setting the `perfrom_actions` parameter to "FALSE", and run the script from SQLPLUS. The procedure will create the SQL script to set up the Streams to directory specified by the `script_directory_object` parameter with the filename by the `script_name` parameter. This script can then be opened and viewed with a standard text editor. This file can then be run as a standalone script. Keeping a copy of these scripts also provides a way to quickly and accurately recreate the Streamed configuration between the two databases from the command line, should the need arise.

Diving in

In this section, we are going to look at the PL/SQL commands needed to configure single-streams replication between our two databases. The scripts created by the EM and `DBMS_STREAMS_ADM.MAINTAIN_*` procedure do pretty much the same thing though there may be some minor differences in order of operations and the secondary version checks which we chose to skip here. The PL/SQL presented here is formatted to be run, stand-alone for each step. This will allow you to "play" with each step, individually. You can download these scripts from the Packt website.

If you would like more information on the PL/SQL packages and SQL commands issued in these scripts you can find it in your *Oracle PL/SQL Packages and Types Reference*, and the *Oracle SQL Language Reference* manuals respectively.

For PL/SQL block structure and coding, please reference your *Oracle PL/SQL Language Reference* manual.

The first step is the creation of the Streams Administrator user and granting of privileges at both the source master and destination target databases. This must be done by a SYSDBA user. The code is in the `create_strmadmin.sql` script and does the following:

- Connects to the source database as SYS
- Creates the STRM_ADMIN user
- Grants DBA, IMP_FULL_DATABASE, EXP_FULL_DATABASE privileges to STRM_ADMIN
- Executes DBMS_STREAMS_AUTH.GRANT_ADMIN_PRIVILEGE for STRM_ADMIN
- Connects to the destination database as SYS
- Creates the STRM_ADMIN user
- Grants DBA, IMP_FULL_DATABASE, EXP_FULL_DATABASE privileges to STRM_ADMIN
- Executes DBMS_STREAMS_AUTH.GRANT_ADMIN_PRIVILEGE for STRM_ADMIN
- Connects at the source database as the new STRM_ADMIN user
- Creates a database link from the source database to the destination database.

For more detailed information on the privileges for the Streams Administrator, reference the "Configure an Oracle Streams Administrator" of the *Oracle Streams Concepts and Administration* manual for 11gR1, or the *Oracle Streams Replication Administrator's Guide* for 11gR2.

```
--create_strmadmin.sql...
set echo on;
ACCEPT src PROMPT 'Enter tnsalias for the source database:'
ACCEPT dba_pwd_src PROMPT 'Enter Password of user "sys" to create
                            Streams Admin at Source : ' HIDE
ACCEPT strm_pwd_src PROMPT 'Enter Password of Streams Admin
            "strm_admin" to be created at Source : ' HIDE
ACCEPT dest PROMPT 'Enter tnsalias for the target database:'
ACCEPT dba_pwd_dest PROMPT 'Enter Password of user "sys" to create
                            Streams Admin at Destination : ' HIDE
ACCEPT strm_pwd_dest PROMPT 'Enter Password of Streams Admin
            "strm_admin" to be created at Destination : ' HIDE

PROMPT connecting as sys at &src
connect sys/&dba_pwd_src@&src as SYSDBA;
PROMPT
PROMPT creating strm_admin user
create user strm_admin identified by &strm_pwd_src;
PROMPT granting privs
```

```
grant DBA, IMP_FULL_DATABASE, EXP_FULL_DATABASE to  strm_admin;
BEGIN
  DBMS_STREAMS_AUTH.GRANT_ADMIN_PRIVILEGE(
     grantee => 'strm_admin',
     grant_privileges => true);
END;
/
COMMIT;
/
PROMPT connecting as sys at &dest
connect sys/&dba_pwd_dest@&dest as SYSDBA;
PROMPT
PROMPT creating strm_admin user
create user strm_admin identified by &strm_pwd_dest;
PROMPT granting privs
grant DBA, IMP_FULL_DATABASE, EXP_FULL_DATABASE to  strm_admin;
BEGIN
  DBMS_STREAMS_AUTH.GRANT_ADMIN_PRIVILEGE(
     grantee => 'strm_admin',
     grant_privileges => true);
END;
/
PROMPT strm_admin create and privs complete
/
COMMIT;
/
```

Next, we connect as `strm_admin` and create a database link from our source database to our target database.

```
connect strm_admin/&strm_pwd_src;

--if the STRM2 dblink already exists you can drop it.
--DROP DATABASE LINK STRM2;

CREATE DATABASE LINK STRM2 connect to  strm_admin identified by
       &strm_pwd_dest using '(DESCRIPTION=(ADDRESS_LIST=(ADDRESS=
                             (PROTOCOL=TCP)(HOST=strm_target)
(PORT=1521)))(CONNECT_DATA=(SID=strm2)(server=DEDICATED)))';
COMMIT;
/
--end code
```

Notice that we used the full TNS connect description rather than the alias for the using parameter? Using the full connect description instead of a TNS alias avoids issues with tnsnames.ora file configurations. This removes any dependency of the database link on tnsnames.ora files that can be changed, moved, or deleted.

Next, we need to add supplemental logging to the tables in the HR schema at the source master database. This needs to be done for each table.

The command to do this is:

```
ALTER TABLE "HR"."<table_name>" ADD SUPPLEMENTAL LOG DATA (PRIMARY
KEY, -FOREIGN KEY, UNIQUE INDEX) COLUMNS';
```

In the setup script generated by the DBMS_STREAMS_ADM.MAINTAIN_* procedure, you will see the command repeated and hard-coded for each table in the schema. The following code block below accomplishes the same actions, but dynamically, so it does not need to be edited if table names change, or if tables are added or dropped. This code is found in the add_supplog_schema.sql script and does the following:

- Sets up a loop for each table name in the specified schema
- Builds and executes the statement to add supplemental logging for each table
- Reports the results of each statement

```
--create_supplog_schema.sql..
ACCEPT sowner PROMPT 'Enter schema owner:'
set serveroutput on
BEGIN
  For tn in (select table_name from dba_tables where owner =
upper('&sowner')) loop
    BEGIN
      EXECUTE IMMEDIATE 'ALTER TABLE "&sowner"."' ||
                                tn.table_name ||
                    '" ADD SUPPLEMENTAL LOG DATA (PRIMARY KEY,
FOREIGN KEY, UNIQUE INDEX) COLUMNS';
      dbms_output.put_line('added supplemental logging for ' ||
                                tn.table_name);
    EXCEPTION WHEN OTHERS THEN
      IF sqlcode = -32588 THEN
       dbms_output.put_line('supplemental logging already exists
                            for ' || tn.table_name);
      ELSE
         RAISE;
      END IF;
    END;
  end loop;
END;
/
--end code
```

Next we set up the capture queue on our source master (STRM1). This code is found in the `create_capture_queue.sql` script. The script should be run as the STRM_ADMIN user and does the following:

- Calls `dbms_streams_adm.set_up_queue` to create the queue
- Verifies queue creation

```
--create_capture_queue.sql...
ACCEPT cqname PROMPT 'Enter Capture Queue Name: ex: SCHEMA_HR'
DECLARE
 uname varchar2(50);
BEGIN
   select user into uname from dual;
   dbms_streams_adm.set_up_queue(
      queue_table => uname ||'.&cqname._CAPTURE_QT',
      storage_clause => NULL,
      queue_name => uname ||'.&cqname._CAPTURE_Q',
      queue_user => uname);
END;
/
column object_name format a30
select object_name, object_type, created from user_objects
where object_name like upper('%&cqname%')
/
--end code
```

Next, create the propagation rules for the schema. Note that the propagation job is created in an enabled state, so we want to disable it until we are finished setting up the apply queue on the destination site. This code is found in the `add_schema_propagation.sql` script. The script should be run as the STRM_ADMIN user and does the following:

- Calls `dbms_streams_adm.add_schema_propagation_rules` to create the Propagation process and job
- Calls `dbms_aqadm.disable_propagation_schedule` to disable the propagation
- Verifies the creation of the Propagation process and rules

```
--add_schema_propagation.sql…
ACCEPT sname PROMPT 'Enter Schema Name:'
ACCEPT qname PROMPT 'Enter Queue Name prefix: (ex: SCHEMA_HR) '

ACCEPT destlink PROMPT 'Enter the DB Link name for
                  the destination DB: (ex: STRM2) '
DECLARE
```

```
   uname varchar2(50);
  gsid varchar2(10) ;
BEGIN
  select user into uname from dual;
  select upper(instance) into gsid from v$thread;

  dbms_streams_adm.add_schema_propagation_rules(
    schema_name => upper('&sname'),
    streams_name => '&qname._PROPAGATION',
    source_queue_name => uname||'.&qname._CAPTURE_Q',
    destination_queue_name => uname||'.&qname._APPLY_Q@&destlink',
    include_dml => TRUE,
    include_ddl => TRUE,
    include_tagged_lcr => TRUE,
    source_database => gsid,
    inclusion_rule => TRUE,
    and_condition => NULL,
    queue_to_queue => TRUE);

  --disable propagation until we are finished
  BEGIN
    dbms_aqadm.disable_propagation_schedule(
      queue_name => uname||'.&qname._CAPTURE_Q',
      destination => '&destlink',
      destination_queue => uname||'.&qname._APPLY_Q');
  EXCEPTION WHEN OTHERS THEN
    IF sqlcode = -24065 THEN NULL;
  -- propagation already disabled
    ELSE RAISE;
    END IF;
  END;
END;
/
--let's verify
set pagesize 150
set linesize 100

select * from dba_propagation
where propagation_name like upper('%&qname.%')
/

select * from dba_streams_schema_rules
where streams_type = 'PROPAGATION'
/
--end code
```

Next we add the schema capture rule. This code is found in the
`add_schema_capture.sql` script. The script should be run as the
`STRM_ADMIN` user and does the following:

- Calls `dbms_streams_adm.add_schema_rule` to create the schema level
  Capture process and rules
- Verifies the creation of the Capture process and rules

```
--add_schema_capture.sql…
ACCEPT sname PROMPT 'Enter Schema Name:'
ACCEPT qname PROMPT 'Enter Queue Name prefix: (ex: SCHEMA_HR) '
DECLARE
 uname varchar2(50);
 gsid varchar2(10) ;
BEGIN
   select user into uname from dual;
   select upper(instance) into gsid from v$thread;

   dbms_streams_adm.add_schema_rules(
     schema_name => '&sname',
     streams_type => 'CAPTURE',
     streams_name => '&qname._CAPTURE',
     queue_name => uname ||'.&qname._CAPTURE_Q',
     include_dml => TRUE,
     include_ddl => TRUE,
     include_tagged_lcr => TRUE,
     source_database => gsid,
     inclusion_rule => TRUE,
     and_condition => NULL);
END;
/

--let's verify
set pagesize 150
set linesize 100

select * from dba_capture
where capture_name like upper('%&qname.%')
/

select * from dba_streams_schema_rules
where streams_type = 'CAPTURE'
/
--end code
```

We do not want to actually start the Capture process until we have everything else in place. This we will do at the end. The script generated by the DBMS_STREAMS_ADM.MAINTAIN_* procedure starts the Capture process here. However, Oracle documentation, and Oracle Streams course material both recommend starting the capture as the last step, as do these authors. In this case, we will do as "they say" not as "they do".

Next, we will want to instantiate the HR schema. We do this using Data Pump to export the HR schema to a dump file that will then be imported into the destination target database. In our example, the HR schema does not exist at our destination site. If it did exist, we would want to drop the HR schema at the destination site so that the Data Pump import is able to identically reproduce it at the destination site.

For detailed information on instantiation, reference the "Instantiation and Oracle Streams Replication" chapter of the *Oracle Streams Replication Administrators Guide*.

First, we will do the Data Pump export. This code is found in the instantiate_exp_schema.sql script. The script will connect as the STRM_ADMIN user and do the following:

- Opens a Data Pump job handle with dbms_datapump.open
- Sets the metadata for the Data Pump job handle with dbms_datapump.metadata_filter
- Sets the filenames to be generated using dbms_datapump.add_file
- Starts the Data Pump export job with dbms_datapump.start_job
- Monitors the job and reports status and completion

```
--instantiate_exp_schema_hr.sql…
ACCEPT sname PROMPT 'Enter Schema Name to instantiate: '
ACCEPT src_dirobj PROMPT 'Enter Source directory Object name:
                                        (DATA_PUMP_DIR:) '
ACCEPT expdump PROMPT 'Enter Export dump file Name
                        (file extension .dmp will be appended): '
ACCEPT stmadm PROMPT 'Enter Stream Admin username: '
ACCEPT stmadmpwd PROMPT 'Enter Stream Admin Password: '
ACCEPT srcsdb PROMPT 'Enter Source SID: '

connect &stmadm/&stmadmpwd@&srcsdb
set serveroutput on
PROMPT 'Opening DataPump Export Job at &srcsdb'
DECLARE
```

```
  -- data pump job handle
   H1                    NUMBER;
   srcsid varchar2(10);
   job_state    VARCHAR2(30) := 'UNDEFINED'; -- job state
   status       ku$_Status; -- data pump status
   no_job       exception;
   pragma       exception_init(no_job, -40717);

BEGIN

   H1 := dbms_datapump.open(
      operation=>'EXPORT',
      job_mode=>'SCHEMA',
      remote_link=>'',
      job_name=>NULL, version=>'COMPATIBLE');

   dbms_output.put_line('setting metadata filter with handle: '
||H1);
   dbms_datapump.metadata_filter(
      handle=>H1,
      name=>'SCHEMA_EXPR',
      value=>'IN (''&sname'')');

--This command specifies the export dump file
   dbms_output.put_line('Adding export dump file name to handle: '
||H1);
   dbms_datapump.add_file(
      handle=>H1,
      filename=>'&expdump..dmp',
      directory=>'&src_dirobj',
      filetype=>dbms_datapump.ku$_file_type_dump_file);

--This command specifies the export log file
   dbms_output.put_line('Adding export log file name');
   dbms_datapump.add_file(
      handle=>H1,
      filename=>'&expdump._exp.log',
      directory=>'&src_dirobj',
      filetype=>dbms_datapump.ku$_file_type_log_file);

--This command starts the export
   dbms_output.put_line('starting DataPump Export Job');
   dbms_datapump.start_job(H1);

   commit;
```

```
      --monitor export job status
        job_state := 'STARTING';
        BEGIN
          WHILE (job_state != 'COMPLETING') AND (job_state != 'STOPPED')
    LOOP
            dbms_output.put_line ('job is: ' || job_state ||' ' ||
                                    to_char(sysdate,'HH24:MI:SS'));
            status := dbms_datapump.get_status(
              handle => h1,
              mask => dbms_datapump.ku$_status_job_error +
                      dbms_datapump.ku$_status_job_status +
                      dbms_datapump.ku$_status_wip,
              timeout => -1);
            job_state := status.job_status.state;
            dbms_lock.sleep(5);
          END LOOP;
        EXCEPTION
          WHEN no_job THEN
            dbms_output.put_line('job finished');
        END;

        DBMS_DATAPUMP.DETACH(handle => h1);

    END;
    /

    PROMPT DataPump Export Operation is finished
    --end code

    --end code
```

Now, we move to the destination site.

First, we need to instantiate the HR schema, and then create the Apply process. We use Data Pump import to instantiate the HR schema and data. It is important to remember that Data Pump will create the objects in the same tablespace in which they reside at the source database. So, our import is going to need the EXAMPLE tablespace. Make sure you create the EXAMPLE tablespace in the destination database if you have not already done so. You can do this through the EM DBConsole. Or, you can issue the create tablespace command.

For example:

```
CREATE SMALLFILE TABLESPACE "EXAMPLE"
DATAFILE 'C:\ORACLE\11GR2\ORADATA\STRM1\EXAMPLE01.DBF' SIZE 100M
AUTOEXTEND ON NEXT 640K MAXSIZE UNLIMITED LOGGING EXTENT MANAGEMENT
LOCAL SEGMENT SPACE MANAGEMENT AUTO;
```

Now that we have our tablespace in place, we can begin the import. This code is found in the `instantiate_imp_schema.sql` script. This will connect as the `STRM_ADMIN` user and do the following:

Check to see if it needs to transport the databfile based on the source and destination directory locations you specify. If these are different, `dbms_file_transfer.put_file` is called.

Note some caveats here:

- Make sure that the file specified for the import file exists in the location defined for the source directory in the destination database.

  If it does not, the `dbms_file_transfer.put_file` will fail with:

  ```
  ORA-19505: failed to identify file"<path\filename>"
  ORA-27041: unable to open file
  OSD-04002: unable to open file
  O/S-Error: (OS 2) The system cannot find the file specified.
  ```

- Make sure that the file specified for the import file does not already exist in the destination directory.

  If it does, the `dbms_file_transfer.put_file` will fail with:

  ```
  ORA-19504: failed to create file "<path\filename>"
  ORA-27038: created file already exists
  ```

  And will use the existing file for the import instead.

- Opens a Data Pump job handle with `dbms_datapump.open`.

- Sets the filenames to be used with `dbms_datapump.add_file`.

- Starts the Data Pump import job with `dbms_datapump.start_job`.

- Monitors the job and reports status and completion.

- Checks the object count for the schema.

  ```
  --instantiate_exp_schema_hr.sql...
  ACCEPT sname PROMPT 'Enter Schema Name to instantiate: '
  ACCEPT src_dirobj PROMPT 'Enter Source directory Object name:
                                        (DATA_PUMP_DIR): '
  ACCEPT dest_dirobj PROMPT 'Enter Destination directory
                           Object name: (DATA_PUMP_IMP_DIR): '
  ACCEPT expdump PROMPT 'Enter Import dump file Name
                      (file extension .dmp will be appended): '
  ACCEPT destdb PROMPT 'Enter Import Destination
                                      DB Sid: (ex: STRM2): '
  ACCEPT stmadm PROMPT 'Enter Stream Admin username: '
  ACCEPT stmadmpwd PROMPT 'Enter Stream Admin Password: '
  ```

```
connect &stmadm/&stmadmpwd@&destdb
set serveroutput on

--we  check to see if the source and destination directory objects
are different.
--If so we need to transfer the dump file from the source to the
destination target database directory Object
PROMPT 'Checking if dump file requires transport from &src_dirobj
to &dest_dirobj'
DECLARE
   dest_sid varchar2(10) := upper('&&destdb');
BEGIN
   --dbms_output.put_line('dest_sid is: ' || dest_sid);
   IF '&src_dirobj' != '&dest_dirobj' THEN
     dbms_file_transfer.put_file(
       source_directory_object => '"DATA_PUMP_DIR"',
       source_file_name => '&expdump..dmp',
       destination_directory_object => '"DATA_PUMP_IMP_DIR"',
       destination_file_name => '&expdump..dmp',
       destination_database => '&destdb');

       commit;
   END IF;
END;
/

PROMPT 'Opening DataPump Import Job at &destdb'

DECLARE
   H1                NUMBER;         -- data pump job handle
   job_state   VARCHAR2(30) := 'UNDEFINED'; -- job state
   status        ku$_Status; -- data pump status
   no_job      exception;
   pragma            exception_init(no_job, -40717);
BEGIN

   H1 := dbms_datapump.open(operation=>'IMPORT',job_mode=>'SCHEMA',
     remote_link=>'',
     job_name=>NULL, version=>'COMPATIBLE');

--This command specifies the import dump file location
   dbms_output.put_line('Adding import dump
                                 file name to handle: ' ||H1);
   dbms_datapump.add_file(
     handle=>H1,
```

```
      filename=>'&expdump..dmp',
      directory=>'&dest_dirobj',
      filetype=>dbms_datapump.ku$_file_type_dump_file);

--This command specifies the import log file location
   dbms_output.put_line('Adding import log
                                    file name to handle: ' ||H1);
   dbms_datapump.add_file(
      handle=>H1,
      filename=>'&expdump._imp.log',
      directory=>'&dest_dirobj',
      filetype=>dbms_datapump.ku$_file_type_log_file);

--This command starts the import job.
   dbms_output.put_line('starting import job with handle: ' ||H1);
   dbms_datapump.start_job(H1);


--monitor export job status
   job_state := 'STARTING';
   BEGIN
      WHILE (job_state != 'COMPLETING') AND (job_state != 'STOPPED')
LOOP
         dbms_output.put_line ('job is: ' || job_state ||' ' ||
                                    to_char(sysdate,'HH24:MI:SS'));
         status := dbms_datapump.get_status(
            handle => h1,
            mask => dbms_datapump.ku$_status_job_error +
                    dbms_datapump.ku$_status_job_status +
                    dbms_datapump.ku$_status_wip,
            timeout => -1);
         job_state := status.job_status.state;
         dbms_lock.sleep(5);
      END LOOP;
   EXCEPTION
      WHEN no_job THEN
         dbms_output.put_line('job finished');
      WHEN OTHERS THEN
         RAISE;
   END;
   --dbms_lock.sleep(10); --give it time to create objs before
checking count

   DBMS_DATAPUMP.DETACH(handle => h1);

END;
```

```
/
--Once the import is complete, verify the HR schema objects exist.
PROMPT DataPump Import operation is finished
exec dbms_output.put_line('check object count at &destdb')
Select count(*) from dba_objects where owner = '&sname'
/
--end code
```

> If the OE user does not exist on the destination database and it did on the source database, you will see grant permission errors in the import log when the import brings in the HR schema object permissions. This is okay. You just want to remember to make sure that the OE gets the grants if you ever decide to create that schema on the destination in the future.

Next, create the apply queue at the destination target. This code is found in the `add_apply.sql` script, it should run as the `STRM_ADMIN` user and do the following:

- Creates the Apply queue with the `dbms_streams_adm.set_up_queue` procedure
- Adds the Apply rule for the schema with the `dbms_streams_adm.add_schema_rules` procedure
- Verifies the creation of the Apply process and rules

```
--add_apply.sql...
ACCEPT sname PROMPT 'Enter Schema Name:'
ACCEPT qname PROMPT 'Enter Queue Name prefix: (ex: SCHEMA_HR) '
ACCEPT srcsdb PROMPT 'Enter the Source Database SID: (STRM1) '
ACCEPT destdb PROMPT 'Enter the Destination Database
                                          SID: (STRM2) '
ACCEPT stmadm PROMPT 'Enter Stream Admin username: '
ACCEPT stmadmpwd PROMPT 'Enter Stream Admin Password: '

connect &stmadm/&stmadmpwd@&destdb
set serveroutput on
DECLARE
 uname varchar2(50);
BEGIN
  select user into uname from dual;

--Create the apply queue
  dbms_output.put_line('Creating &qname._apply queue');
  dbms_streams_adm.set_up_queue(
    queue_table => uname || '.&qname._APPLY_QT',
    storage_clause => NULL,
    queue_name => uname || '.&qname._APPLY_Q',
```

```
      queue_user => uname);
    dbms_output.put_line('sleep 10 secs');
    dbms_lock.sleep(10);
  --give it time to create the queue before we create rules

  --Add the schema apply rules
    dbms_output.put_line('adding apply rules for source &srcsdb');
    dbms_streams_adm.add_schema_rules(
      schema_name => '&sname',
      streams_type => 'APPLY',
      streams_name => '&qname._APPLY',
      queue_name => uname || '.&qname._APPLY_Q',
      include_dml => TRUE,
      include_ddl => TRUE,
      include_tagged_lcr => TRUE,
      source_database => '&srcsdb',
      inclusion_rule => TRUE,
      and_condition => NULL);
END;
/

--verify the queue and rule creation
set pagesize 150
set linesize 100

select * from dba_apply
where apply_name like upper('%&qname.%')
/

select * from dba_streams_schema_rules
where streams_type = 'APPLY'
/
```

By using the `dbms_streams_adm.add_schema_rules` procedure to add our Capture process at the source-master database, we automatically prepared our schema object SCN instantiation value. This means that the `dbms_streams_adm.add_schema_rules` already made a call to the `dbms_capture_adm.prepare_schema_instantiation` procedure for us.

If we had used `dbms_capture_adm`, we would need to call the `dbms_capture_adm.prepare_schema_instantiation` procedure explicitly.

As we used Data Pump export/import to instantiate our schema at the destination target database, the instantiation SCN has also been set for us.

If we had used other instantiation methods, we would need to call
`DBMS_APPLY_ADM.SET_TABLE_INSTANTIATION_SCN` manually.

 For more information on instantiation methods and setting the capture and apply instantiation SCN, please refer the "Instantiation and Oracle Streams Replication" chapter in your *Oracle Streams Replication Administrator's Guide*.

With our instantiation SCNs synchronized, we are now ready to start our Apply process at our destination database, our Propagation process at our source database, and finally our Capture process at our source database; in that order. We do it in this order to allow the apply and Propagation processes time to "ramp up" before getting work from the Capture process. This code is found in the `start_it_all_up.sql` script. The script runs as the `STRM_ADMIN` user and does the following:

- Connects to the destination database
- Starts the Apply process with `dbms_apply_adm.start_apply`
- Connects to the source database
- Starts the Propagation process with `dbms_aqadm.enable_propagation_schedule`
- Starts the Capture process with `dbms_capture_adm.start_capture`
- Verifies the status of the processes

First, we start at our destination database and start the Apply process.

```
--start_it_all_up.sql…
ACCEPT destdb PROMPT 'Enter Destination DB tnsalias: (ex: STRM2): '
ACCEPT stmadm PROMPT 'Enter Stream Admin username: '
ACCEPT stmadmpwd PROMPT 'Enter Stream Admin Password: '
ACCEPT srcsdb PROMPT 'Enter Source tnsalias: (ex: STRM1): '
ACCEPT qname PROMPT 'Enter Queue Name prefix: (ex: SCHEMA_HR) '

--First connect to the destination database and start the Apply
process.

PROMPT 'connecting to &destdb as &stmadm and starting &qname._APPLY'
connect &stmadm/&stmadmpwd@&destdb
BEGIN
  dbms_apply_adm.start_apply(
    apply_name => '&qname._APPLY');
```

```
    dbms_lock.sleep(10); --give it time to start
EXCEPTION WHEN OTHERS THEN
  IF sqlcode = -26666 THEN NULL;  -- APPLY process already running
  ELSE RAISE;
  END IF;
END;
/
```

Next, connect to the source database and start the Propagation process.

```
--NOTE:  this code assumes the db link name is the same as the
tnsalias
--        if this is not the case, you will need to accommodate for the
--        destination parameter in the enable_propagation_schedule call

PROMPT 'connecting to &srcsdb as &stmadm
connect &stmadm/&stmadmpwd@&srcsdb
PROMPT 'starting &qname._PROPAGATION'
BEGIN
  dbms_aqadm.enable_propagation_schedule(
    queue_name => '&stmadm..&qname._CAPTURE_Q',
    destination => '&destdb',
    destination_queue => '&stmadm..&qname._APPLY_Q');

    dbms_lock.sleep(10); --give it time to start

EXCEPTION WHEN OTHERS THEN
  IF sqlcode = -24064 THEN NULL; -- propagation already enabled
  ELSE RAISE;
  END IF;
END;
/

--Finally, start the Capture process
PROMPT starting &qname._CAPTURE'
BEGIN
  dbms_capture_adm.start_capture(
    capture_name => '&qname._CAPTURE');

  dbms_lock.sleep(10); --give it time to start
EXCEPTION WHEN OTHERS THEN
  IF sqlcode = -26666 THEN NULL;  -- CAPTURE process already running
  ELSE RAISE;
  END IF;
END;
/
```

```
select apply_name || ' is ' ||status apply_status from dba_
apply@&destdb
where apply_name like upper('%&qname.%')
/

select propagation_name || ' is ' ||status apply_status from dba_
propagation
where propagation_name like upper('%&qname.%')
/

select capture_name || ' is ' ||status apply_status from dba_capture
where capture_name like upper('%&qname.%')
/
--end code
```

The process for setting up single-source replication from STRM1 to STRM2 is now complete.

The proof is in the pudding (or propagation in this case)

Now that we have created our single source environment, let us see if it works!

We will log into SQLPlus as the HR user at our source master (STRM1) and create a record in the employee table.

We will then log into SQLPlus as the HR user at our destination target (STRM2) and see if the new record appears.

In this screenshot for our STRM1 SQLPlus session, we will do the following:

- We first show the current user and the global name of our instance to verify where we are
- We then show that there are no records in the employee table for last name "McKinnell"
- We then insert a "McKinnell" record into the employee table at STRM1 and commit

- We then show that there is now a record in the employee table for last name "McKinnell"

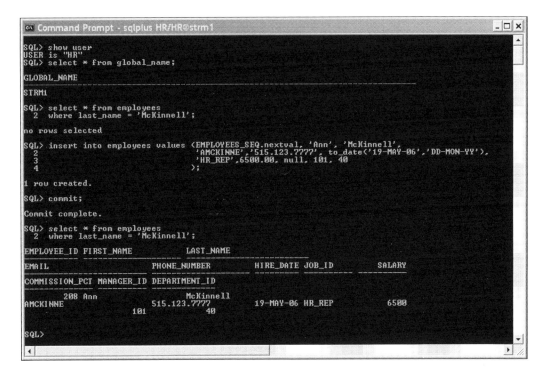

In this screenshot for our `STRM2` `SQLPlus` session, we first show the current user and the global name of our instance to verify where we are.

We then show that there are no records in the employee table that has "McKinnell" for the `last_name`.

After we insert the "McKinnell" record into the employee table at STRM1 and commit, we rerun the select at STRM2 to see if the record is now there.

```
Command Prompt - sqlplus HR/HR@strm2

SQL> show user
USER is "HR"
SQL> select * from global_name;

GLOBAL_NAME
--------------------------------------------------------------------------------
STRM2

SQL> select * from employees
  2  where last_name = 'McKinnell';

no rows selected

SQL> select * from employees
  2  where last_name = 'McKinnell';

EMPLOYEE_ID FIRST_NAME          LAST_NAME
--------------------------------------------------------------------------------
EMAIL                     PHONE_NUMBER          HIRE_DATE JOB_ID        SALARY
--------------------------------------------------------------------------------
COMMISSION_PCT MANAGER_ID DEPARTMENT_ID
--------------------------------------------------------------------------------
        208 Ann                 McKinnell
AMCKINNE                  515.123.7777          19-MAY-06 HR_REP          6500
                    101            40

SQL>
```

Voila! Our record has been replicated.

Sequences and triggers and Apply

Have you noticed there is a sequence being used for the employee ID? Aren't there special rules for replicating with sequences? There are indeed. However, in our example, they don't affect us. The LCR is created with the value generated by the sequence, not the call to the sequence itself. So, the insert statement actually sent to STRM2 has "208" hard coded as the employee ID. As this is a single source, uni-directional configuration we don't need to worry about what the other sequence is doing as it will/should never be used for values in this table. If you wish to be safe, you can even drop the table PK sequences on the destination site. However, as you will see in the next chapter, be very careful with sequences in a multi-master configuration.

What would happen if we had a before insert trigger on the table that populates the employee_id value from the local employees_seq? Would the trigger end up overwriting the "208" with the local sequence next value? In this case, it would not. The reason is that the Apply process will not fire triggers on the receiving site table by default. This keeps us from potentially duplicating changes that will be generated, captured, and propagated to the destination as a result of the same triggers firing at the source site.

Let's take this one step further. What if we are not replicating the tables that are updated by the triggers at the source site? How do those changes get made at the receiving site if the triggers aren't fired by the Apply process? To force our Apply process to fire table triggers on apply, we have to specify a special "fire flag". To do this we use the DBMS_DDL.SET_TRIGGER_FIRING_PROPERTY. This procedure accepts a trigger owner and name, and a fire_once Boolean indicating if a trigger should fire more than once. Be careful with how you interpret this Boolean. It logically acts as a double negative and can be confusing. If the value is TRUE (default), the trigger will only fire once, and thus does NOT fire if the action is a result of an Apply process. If the value is FALSE, the trigger will fire more than once allowing the Apply process to fire the trigger. So, in this particular case we want to set the fire_once value to false so the Apply process will fire the trigger.

```
exec DBMS_DDL.SET_TRIGGER_FIRING_PROPERTY
    trig_owner => 'HR',
    trig_name  => 'HRID_TRIGGER',
    fire_once  =>  FALSE);
```

 This example references a fictitious trigger. It really doesn't exist in the schema.

Other levels at which to replicate

In the example that we have used in this chapter, we replicated at the schema level. As mentioned earlier, it is possible to replicate at the table level, the tablespace level, and the entire database (also known as global).

The principle for creating the different levels of replication are pretty much the same as those we used in the schema level setup. You just use different subprograms of the DBMS_STREAMS_ADM package.

Subprogram	Description
ADD_GLOBAL_PROPAGATION_RULES Procedure	Adds global rules to the appropriate positive/negative rule set for the specified Propagation process.
	The rules propagate changes for the entire database.
	Creates the specified Propagation process if it does not exist.

Subprogram	Description
ADD_GLOBAL_RULES Procedure	Adds global rules to the appropriate positive/negative rule set for the specified Capture/Apply process.
	The rules capture/apply changes for the entire database.
	Creates the specified Capture/Apply process if it does not exist.
MAINTAIN_GLOBAL Procedure	Configures Streams replication at the database level between two databases.
	Calls ADD_GLOBAL_PROPAGATION_RULES and
	ADD_GLOBAL_RULES
	Uses Data Pump Full Export/Import to Instantiate.
ADD_SCHEMA_PROPAGATION_RULES Procedure	Adds schema level rules to the appropriate positive/negative rule set for the specified Propagation process.
	The rules propagate changes for the specified schema.
	Creates the specified Propagation process if it does not exist.
ADD_SCHEMA_RULES Procedure	Adds schema level rules to the appropriate positive/negative rule set for the specified Capture/Apply process.
	The rules capture/apply changes to the specified schema.
	Creates the specified Capture/Apply process if it does not exist.
MAINTAIN_SCHEMAS Procedure	Configures Streams replication for the specified schema(s) between two databases.
	Calls ADD_SCHEMA_PROPAGATION_RULES and
	ADD_SCHEMA_RULES
	Uses Data Pump SCHEMA Export/Import to Instantiate.
ADD_SUBSET_PROPAGATION_RULES Procedure	Adds table row level subset rules to the appropriate positive/negative rule set for the specified Propagation process.
	The rules propagate changes for the specified table row level subset data.
	Creates the specified Propagation process if it does not exist.

Subprogram	Description
ADD_SUBSET_RULES Procedure	Adds table row level subset rules to the appropriate positive/negative rule set for the specified Capture/Apply process.
	The rules capture/apply changes to the specified table row level subset data.
	Creates the specified Capture/Apply process if it does not exist.
ADD_TABLE_PROPAGATION_ RULES Procedure	Adds table rules to the appropriate positive/negative rule set for the specified Propagation process.
	The rules propagate changes to the specified table.
	Creates the specified Propagation process if it does not exist.
ADD_TABLE_RULES Procedure	Adds table rules to the appropriate positive/negative rule set for the specified Capture/Apply process.
	The rules capture/apply changes to the specified table.
	Creates the specified Capture/Apply process if it does not exist.
MAINTAIN_TABLES Procedure	Configures Streams replication for the specified table(s) between two databases.
	Calls ADD_TABLE_PROPAGATION_RULES and
	ADD_TABLE_RULES.
	Uses Data Pump Table Export/Import to Instantiate.
MAINTAIN_SIMPLE_TTS Procedure	Clones a single tablespace from the source database.
	Uses Data Pump to instantiate the tablespace at the destination database.
	Calls ADD_TABLE_PROPAGATION_RULES and
	ADD_TABLE_RULES.

 For more information on the DBMS_STREAMS_ADM package subprograms, refer to your *Oracle PL/SQL Packages and Types Reference* manual.

A note about the DBMS_STREAMS_ADM.MAINTAIN_* scripts.

These scripts can be used to generate setup scripts similar to those we have already seen in this chapter. The EM DBConsole actually makes a call to these subprograms to accomplish the Streams configuration tasks. These subprograms each go about the configuration differently, depending on parameter values and the replication level being configured. Therefore, we would recommend that before using these subprograms to configure your Streamed environment, to first run the subprogram with the `perform_actions` parameter set to FALSE so that you can generate and review the scripts to familiarize yourself with what the scripts will be doing, prior to actually doing it.

The beauty of DBMS_STREAMS_ADM.MAINTAIN_*

As mentioned earlier, the EM setup wizard generates a PL/SQL block with a call to the appropriate `DBMS_STREAMS_ADM.MAINTAIN_*` subprogram. This PL/SQL block can be run manually from SQLPLUS if you wish. These scripts can save you a lot of time and headaches.

What happens if the `DBMS_STREAMS_ADM.MAINTAIN_*` scripts fail? How do you recover? The beauty of the `DBMS_STREAMS_ADM.MAINTAIN_*` scripts is that they record their progress in the database and "know" where it left off. If the script fails, it will raise an error and add an entry in the `DBA_RECOVERABLE_SCRIPT` view (and other `DBA_RECOVERABLE_SCRIPT` views). You can then use the `DBMS_STREAMS_ADM.RECOVER_OPERATION` procedure to do the following:

- Rollback the build: This undoes the build and purges the script metadata.
- Purge the build without rolling back: Leaves everything as it is, just purges the script metadata (you will need to clean up manually: See `DBMS_STREAMS_ADM.REMOVE_STREAMS_CONFIGURATION`).
- Forward the build: You will first need to correct the error condition. The forward will start with the command that erred, and if the command is successful, it will continue the build from that point.

If you want to use the forward recover, do *not* rollback or purge.

The caveat here is that `DBMS_STREAMS_ADM.RECOVER_OPERATION` will only recover a Streams build done through a `DBMS_STREAMS_ADM.MAINTAIN_*` procedure.

The `DBMS_STREAMS_ADM.MAINTAIN_*` scripts also provide an excellent baseline with which to begin scripting a custom Streams topology.

Summary

In this chapter, we demonstrated how to set up a single-source (uni-directional) streamed environment.

We demonstrated how to use the EM DBConsole Streams "Wizard" to configure your streamed environment and/or generate scripts that you can run manually.

We walked through the steps to manually configure your streamed environment using PL/SQL code and provided code examples.

We addressed the different DBMS_STREAM_ADM subprograms that can be used to configure different levels of streaming. These being table level, schema level (as in our example), tablespace level, and global (database) level. We also touched on the use of the DBMS_STREAM_ADM.MAINTENANCE_* subprograms that are called by EM DBConsole to configure Streams and/or generate scripts, and the importance of understanding how these subprograms work "under the covers".

We also discussed sequence and trigger calls, what we can expect, and how to control them in a streamed environment.

In the next chapter, we will demonstrate how to stream both ways. Like canoeing up-stream, it takes a bit more work, but using the paddle helps.

5
N-Way Replication

Now is the real fun N-way replication. N-way replication refers to a Streams environment where there are multiple sources. In this chapter, we will still use the STRM1 and STRM2 databases but with a little twist; making both databases the source. By making both STRM1 and STRM2 sources, we need to first consider a couple of unique situations and do a little more pre-planning, specifically for N-Way replication.

The concepts and techniques used to configure a 2-way replication can then be used to scale to N-way replication. We all need to crawl before we run, the better you crawl (understand) this chapter, the easier it will be to scale up to N-way replication. Pay close attention and learn the technique so that you can implement it well.

This chapter will cover the following:

- Planning for N-way replication
- Technique to avoid conflict
- The setup
    - Configure replication from STRM1 to STRM2
    - Configure replication from STRM2 to STRM1
- Configure conflict resolution
- Expanding the example
- Rinse and repeat

Warning: In this chapter, you should be familiar with the concepts presented earlier in this book. We highly recommend that you DO NOT start with this chapter unless you have completed a couple of single-source configurations and are comfortable with the Streams processes and terms.

We need to repeat this—Streams is not Failover.

We need to repeat this—Streams is not Failover.

No, that is not a typo. The authors are passionate about Streams and want to see you successfully implement it. To successfully implement Streams, you need to know not to step into the trap of using it for Failover.

Both authors have done some work where Failover was the requirement. Streams is not a Failover solution. Failover is handled by Oracle Data Guard, *NOT* Oracle Streams. Streams is about distributing the data to multiple locations. On more than one occasion, Streams was used as a Failover technology because it can distribute data to multiple locations. Do not fall into the trap of using the wrong tool for the wrong job. Streams distributes (replicates) data. As such, there will always be some difference between the databases in a Streams environment. All replication technology has this problem. The only time where all of the databases are in sync is, when there is *no* activity and all replication has been applied to all target locations.

If you need Failover, then use the proper tool. Oracle Data Guard is for Failover. It has the necessary processes to guarantee a different level of failover from a primary site to a secondary site, whereas Streams is a Replication tool that distributes data. Just remember the following, when there is a discussion of Replication and Failover that comes up:

- Streams distributes data, it is built for replication
- Data Guard is built for Failover

Pre-planning for N-way replication

When we set up N-way replication, we must consider the possibility of a collision of data. Since we have multiple sources of data, it is possible for the exact same data to be inputted on any or all of the sources at the exact same time. When this happens, it is a conflict. This example is just one type of conflict that can happen in N-way replication environments. The types of conflict that can occur are as follows:

- **Update conflict**: When transactions from different databases try to update the same row at nearly the same time.
- **Delete conflict**: When one transaction deletes a row and the next transaction tries to update or delete the row. Transactions originate from different databases.

- **Unique conflict**: When transactions from different databases violate a primary or unique constraint, the first transaction is accepted. The second transaction obtains the conflict.
- **Foreign key conflict**: This happens when a transaction from a Source tries to insert a child record before the parent record exists.

The good news is that Oracle has provided built-in conflict resolution in Streams that solves the most common situations. The built-in solutions are as follows:

- OVERWRITE
- DISCARD
- MAXIMUM
- MINIMUM

We will provide an example of conflict resolution after we build our N-way replication. In our case, we will use MAXIMUM.

As part of the pre-planning for N-way replication, we highly suggest creating a simple table such as the Setup Table.

Avoiding conflict

As conflict requires additional pre-planning and configuration, one begins to wonder, "Are there techniques so that we can configure N-way replication without the possibility of conflict?" The simple answer to the question is "Yes". The not-so-simple answer is that there is some configuration magic that needs to be done and the devil is in the details.

Limiting who and what can be updated is one method of avoiding conflict. Think of it this way— there is no conflict if we agree to who and what can update the specific data. User 1 can only update his specific data and no one else can do that. Similarly, user 2 can only update his specific data. So, user 1 and user 2 can never cause a conflict. Now this may be a little bit difficult depending on the application. This can be implemented with the use of offset sequences. One sequence produces only odd values, and another produces only even values. We could also use a combination of sequence and some unique characteristics of the database.

The setup

Here is the big picture for this chapter. We will create a new user and tablespace to isolate all the examples used in this chapter. That user's schema will contain one table replicated between STRM1 and STRM2 database. Both STRM1 and STRM2 are sources. STRM1 is the source for STRM2 and vice-versa. The Streams Administrator will configure the Streams environment. Conflict resolution will handle the situation where the exact same data inputted on one or more sources at the same time. The conflict resolution will use the built-in MAXIMUM confliction resolution handler.

The set-up table is given as follows:

Description	Value
New User	LEARNING
Table	EMPLOYEE
New Tablespace	LEARNING
Replication Type	N-Way
Conflict Resolution	MAXIMUM
Streams Administrator	STRM_ADMIN on both STRM1 & STRM2
Databases	STRM1 & STRM2

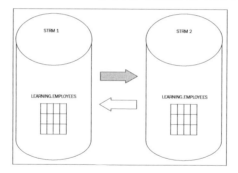

This chapter is heavy on the PL/SQL and does not use DB Control or Grid Control to set up Streams. As such, this is a deeper dive into what actually is going on under the covers. There is an extensive use of comments in the provided code and images to help you understand and visualize what Streams is doing. The set-up here is to make sure you learn, understand, and are able to implement N-way replication by providing a working example that is extendable.

All code in this chapter ran against a Beta of Oracle 11*g* R2 on both Windows and Linux 32 bit. The authors have made efforts to make the code reusable with slight modification.

Preliminary setup

Please refer to Chapter 3, *Prepare the Rafts and Secure Your Gear: The pre-work before configuring Oracle 11g Streams*, for a full explanation on how to configure the database for Streams. For this chapter, the preliminary setup involves:

On both STRM1 and STRM2:

- Create Tablespace for User "Learning"
- Create User "Learning"
- Create Table "Employees" and ADD SUPPLEMENTAL LOG
- Create Trigger on "Employees" table to record when data was inserted or updated
- Load data for table "Employees"
- If not already done
    - Create strm_admin using a DBA account.
        - Tablespace for Streams Administrator
        - Create Streams Administrator reuse from Chapter 4, *Single-Source Configuration.*
            - Clear out previous configuration
            - Drop and recreate Streams Administrator
    - Check TNSNAMES.ORA
        - The tnsnames.ora file on the STRM1 host should have an STRM2 entry
        - The tnsnames.ora file on the STRM2 host should have an STRM1 entry
    - Make sure that the parameter global_names is set to TRUE on both databases.
      ```
      select name, value
      from v$parameter
      where name = 'global_names';
      ```
    - Global names
      ```
      select * from global_name;
      ```
    - DBLINKS
        - Create Private DB link as STRM_ADMIN
- Grant permissions to Streams Administrator for the table "Employees"

`Scripts_5_1_PSU.sql` provides the setup for the above. The script does not include the steps:

- ° Check `TNSNAMES.ORA`

  - The `tnsnames.ora` file on the `STRM1` host should have an `STRM2` entry
  - The `tnsnames.ora` file on the `STRM2` host should have an `STRM1` entry

- ° Make sure that the parameter `global_names` is set to `TRUE` on both databases.

  ```
  select name,
  value from v$parameter
  where name = 'global_names';
  ```

- ° Global names

  ```
  select * from global_name;
  ```

- ° DBLINKS

  - Create Private DB Link as `STRM_ADMIN`

Carefully review `Scripts_5_1_PSU.sql` and modify what you deem appropriate. Then use an account with DBA privileges to run `Scripts_5_1_PSU.sql` script. At the minimum, you will need to modify the creation of the tablespaces.

At this point, both `STRM1` and `STRM2` are set up according to the setup table with the exception of the implementation of conflict resolution. Now, we will configure Streams first on `STRM1` then on `STRM2`. Check scripts will also be run to confirm that the configuration of Streams is going well.

In a Streams environment, you connect to more than one database at a time while performing Streams administration. To make things easier, we highly suggest changing your `glogin.sql` script located in your `$ORACLE_HOME/SQLPLUS/admin`. The following code will change the prompt from the default `SQL>` to the `USER@GLOBAL_NAME>`. In our case we will see:

STRM_ADMIN@STRM1.US.APGTECH.COM>

STRM_ADMIN@STRM2.US.APGTECH.COM>

when we are logged into `STRM1` and `STRM2` as `STRM_ADMIN` respectively.

When logged into the database as DBA, the login prompt will reflect

DBA1@STRM1.US.APGTECH.COM>

DBA1@STRM1.US.APGTECH.COM>

showing DBA1 being logged into STRM1 and STRM2 respectively.

```
----------------------------------------------------------
-- start: change the sql prompt
-- to reflect user@global_name
-- Code for modifying glogin.sql
-- Append to the end of the glogin.sql
   set termout off
   col gname new_value prompt_gname
   select global_name gname from global_name;
   set sqlprompt "&&_USER'@'prompt_gname> "
   set termout on
-- end: change the sql prompt
----------------------------------------------------------
```

STRM_ADMIN is used to run all of the scripts to set up for Streams. If necessary, a DBA account may be used. The login prompt will reflect the logged-in user and at what database. STRM_ADMIN does have DBA role and privileges, but we suggest opening a separate session and using a different user for simplicity. The code for the next two sections is in the files Scripts_5_1_STRM1_STRM2.sql and Scripts_5_1_STRM2_STRM1.sql.

Streaming STRM1 to STRM2

If you are reusing the Streams set up from Chapter 4, *Single-Source Configuration*, please run the following to clear out all previous configurations. This will destroy the previous configuration! If you are starting with a new STRM_ADMIN account with no previous configuration, skip this step.

```
STRM_ADMIN@STRM1.US.APGTECH.COM>
EXEC DBMS_STREAMS_ADM.REMOVE_STREAMS_CONFIGURATION();
```

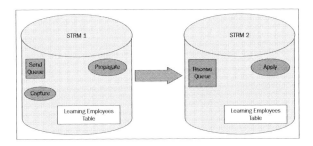

Let us step back and plan the set up of Streams between STRM1 and STRM2.

On STRM1, log in as STRM_ADMIN

-- ADD THE QUEUE: A good queue name is STREAMS_CAPTURE_Q

-- ADD THE CAPTURE RULE

-- ADD THE PROPAGATION RULE

-- INSTANTIATE TABLE ACROSS DBLINK

-- DBLINK TO DESTINATION is STRM2.US.APGTECH.COM

-- SOURCE is STRM1.US.APGTECH.COM

On STRM2 log in as STRM_ADMIN

-- ADD THE QUEUE: A good queue name is STREAMS_APPLY_Q

-- ADD THE APPLY RULE

Start everything up and test the Stream on STRM1

Then, check to see if the record is Stream'ed to STRM2.

 We take the additional step of performing a commit after each running of a procedure. Although not technically needed, we use it as a precaution.

-- On STRM1, log in as STRM_ADMIN

-- ADD THE QUEUE: A good queue name is STREAMS_CAPTURE_Q

```
-- STRM_ADMIN@STRM1.US.APGTECH.COM>
BEGIN
  DBMS_STREAMS_ADM.SET_UP_QUEUE(
    queue_table => '"STREAMS_CAPTURE_QT"',
    queue_name  => '"STREAMS_CAPTURE_Q"',
    queue_user  => '"STRM_ADMIN"');
END;
/
commit;

-- ADD THE CAPTURE RULE
-- STRM_ADMIN@STRM1.US.APGTECH.COM>
BEGIN
 DBMS_STREAMS_ADM.ADD_TABLE_RULES(
```

```
    table_name    => '"LEARNING.EMPLOYEES"',
    streams_type => 'capture',
    streams_name => '"STREAMS_CAPTURE"',
    queue_name    => '"STRM_ADMIN"."STREAMS_CAPTURE_Q"',
    include_dml   => true,
    include_ddl   => true,
    include_tagged_lcr => false,
    inclusion_rule    => true);
END;
/
commit;

-- ADD THE PROPAGATION RULE
-- STRM_ADMIN@STRM1.US.APGTECH.COM>
BEGIN
DBMS_STREAMS_ADM.ADD_TABLE_PROPAGATION_RULES(
table_name         => '"LEARNING.EMPLOYEES"',
streams_name       => '"STREAMS_PROPAGATION"',
source_queue_name =>
          '"STRM_ADMIN"."STREAMS_CAPTURE_Q"',
destination_queue_name =>
          '"STRM_ADMIN"."STREAMS_APPLY_Q"@STRM2.US.APGTECH.COM',
include_dml           => true,
include_ddl           => true,
source_database       => 'STRM1.US.APGTECH.COM',
inclusion_rule        => true);
END;
/
COMMIT;

-- INSTANTIATE TABLE ACROSS DBLINK
-- STRM_ADMIN@STRM1.US.APGTECH.COM>
DECLARE
-- Variable to hold instantiation System Change Number
  iscn  NUMBER;
BEGIN
  iscn := DBMS_FLASHBACK.GET_SYSTEM_CHANGE_NUMBER();
DBMS_APPLY_ADM.SET_TABLE_INSTANTIATION_SCN@STRM2.US.APGTECH.COM(
    source_object_name    => 'LEARNING.EMPLOYEES',
    source_database_name  => 'STRM1.US.APGTECH.COM',
    instantiation_scn     => iscn);
END;
/
COMMIT;
```

-- On STRM2 log in as STRM_ADMIN

-- ADD THE QUEUE a good queue name is STREAMS_APPLY_Q

```
-- STRM_ADMIN@STRM2.US.APGTECH.COM>
BEGIN
  DBMS_STREAMS_ADM.SET_UP_QUEUE(
    queue_table => '"STREAMS_APPLY_QT"',
    queue_name  => '"STREAMS_APPLY_Q"',
    queue_user  => '"STRM_ADMIN"');
END;
/
COMMIT;

-- ADD THE APPLY RULE
-- STRM_ADMIN@STRM2.US.APGTECH.COM>
BEGIN
  DBMS_STREAMS_ADM.ADD_TABLE_RULES(
    table_name         => '"LEARNING.EMPLOYEES"',
    streams_type       => 'apply',
    streams_name       => '"STREAMS_APPLY"',
    queue_name         => '"STRM_ADMIN"."STREAMS_APPLY_Q"',
    include_dml        => true,
    include_ddl        => true,
    include_tagged_lcr => false,
    inclusion_rule     => true);
END;
/
commit;
```

Start everything up and test.

```
-- STRM_ADMIN@STRM2.US.APGTECH.COM>
BEGIN
  DBMS_APPLY_ADM.SET_PARAMETER(
    apply_name => 'STREAMS_APPLY',
    parameter  => 'disable_on_error',
    value      => 'n');
END;
/
COMMIT;

-- STRM_ADMIN@STRM2.US.APGTECH.COM>
DECLARE
    v_started number;
```

```
BEGIN
SELECT DECODE(status, 'ENABLED', 1, 0) INTO v_started
 FROM DBA_APPLY where apply_name = 'STREAMS_APPLY';
 if (v_started = 0) then
  DBMS_APPLY_ADM.START_APPLY(apply_name => '"STREAMS_APPLY"');
 end if;
END;
/
COMMIT;

-- STRM_ADMIN@STRM1.US.APGTECH.COM>
DECLARE
    v_started number;
BEGIN
SELECT DECODE(status, 'ENABLED', 1, 0) INTO v_started
FROM DBA_CAPTURE where CAPTURE_NAME = 'STREAMS_CAPTURE';
if (v_started = 0) then
  DBMS_CAPTURE_ADM.START_CAPTURE(capture_name =>
                                '"STREAMS_CAPTURE"');
end if;
END;
/
```

Then on STRM1,

```
-- STRM_ADMIN@STRM1.US.APGTECH.COM>
ACCEPT fname  PROMPT 'Enter Your First Name:'
ACCEPT lname  PROMPT 'Enter Your Last Name:'
Insert into LEARNING.EMPLOYEES (EMPLOYEE_ID, FIRST_NAME, LAST_NAME,
TIME) Values (5, '&fname', '&lname', NULL);
dbms_lock.sleep(10); --give it time to replicate
```

 On the first record we have found that the Streams take a while to "warm up". That is why we used `dbms_lock` above. Once Streams is up and running it runs and runs and runs.

Then on STRM2, search for the record.

```
-- STRM_ADMIN@STRM2.US.APGTECH.COM>
Select * from LEARNING.EMPLOYEES;
```

If everything is working, now is a good time for a break before moving on to the next section. In the next section, we will set up the reverse STRM2 to STRM1.

Streaming STRM2 to STRM1

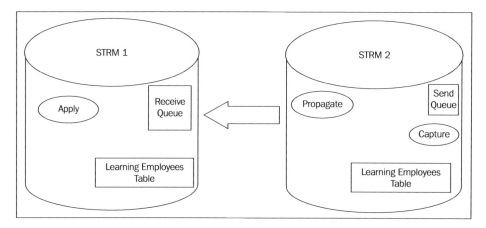

Now the plan for setting up Streams for STRM2. It is the mirror image of what we have done above, except for the test part.

On STRM2, log in as STRM_ADMIN.

-- ADD THE QUEUE, a good queue name is STREAMS_CAPTURE_Q

-- ADD THE CAPTURE RULE

-- ADD THE PROPAGATION RULE

-- INSTANTIATE TABLE ACROSS DBLINK

-- DBLINK TO DESTINATION is STRM1.US.APGTECH.COM

-- SOURCE is STRM2.US.APGTECH.COM

On STRM1 log in as STRM_ADMIN.

-- ADD THE QUEUE: A good queue name is STREAMS_APPLY_Q

-- ADD THE APPLY RULE

Start everything up and test the Stream on STRM2.

Then check to see if the record is STREAM'ed to STRM1.

-- On STRM2 log in as STRM_ADMIN

-- ADD THE QUEUE :A good queue name is STREAMS_CAPTURE_Q

```
-- STRM_ADMIN@STRM2.US.APGTECH.COM>
BEGIN
  DBMS_STREAMS_ADM.SET_UP_QUEUE(
    queue_table => '"STREAMS_CAPTURE_QT"',
    queue_name  => '"STREAMS_CAPTURE_Q"',
    queue_user  => '"STRM_ADMIN"');
END;
/
commit;

-- ADD THE CAPTURE RULE
-- STRM_ADMIN@STRM2.US.APGTECH.COM>
BEGIN
  DBMS_STREAMS_ADM.ADD_TABLE_RULES(
    table_name        => '"LEARNING.EMPLOYEES"',
    streams_type      => 'capture',
    streams_name      => '"STREAMS_CAPTURE"',
    queue_name        => '"STRM_ADMIN"."STREAMS_CAPTURE_Q"',
    include_dml       => true,
    include_ddl       => true,
    include_tagged_lcr => false,
    inclusion_rule    => true);
END;
/
commit;

-- ADD THE PROPAGATION RULE
-- STRM_ADMIN@STRM2.US.APGTECH.COM>
BEGIN
DBMS_STREAMS_ADM.ADD_TABLE_PROPAGATION_RULES(
table_name        => '"LEARNING.EMPLOYEES"',
streams_name      => '"STREAMS_PROPAGATION"',
source_queue_name =>
          '"STRM_ADMIN"."STREAMS_CAPTURE_Q"',
destination_queue_name =>
          '"STRM_ADMIN"."STREAMS_APPLY_Q"@STRM1.US.APGTECH.COM',
include_dml       => true,
include_ddl       => true,
source_database   => 'STRM2.US.APGTECH.COM',
inclusion_rule     => true);
END;
/
COMMIT;
```

Because the table was instantiated from STRM1 already, you can skip this step.

```
-- INSTANTIATE TABLE ACROSS DBLINK
-- STRM_ADMIN@STRM2.US.APGTECH.COM>
DECLARE
  iscn  NUMBER; -- Variable to hold instantiation SCN value
BEGIN
  iscn := DBMS_FLASHBACK.GET_SYSTEM_CHANGE_NUMBER();
DBMS_APPLY_ADM.SET_TABLE_INSTANTIATION_SCN@STRM1.US.APGTECH.COM(
    source_object_name     => 'LEARNING.EMPLOYEES',
    source_database_name   => 'STRM1.US.APGTECH.COM',
    instantiation_scn      => iscn);
END;
/
COMMIT;
```

-- On STRM1, log in as STRM_ADMIN.

```
-- ADD THE QUEUE, a good queue name is STREAMS_APPLY_Q
-- STRM_ADMIN@STRM1.US.APGTECH.COM>
BEGIN
  DBMS_STREAMS_ADM.SET_UP_QUEUE(
    queue_table => '"STREAMS_APPLY_QT"',
    queue_name  => '"STREAMS_APPLY_Q"',
    queue_user  => '"STRM_ADMIN"');
END;
/
COMMIT;

-- ADD THE APPLY RULE
-- STRM_ADMIN@STRM1.US.APGTECH.COM>
BEGIN
  DBMS_STREAMS_ADM.ADD_TABLE_RULES(
    table_name          => '"LEARNING.EMPLOYEES"',
    streams_type        => 'apply',
    streams_name        => '"STREAMS_APPLY"',
    queue_name          => '"STRM_ADMIN"."STREAMS_APPLY_Q"',
    include_dml         => true,
    include_ddl         => true,
    include_tagged_lcr  => false,
    inclusion_rule      => true);
END;
/
commit;
```

Start everything up and Test.

```
-- STRM_ADMIN@STRM1.US.APGTECH.COM>
BEGIN
  DBMS_APPLY_ADM.SET_PARAMETER(
    apply_name   => 'STREAMS_APPLY',
    parameter    => 'disable_on_error',
    value        => 'n');
END;
/
COMMIT;

-- STRM_ADMIN@STRM1.US.APGTECH.COM>
DECLARE
    v_started number;
BEGIN
SELECT DECODE(status, 'ENABLED', 1, 0) INTO v_started
 FROM DBA_APPLY where apply_name = 'STREAMS_APPLY';
 if (v_started = 0) then
  DBMS_APPLY_ADM.START_APPLY(apply_name => '"STREAMS_APPLY"');
 end if;
END;
/
COMMIT;

-- STRM_ADMIN@STRM2.US.APGTECH.COM>
DECLARE
    v_started number;
BEGIN
SELECT DECODE(status, 'ENABLED', 1, 0) INTO v_started
 FROM DBA_CAPTURE where CAPTURE_NAME = 'STREAMS_CAPTURE';
 if (v_started = 0) then
  DBMS_CAPTURE_ADM.START_CAPTURE(capture_name => '"STREAMS_CAPTURE"');
 end if;
END;
/
```

Then on STRM2:

```
-- STRM_ADMIN@STRM2.US.APGTECH.COM>
ACCEPT fname  PROMPT 'Enter Your Mom's First Name:'
ACCEPT lname  PROMPT 'Enter Your Mom's Last Name:'
Insert into LEARNING.EMPLOYEES (EMPLOYEE_ID, FIRST_NAME, LAST_NAME,
TIME) Values (5, '&fname', '&lname', NULL);
dbms_lock.sleep(10); --give it time to replicate
```

On the first record we have found the Streams take a while to "warm up". That is why we used `dbms_lock` above. Once Streams is up and running, it runs and runs and runs.

Then on STRM1, search for the record.

```
-- STRM_ADMIN@STRM1.US.APGTECH.COM>
Select * from LEARNING.EMPLOYEES;
```

We now have N-way replication.

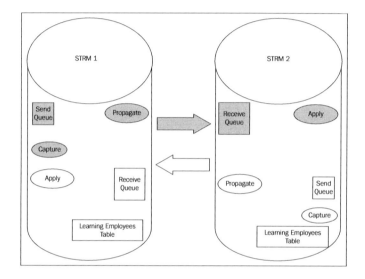

But wait, what about conflict resolution?

Good catch; all of this was just to set up N-way replication. In this case, it is a 2-way replication. It will work the majority of the time; that is until there is conflict. Conflict resolution needs to be set up and in this example the supplied/built-in conflict resolution handler MAXIMUM will be used. Now, let us cause some CONFLICT! Then we will be good people and create the conflict resolution and ask for world peace while we are at it!

Conflict resolution

Conflict between User 1 and User 2 has happened. Unbeknown to both of them, they have both inserted the exact same row of data to the same table, at roughly the same time. User 1's insert is to the STRM1 database. User 2's insert is to the STRM2 database.

Normally the transaction that arrives second will raise an error. It is most likely that the error will be some sort of primary key violation and that the transaction will fail. We do not want that to happen. We want the transaction that arrives last to "win" and be committed to the database.

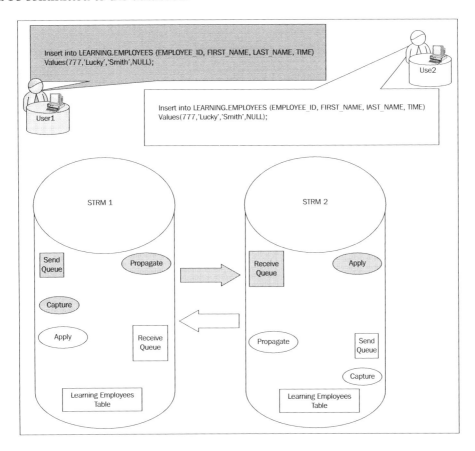

At this point, you may be wondering "How do I choose which conflict resolution to use?" Well, you do not get to choose, the Business Community that you support will determine the rules most of the time. They will tell you how they want conflict resolution handled. Your responsibility is to know what can be solved with built-in conflict resolutions and when you will need to create custom conflict resolution.

Going back to User 1 and User 2. In this particular case, User 2's insert arrives later than User 1's insert. Now the conflict resolution is added using the DBMS_APPLY_ADM package, specifically the procedure DBMS_APPLY_ADM.SET_UPDATE_CONFLICT_ HANDLER which instructs the APPLY process on how to handle the conflict.

`Scripts_5_1_CR.sql` shows the conflict resolution used to resolve the conflict between User 1 and User 2. Since it is part of the APPLY process, this script is run by the Streams Administrator. In our case, that would be STRM_ADMIN. This type of conflict can occur on either STRM1 or STRM2 database, so the script will be run on both databases. The numbers to the left are there for reference reasons. They are not in the provided code.

```
-- Scripts_5_1_CR.sql

1.  DECLARE
2.  cols DBMS_UTILITY.NAME_ARRAY;
3.  BEGIN
4.  cols(0) := 'employee_id';
5.  cols(1) := 'first_name';
6.  cols(2) := 'last_name';
7.  cols(3) := 'time';
8.  DBMS_APPLY_ADM.SET_UPDATE_CONFLICT_HANDLER(
9.  object_name => 'learning.employees',
10. method_name => 'MAXIMUM',
11. resolution_column => 'time',
12. column_list => cols);
13. END;
14. /
15. Commit;
```

So what do these 15 magical lines do to resolve conflict?

Let us break it down piece by piece logically first, and look at the specific syntax of the code. Oracle needs to know where to look when a conflict happens. In our example, that is the `learning.employees` table. Furthermore, Oracle needs more than just the table name. It needs to know what columns are involved. Line 9 informs Oracle of the table. Lines 1 -7 relate to the columns. Line 8 is the actual procedure name.

What Oracle is supposed to do when this conflict happens, is answered by Line 10. Line 10 instructs Oracle to take the MAXIMUM of the `resolution_column` and use that to resolve the conflict. Since our resolution column is `time`, the last transaction to arrive is the "winner" and is applied.

Extending the example

This chapter has covered the concepts needed to implement N-way replication. The provided code made it tangible. Now, what does it take to go to the next level?

Start with the conflicts. In this case we used the built-in MAXIMUM conflict resolution handler. In your case, start with the business units that you are supporting and learn the business use cases. Then drive down to the tables involved in the transactions from the uses cases. Setting up conflict resolution is implemented at the table level. But you need to think at the transaction level.

The example in this chapter is for a table. Taking this skeleton code you can move up to schema level by using the related schema-level procedure. For example, we used the following in this chapter:

Table level:

```
DBMS_STREAMS_ADM.ADD_TABLE_RULES
DBMS_STREAMS_ADM.ADD_TABLE_PROPAGATION_RULES
DBMS_APPLY_ADM.SET_TABLE_INSTANTIATION_SCN
DBMS_STREAMS_ADM.ADD_TABLE_RULES
```

by changing it to Schema level:

```
DBMS_STREAMS_ADM.ADD_SCHEMA_RULES
DBMS_STREAMS_ADM.ADD_SCHEMA_PROPAGATION_RULES
DBMS_APPLY_ADM.SET_SCHEMA_INSTANTIATION_SCN
DBMS_STREAMS_ADM.ADD_SCHEMA_RULES
```

By making minor syntax changes, you can quickly start Stream'ing at the schema level. Please refer to Chapter 4 on using Data Pump to export and import a schema.

Rinse and repeat

You may have noticed that setting up Streams for N-way replication can be confusing. We suggest that you establish the conflict resolution solution with the business units first. Then document it with something as simple as the setup table. Remember to plan thinking about the transaction and then implement conflict resolution at table level. Your implementation documentation should be both visual and in text. During the actual implementation, start with one host and complete and test before moving to the next host.

Summary

Building N-way replication is about making sure it is exactly what you need. Misusing N-way replication as a Failover technology is a trap that you need to avoid at all cost. Remember, replication is about distributing data while Failover (technology) is about disaster recovery.

Planning for N-way replication starts with conflict resolution. Working with your Business Units is a must, and setting and managing expectations needs to be done before any discussion of implementation. The use of Use Case scenarios driven down to transactions, then to tables involved in those transactions is one method to promote discussions with the Business Units.

Document your solution prior to implementation. Use the documentation as your implementation plan. Implementing N-way replication is easy when you are organized and have the steps defined and in order ahead of time. As part of the documentation/implementation plan, we recommend the use of a simple table, such as the Setup Table, and deciding ahead of time the order of implementation. This answers the question of "Where do we start and what next?" So, identify which host to start with and the order of implementation is important to avoid confusion during implementation.

Now, go and take a break before going into Chapter 6, *Get Fancy with Streams Advanced Configurations*, which looks at advanced configurations.

6

Get Fancy with Streams Advanced Configurations

Our previous chapters have presented examples for configuring your basic Streams environments. The configuration ensures the flow of data remains calm and consistent. Now that we have gotten our feet wet in the calm of the current, we understand the underlying principles that we can now build on to move into some white water. This chapter reviews the advanced functionality of Oracle Streams that provides flexibility and maneuverability of data throughout a diverse environment. Please note here that the Authors' intent is to provide a quick reference to these functionalities. In order to attempt to present the myriad of possible scenarios that can be addressed with these functionalities would be similar to attempting to empty Lake Michigan with a two gallon bucket! While the thought of seeing in how many ways we can combine these advanced features to create a totally awesome "water park" of Streams is tempting, the Authors have opted to provide an overview of the advanced features of Streams, with some basic examples of usage, and direction to Oracle documentation allowing our readers to choose which eddies, rapids, and forks they wish to further explore.

In this chapter, we take a quick look at the following advanced features of Streams:

- Synchronous Capture
- Subsetting
- Tags
- Rules (basic structure and user defined)
- Down-Stream Capture
- Streams change tables
- Automated propagation split and merge
- Heterogeneous replication basics
- XSTREAMS basics

Many of the advanced features addressed in this chapter have been introduced in Chapter 1, *All the Pieces: The Parts of an Oracle 11g Streams Environment*. Understanding how each feature interacts with the Streams' core components and other features is paramount to not only successfully implementing the feature in your design, but also in controlling the result.

Synchronous Capture—straight to the Queue

As mentioned in Chapter 1, Synchronous Capture allows you to capture a DML data change (insert, update, delete, and merge) at the source when it is committed, rather than having LogMiner capture the change from the redo. While this can provide performance gains, it does so at the cost of some flexibility; as seen in the restrictions listed in Chapter 1. But remember, Synchronous Capture is NOT Synchronous replication as we explain in Chapter 1.

A Synchronous Capture process is a Streams client that uses internal mechanisms (think table triggers) to capture DML changes at the time they are committed to a table. The DML change is converted to an LCR format and enqueued to the capture queue. To avoid duplicating the capture of the same DML, it is highly recommended that you do not configure Synchronous Capture and regular Capture on the same table.

Synchronous Capture rules can only be added to a ruleset via DBMS_STREAMS_ADM.ADD_TABLE_RULES or DBMS_STREAMS_ADM.ADD_TABLE_RULES. Attempts to create or add Synchronous Capture rules with any other package procedure will cause the rules to be ignored. For a Synchronous Capture rule, you specify sync_capture as the value for the streams_type parameter.

Synchronous Capture rules can only be added to positive rulesets (inclusion_rule = TRUE).

```
BEGIN
  DBMS_STREAMS_ADM.ADD_TABLE_RULES (
    table_name      =>  'hr.employees',
    streams_type    =>  'sync_capture',
    streams_name    =>  'capture_sync1',
    queue_name      =>  'strm_admin.HR_CAPTURE_Q',
    include_dml     =>  TRUE,
    inclusion_rule  =>  TRUE    --default
  );
END;
/
```

The above creates a Synchronous Capture Ruleset with the name of RULESET$_122 and Synchronous Capture with the name CAPTURE_SYNC1. Please note that in your environment, you may have a different numeric value for your ruleset. You can view information for Synchronous Capture using the DBA_SYNC_CAPTURE view:

```
SQL> select * from dba_sync_capture;

CAPTURE_NAME                    QUEUE_NAME                      QUEUE_
OWNER
------------------------------- ------------------------------- ---------
-------------
RULE_SET_NAME                   RULE_SET_OWNER                  CAPTURE_
USER
------------------------------- ------------------------------- --------
---
CAPTURE_SYNC1                   HR_CAPTURE_Q                    STRM_
ADMIN
RULESET$_122                    STRM_ADMIN                      STRM_
ADMIN
```

We also see a new rule, EMPLOYEES121 associated with the ruleset in DBA_RULE_SET_RULES:

```
SQL> select rule_set_owner, rule_set_name, rule_owner,
  2  rule_name, rule_set_rule_enabled, rule_set_rule_comment
  3  from dba_rule_set_rules
  4  where rule_set_name = 'RULESET$_122'
  5  ;
RULE_SET_OWNER  RULE_SET_NAME   RULE_OWNER
--------------- --------------- ---------------
RULE_NAME                       RULE_SET
------------------------------- --------
RULE_SET_RULE_COMMENT
-----------------------------------------------
STRM_ADMIN      RULESET$_122    STRM_ADMIN
EMPLOYEES121                    ENABLED
"STRM_ADMIN"."RULESET$_122"
```

And the EMPLOYEES121 rule information in DBA_RULES

```
SQL> select rule_owner, rule_name, rule_condition
  2  from dba_rules where rule_name = 'EMPLOYEES121';

RULE_OWNER      RULE_NAME
--------------- ---------------------
RULE_CONDITION
----------------------------------
```

```
STRM_ADMIN        EMPLOYEES121
(((:dml.get_object_owner() = 'HR' and
:dml.get_object_name() = 'EMPLOYEES'))
 and :dml.is_null_tag() = 'Y' )
```

Rulesets can be assigned to one or more Oracle Streams Clients. If you wish to assign a Synchronous Capture ruleset to additional Oracle Synchronous capture clients, once it has been created using one of the two above-mentioned DBMS_STREAMS_ADM and rule procedures, you can use the DBMS_CAPTURE_ADM.ALTER_SYNC_CAPTURE to add that ruleset to the specified Synchronous Capture client as well.

```
BEGIN
  DBMS_CAPTURE_ADM.ALTER_SYNC_CAPTURE(
    capture_name  => 'CAPTURE_SYNC2',
    rule_set_name => 'RULESET$_122');
END;
/
```

 Note: CAPTURE_SYNC2 would be Synchronous Capture process previously created using the DBMS_STREAMS_ADM.ADD_TABLE_RULES or the DBMS_STREAMS_ADM.ADD_SUBSET_RULES.

Once a Synchronous Capture ruleset is created, its conditions can be modified using the DBMS_RULE_ADM package.

 WARNING: Do not modify the :dml.get_object_name and :dml.get_object_owner conditions of a Synchronous Capture rule. This could cause the Synchronous Capture rule to not capture changes. However, other conditions can be added, deleted, or modified as desired.

As with regular capture, there can be only one capture user associated with a Synchronous Capture client. That capture user for Synchronous Capture requires explicit execute privileges to perform any custom rule-based transformations (this includes all transformation functions and all packages/procedures/functions invoked by any transformation functions), execute privilege on the synchronous capture rule set, and enqueue privileges on the associated capture queue.

If you decide that you wish to remove a Synchronous Capture rule from a ruleset, you can do so by using the DBMS_STREAMS_ADM.REMOVE_RULE procedure.

```
BEGIN
  DBMS_STREAMS_ADM.REMOVE_RULE(
    rule_name      => 'EMPLOYEES121',
    streams_type   => 'sync_capture',
```

```
      streams_name      => 'capture_sync2',
   );
END;
/
```

You can convert a regular Capture process to a Synchronous Capture process and vice versa, but restrictions do apply. For information on these restrictions, please refer to the *Switching From a Capture Process to a Synchronous Capture* and *Switching from a Synchronous Capture to a Capture Process* sections of Chapter 15, in the *Oracle Streams Concepts and Administration Guide*.

> For more information on Synchronous Capture, please refer to the *Implicit Capture with Synchronous Capture* section in Chapter 2, *Managing a Synchronous Capture* section in Chapter 15, and *Monitoring a Synchronous Capture* section in Chapter 24 of the *Oracle Streams Concepts and Administration Manual 11gR2*. For more information on the DBMS_ STREAMS_ADM and DBMS_CAPTURE_ADM subprograms mentioned, please refer to the *Oracle PL/SQL Packages and Types References Manual*.

Subsetting—the micro side of replication

In the previous chapters, we looked at replicating whole table via table level and schema level replication. There may be times when you only what to replicate a subset of rows in a table to a site. Say for instance, your corporate headquarter's database has HR table data for all departments, but you only want to send HR data specific to location_id to that location's database. You can do this with subsetting rules. Subsetting is considered a table level replication, but includes a filter parameter that is applied to the process to include only those LCRs that meet that filter criteria. Along with the ADD GLOBAL, SCHEMA, and TABLE rules of the DBMS_STREAMS_ADM package, the ADD_SUBSET_RULE can be defined for the Capture, Propagation, and/or Apply process.

Subsetting will generate rather complex rule_conditions depending on the dml operation it is associated with. Because of this, it is recommended that Subset rules only be assigned to positive rulesets. Assigning Subset rules to negative rule sets could yield unexpected results.

An example use of the ADD_SUBSET_RULE is described below.

The HR.EMPLOYEES table has a department column DEPARTMENT_ID that references the HR.DEPARTMENTS table. The HR.DEPARTMENTS table in turn has a column that references the HR.LOCATIONS table.

Depending on how you have configured your Streams environment and your business rules, you may find that it is more advantageous to put the subset rule on the Propagation process, rather than the Apply process. Or you may find it more advantageous to put the subset rule on the Capture process. It all depends on what is most efficient for your environment. For our example, we are going to assume that we have created a capture queue (1500_CAPT_Q) that captures changes only for a particular location—let's pick San Francisco, whose location ID is 1500. For the HR.EMPLOYEE table, we only want to capture HR records that are associated with LOCATION_ID 1500 for our capture queue 1500_CAPT_Q.

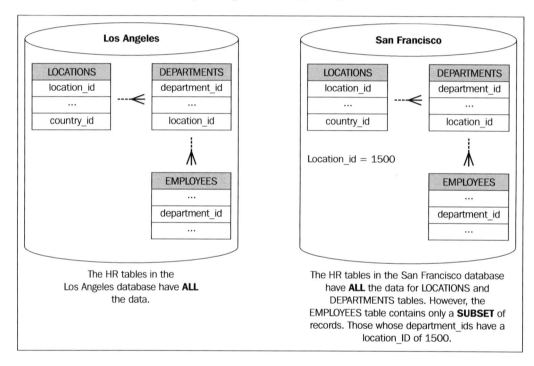

The HR tables in the
Los Angeles database have **ALL**
the data.

The HR tables in the San Francisco database
have **ALL** the data for LOCATIONS and
DEPARTMENTS tables. However, the
EMPLOYEES table contains only a **SUBSET** of
records. Those whose department_ids have a
location_ID of 1500.

The main thing to keep in mind here is that the dml_condition works best with simpler evaluations formatted as they would be for the where clause of a SQL statement, but just not actually including the where key word. You also want the evaluation field(s) to be in the table you are sub-setting. Also make sure that supplemental logging has been enabled for the fields referenced in the dml_condition. We will see why when we look at the actual rule condition created. Now, if the table we were sub-setting were the HR.DEPARTMENTS table, we could simply supply the dml_condition as such:

```
dml_condition => 'location_id = 1500'
```

But not so fast (in a couple of ways)! The table we want to sub-set is the
HR.EMPLOYEES table. It does not have a location_id. It does have a department_id
from which we can derive the location_id, but it is a table "down the line". So, for
a select statement to yield a result to determine if an employee record belongs to
location_id 1500, we would need something like this in the where clause:

```
department_id in (select department_id
                  from hr.departments
                  where location_id = 1500)
```

Unfortunately the dml_condition does not handle complex filters such as this very
well at all. Thus, we have to simplify the call for the dml_condition and allow it
to return an "easy" value to evaluate. Sounds like a job for Super-Function! We can
create a function that returns Y if the employee_id is related to the location id we are
looking for, and N if it is not. We can then pass in the simplified function call with
desired return value to the dml_condition to include in the rule_condition just
as we might in the where clause of a SQL statement. Please note, even though the
dml_condition is in a simplified format, you may still experience a noticeable
slow-down of change capture (the other part of the "not so fast"—it really can be
"not so fast"). It is highly recommended that you test the performance of a complex
capture such as this and determine if performance impacts are acceptable. If not,
look at using Tags (discussed later) and and_conditions as alternatives.

The complete code to set up a Single-Source Subsetting on the HR.EMPLOYEE table
can be found in the SubSetting.sql code file. In the following discussion, we are
only going to delve into the creation of the Subset Capture process creation to get a
good understanding of how the dml_condition can be used for complex conditions.
So, synch up your life-vest; here we go.

First we want to make sure the capture user STRM_ADMIN has the necessary privileges
to select the data in question via PL/SQL. This means explicitly granting all
privileges on HR.EMPLOYEES, HR.DEPARTMETNS, AND HR.LOCATIONS to STRM_ADMIN.
If STRM_ADMIN were only to be the Capture user, then the SELECT privileges on the
above tables would suffice.

```
grant all on hr.employees to strm_admin;
grant all on hr.departments to strm_admin;
grant all on hr.locations to strm_admin;
```

Next, we create a function under the STRM_ADMIN schema that performs the complex evaluation for us and returns either a Y if the employee_id belongs to location_id 1500, and N if it does not. The function will also return N in the case of error. To make the function **reusable**, we will also pass in the location_id value we want to evaluate against so that it is not limited to just 1500. If you choose to create the function under a different schema, be sure to explicitly grant EXECUTE on the function to the STRM_ADMIN user. Using a PL/SQL function allows us to code the complex SQL needed to return the location_id associated with the employee_id in question. The employee_id is a column in the HR.EMPLOYEE table, so we use it in the dml_condition to pass to the function. We could use the department_id instead, but let's stick with the employee_id for this example:

```
create or replace function chk_emp_loc (hrid in number,
                                        schkloc in number)
return varchar2 is get_loc number;
begin
  select location_id into get_loc from hr.departments
  where department_id = (select department_id from hr.employees
                         where employee_id = hrid);
  if get_loc = chkloc then
    return 'Y';
  else
    return 'N';
  end if;
  exception
    when others then
      return 'N';
end;
/
```

Now, all we have to do is use the evaluation of the function return value in the dml_condition. We create our Subset Rule as follows:

```
BEGIN
DBMS_STREAMS_ADM.ADD_SUBSET_RULES(
table_name        => 'hr.employees',
dml_condition     => 'strm_admin.chk_emp_loc(employee_id, 1500) =
''Y''',
streams_type      => 'capture',
streams_name      => 'capture_1500',
queue_name        => 'STRM_ADMIN.HR_CAPTURE_Q',
include_tagged_lcr => false,
source_database   => 'STRM1');
END;
/
```

You may have noticed that the ADD_SUBSET_RULES procedure has three out
parameters at the end of the procedure. These allow the procedure to report back the
DML rule names created should you wish to view them after the rules are created. The
procedure itself is an overloaded procedure (as shown below). If you do not need
this information, you can simply leave them out of the parameter list:

```
DBMS_STREAMS_ADM.ADD_SUBSET_RULES(
    table_name          IN    VARCHAR2,
    dml_condition       IN    VARCHAR2,
    streams_type        IN    VARCHAR2 DEFAULT 'apply',
    streams_name        IN    VARCHAR2 DEFAULT NULL,
    queue_name          IN    VARCHAR2 DEFAULT 'streams_queue',
    include_tagged_lcr  IN    BOOLEAN DEFAULT FALSE,
    source_database     IN    VARCHAR2 DEFAULT NULL,
    insert_rule_name    OUT   VARCHAR2,
    update_rule_name    OUT   VARCHAR2,
    delete_rule_name    OUT   VARCHAR2);
DBMS_STREAMS_ADM.ADD_SUBSET_RULES(
    table_name          IN    VARCHAR2,
    dml_condition       IN    VARCHAR2,
    streams_type        IN    VARCHAR2 DEFAULT 'apply',
    streams_name        IN    VARCHAR2 DEFAULT NULL,
    queue_name          IN    VARCHAR2 DEFAULT 'streams_queue',
    include_tagged_lcr  IN    BOOLEAN  DEFAULT FALSE,
    source_database     IN    VARCHAR2 DEFAULT NULL);
```

Once you have created the Sub-Setting Rule for the table, you can view the
sub-setting condition as well as the rule_condition generated in the
DBA_STREAMS_TABLE_RULES view:

```
set long 1000
column rule_condition format a75;

select streams_name, table_owner || '.' || table_name tablename,
       subsetting_operation action, rule_name, dml_condition,
       rule_condition
 from dba_streams_table_rules
 where streams_name = 'CAPTURE_1500'
 order by rule_name;

STREAMS_NAME     TABLENAME           ACTION RULE_NAME
---------------  --------------      ------ --------------

DML_CONDITION||CHR(13)||CHR(10)
-----------------------------------------------------------

RULE_CONDITION
-----------------------------------------------------------
```

```
CAPTURE_1500    HR.EMPLOYEES    INSERT EMPLOYEES127
strm_admin.chk_emp_loc(employee_id, 1500) = 'Y'
:dml.get_object_owner()='HR' AND :dml.get_object_name()=
'EMPLOYEES' AND :dml.is_null_tag()='Y' AND :dml.get_source_datab
ase_name()='STRM1' AND :dml.get_command_type() IN ('UPDATE',
'INSERT') AND (:dml.get_value('NEW','"EMPLOYEE_ID"') IS NOT
NULL) AND ("STRM_ADMIN"."CHK_EMP_LOC"(:dml.get_value('NEW','
"EMPLOYEE_ID"').AccessNumber(),1500)='Y') AND (:dml.get_comm
and_type()='INSERT' OR ((:dml.get_value('OLD','"EMPLOYEE_ID"
') IS NOT NULL) AND NOT EXISTS (SELECT 1 FROM SYS.DUAL WHERE
 ("STRM_ADMIN"."CHK_EMP_LOC"(:dml.get_value('OLD','"EMPLOYEE
_ID"').AccessNumber(),1500)='Y'))))


CAPTURE_1500    HR.EMPLOYEES    UPDATE EMPLOYEES128
strm_admin.chk_emp_loc(employee_id, 1500) = 'Y'
:dml.get_object_owner()='HR' AND :dml.get_object_name()=
'EMPLOYEES' AND :dml.is_null_tag()='Y' AND :dml.get_source_datab
ase_name()='STRM1' AND :dml.get_command_type()='UPDATE' AND
(:dml.get_value('NEW','"EMPLOYEE_ID"') IS NOT NULL) AND (:dm
l.get_value('OLD','"EMPLOYEE_ID"') IS NOT NULL) AND ("STRM_A
DMIN"."CHK_EMP_LOC"(:dml.get_value('OLD','"EMPLOYEE_ID"').Ac
cessNumber(),1500)='Y') AND ("STRM_ADMIN"."CHK_EMP_LOC"(:dml
.get_value('NEW','"EMPLOYEE_ID"').AccessNumber(),1500)='Y')


CAPTURE_1500    HR.EMPLOYEES    DELETE EMPLOYEES129
strm_admin.chk_emp_loc(employee_id, 1500) = 'Y'
:dml.get_object_owner()='HR' AND :dml.get_object_name()=
'EMPLOYEES' AND :dml.is_null_tag()='Y' AND :dml.get_source_datab
ase_name()='STRM1' AND :dml.get_command_type() IN ('UPDATE',
'DELETE') AND (:dml.get_value('OLD','"EMPLOYEE_ID"') IS NOT
NULL) AND ("STRM_ADMIN"."CHK_EMP_LOC"(:dml.get_value('OLD','
"EMPLOYEE_ID"').AccessNumber(),1500)='Y') AND (:dml.get_comm
and_type()='DELETE' OR ((:dml.get_value('NEW','"EMPLOYEE_ID"
') IS NOT NULL) AND NOT EXISTS (SELECT 1 FROM SYS.DUAL WHERE
 ("STRM_ADMIN"."CHK_EMP_LOC"(:dml.get_value('NEW','"EMPLOYEE
_ID"').AccessNumber(),1500)='Y'))))
```

Let's examine the UPDATE action `rule_condition` (we will get into rules in more depth later in the chapter): each condition must evaluate to TRUE for the rule to capture the change (Positive Rule Set). Each condition acts very much like the conditions in a SQL statement WHERE clause, and could be considered synonymous with the WHERE clause.

The first conditions are pretty straight forward. The change has to be an UPDATE for the HR.EMPLOYEE table, with a null tag, and source database being STRM1.

```
:dml.get_object_owner()='HR' AND
:dml.get_object_name()='EMPLOYEES' AND
:dml.is_null_tag()='Y' AND
:dml.get_source_database_name()='STRM1' AND :dml.get_command_
type()='UPDATE'
```

The next set of evaluations, as stated in the following, check to make sure the primary key column has a value:

```
AND
(:dml.get_value('NEW','"EMPLOYEE_ID"') IS NOT NULL) AND
(:dml.get_value('OLD','"EMPLOYEE_ID"') IS NOT NULL)
```

And finally, our dml_condition evaluation. Notice the column employee_id has been extended to use the LCR$_ROW_RECORD Type nomenclature.

```
AND
("STRM_ADMIN"."CHK_EMP_LOC"(:dml.get_value('OLD','"EMPLOYEE_ID"').
AccessNumber(),1500)='Y') AND
("STRM_ADMIN"."CHK_EMP_LOC"(:dml.get_value('NEW','"EMPLOYEE_ID"').
AccessNumber(),1500)='Y')
```

For more information on LRC Types and Member functions, please refer to the *Logical Change Record Types* chapter in the *Oracle Database PL/SQL Packages and Types Reference Manual*.

You will see more verbose checking on the primary key columns with the INSERT and DELETE statements to address additional existing record checks. It is possible for an UPDATE statement to be converted into an INSERT or DELETE statement depending on the situation.

For more information on Subset rule evaluation for different DML operations, please refer to the DBMS_STREAMS_ADM. ADD_SUBSET_RULES usage notes in the Oracle Database PL/SQL Packages and Types Reference Manual.

The resulting Capture should capture only those changes for `location_id` 1500 that can then be propagated to the Location 1500 database and applied.

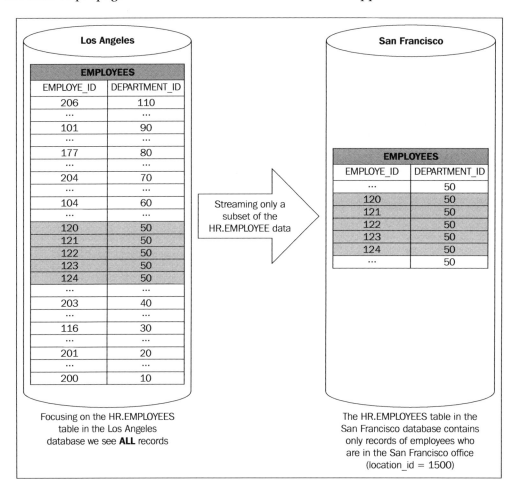

Focusing on the HR.EMPLOYEES table in the Los Angeles database we see **ALL** records

The HR.EMPLOYEES table in the San Francisco database contains only records of employees who are in the San Francisco office (location_id = 1500)

Because Sub-Setting is at the table level, you will want to do this for every table in the HR schema for which you wish to subset data by the `location_id`. The previous example is just one such example.

Tag!—you're it

For eons, mankind has used a wonderful, yet simplistic method to mark, differentiate, and/or identify objects. What is this method? They put a tag on it. We put tags on retail merchandise to mark a price, size, inventory id, and so on. We put little tags on maps to show where something of significance has happened. We put tags on presents. We even put tags on toes (morbid, but true). Whatever the reason may be, we tag it. These tags make it easier for us to identify something "special" about the object. Oracle Streams is no different. Streams uses tags on LCRs to help the various Streams processes identify changes that need "special" handling. This tag is of a raw data type and can store a value up to 2000 bytes. If you are familiar with the use of the DBMS_REPUTIL.FROM_REMOTE procedure in advanced replication triggers, you are already familiar with the default usage for a Streams tag.

The default behaviour of tags

Every entry in the redo logs has a tag associated with it. The default value of the tag is set to null when a change is recorded in the redo. When the Capture process evaluates a change it has retrieved from the redo, by default it looks for a null value tag. If the tag is null, the Capture process builds an LCR from the change. When the Capture process builds an LCR from a redo transaction, it includes the null value of the tag. When the LCR is propagated and applied at the receiving site, the Apply process does something special to set the value of the tag that will be included with the redo log entry that resulted from the Apply process of the change at the target database. The Apply process sets the value of the redo tag to the hexadecimal equivalent of "00"—double zero (how you ask? the dbms_streams.set_tag procedure might be a clue here—more on this in the next section). Now, if there is a Capture process at the Apply site, the change is ignored because it has a non-null tag value. Thus Streams gives us a default mechanism that keeps the change from cycling back to the source from whence it came. Just like the DBMS_REPUTIL.FROM_REMOTE procedure call in the advanced replication trigger.

Making tags work for you

You can set the value of a redo entry tag either when the original change is recorded in the redo log at the source database, or when the Apply process applies the change at the destination database. You can also configure your capture, propagate, and Apply processes to evaluate the value of the tag to determine if the process should or should not process the LCR at that stage of the replication. You can also reference these tag values in rules and apply handlers. This allows a great amount of flexibility with how you can manipulate an LCR throughout the replication process based on that tag value. To capture or not to capture; where to propagate; what to apply and how. The combinations are limited only by your imagination (ok, that and the statistical limit of values that can be set, but hey there's a lot you can do in 2000 bytes).

Setting the tag value

You can set the value of a tag at the time the change is made at the source database by first calling the DBMS_STREAMS.SET_TAG function for the session, and then making the change.

```
Begin
  DBMS_STREAMS.SET_TAG(HEXTORAW('22'));
  Insert into oe.promotions values (3,'Local Sale');
  Commit;
End;
/
```

You can also set the value of the tag for the change at the apply site by specifying a value for the APPLY_TAG with the DBMS_APPLY_ADM.CREATE_APPLY or DBMS_APPLY_ADM.ALTER_APPLY procedures:

```
DBMS_APPLY_ADM.CREATE_APPLY(
    queue_name               IN   VARCHAR2,
    apply_name               IN   VARCHAR2,
    rule_set_name            IN   VARCHAR2   DEFAULT NULL,
    message_handler          IN   VARCHAR2   DEFAULT NULL,
    ddl_handler              IN   VARCHAR2   DEFAULT NULL,
    apply_user               IN   VARCHAR2   DEFAULT NULL,
    apply_database_link      IN   VARCHAR2   DEFAULT NULL,
    apply_tag                IN   RAW        DEFAULT '00',
    apply_captured           IN   BOOLEAN    DEFAULT FALSE,
    precommit_handler        IN   VARCHAR2   DEFAULT NULL,
    negative_rule_set_name   IN   VARCHAR2   DEFAULT NULL,
    source_database          IN   VARCHAR2   DEFAULT NULL);
```

Notice that the default for the apply_tag parameter is '00' for the CREATE_APPLY procedure, as we discussed earlier in this chapter:

```
DBMS_APPLY_ADM.ALTER_APPLY(
                       apply_name IN  VARCHAR2,
                       apply_tag  IN  RAW DEFAULT NULL);
```

Notice that the default for the apply_tag parameter is null for the ALTER_APPLY procedure. This means that if you do not explicitly supply a value, the parameter value will not be changed. It does not mean that the value will be changed to null. This being the case, what if you really want the value of the tag to be null? This is where the remove_apply_tag parameter steps up:

```
DBMS_APPLY_ADM.ALTER_APPLY(
                    apply_name          IN   VARCHAR2,
                    remove_apply_tag    IN   BOOLEAN DEFAULT FALSE);
```

If the `remove_apply_tag` is set to true, then the Apply process sets the value of the tag to null when it generates redo. This comes in very handy when you want to configure an "apply forward" directed network streamed configuration.

If the `remove_apply_tag` is set to false (the default), then the apply sets the tag to the value specified for the `apply_tag` parameter.

Evaluating tags at the replication process rule level

When you configure capture, propagation, and Apply processes, you are actually adding rule conditions. These rules tell the process of how to handle an LCR. As mentioned earlier, if created with one of the `DBMS_STREAMS_ADM.ADD_*_RULE`, by default, the capture, propagate, and Apply processes only handle LCR's with null tags, and the Apply processes sets the tag to '00' when it applies a change. First, you want to tell the rule that you want non-null tagged LCRs considered as well as null tags (not ignored as is the default). You do this with the `INCLUDE_TAGGED_LCR`. Next, you want to make sure the rule knows not to let the non-null tag override the expected behavior of the rule set evaluation. You do this with the `INCLUSION_RULE` parameter. Finally, you let the rule know what the evaluation on the non-null tag should be. This is set by the `AND_CONDITION` parameter. Let's dig into this a little deeper.

INCLUDE_TAGGED_LCR

This parameter tells the process whether or not to consider non-null tagged LCR's for replication.

If the value is set to `FALSE`, the rule includes a condition for the process to only look for LCRs with a null tag. If the tag is not null, then ignore the LCR.

If the value is set to `TRUE`, the rule is for the process to consider null and non-null tags. In actuality, it removes the piece of the rule that evaluates if the tag is set, thus making all tags a candidate for additional rule evaluation.

Make sure associated Capture, Propagate, and Apply processes have the same `INCLUDE_TAGGED_LCR` value. If these values are not synchronized between the associated processes, non-null tagged LCR's may be ignored when expected to be replicated, leading to unexpected behavior from one process to the next.

INCLUSION_RULE

If this parameter is set to `TRUE`, this rule becomes part of the positive rule set. This means that if the LCR evaluates to true for this rule, it is processed. If it evaluates to false, it is ignored.

If this parameter is set to false, this rule becomes part of the negative rule set. This means that if the LCR evaluates to true for this rule, it is ignored. If it evaluates to false, it is processed. This is just the opposite from the LCR evaluating true for a positive rule.

A good rule of thumb here is that if this parameter is set to FALSE, meaning it is a negative rule, then set the INCLUDE_TAGGED_LCR = TRUE. The reason is that if the negative rule evaluates to TRUE, we would expect the LCR to be ignored. However, if the INCLUDE_TAGGED_LCR is set to false, and the LCR tag is null, the overall rule will replicate the LCR. By setting INCLUDE_TAGGED_LCR=TRUE, you can use the value of the tag as a "tie-breaker".

AND_CONDITION

This parameter is a string that is appended to the rule conditions defined by the other parameters. Think of these rule conditions as where clauses. This last one allows you to add additional conditions to the where clause with the AND operator. This condition uses the :lcr object reference. When entering this value, remember it is a string. If you have single quotes within the string, make sure you escape them as you would with any PL/SQL string; for example:

```
and_condition    => ':lcr.get_tag = HEXTORAW(''22'')'
```

A word of warning! Make sure your AND_CONDITION corresponds with the INCLUSION_RULE setting. Here is why:

```
dbms_streams_adm.add_schema_rules(
                              inclusion_rule => FALSE,
                and_condition => ':lcr.get_tag = HEXTORAW(''22'')');
```

The above rule tells the process that if the LCR tag is equal to 22, *don't* process the LCR. This is because the INCLUSION_RULE is set to FALSE, which means that the rule is a negative rule, and will NOT process the change if the tag value equal to 22 evaluates to TRUE (we have a positive negative).

```
dbms_streams_adm.add_schema_rules(
    inclusion_rule => TRUE,
    and_condition => ':lcr.get_tag = HEXTORAW(''22'')');
```

Setting the INCLUSION_RULE = TRUE in the rule tells the process that if the LCR tag is equal to 22 then process the LCR. This means that the rule is a positive rule, and will process the change if the tag value equal to 22 evaluates to TRUE (we have a positive positive).

LCR subprograms

Below is a list of LCR subprograms common to both DDL and DML that might be used in the `AND_CONDITION`. For a full list, please refer to *Oracle's PL/SQL Packages and Types Reference* manual:

Subprogram/Member Functions	Description
GET_COMMAND_TYPE	Returns the command type of the LCR
GET_COMMIT_SCN	Returns the LCR commit system change number (SCN) at the time it is Applied (or erred) at the destination database.
GET_COMPATIBLE	Returns the minimal database version compatibility required to support the LCR
GET_EXTRA_ATTRIBUTE	Returns the value for the specified extra attribute in the LCR
GET_OBJECT_NAME	Returns the name of the object that is changed by the LCR
GET_OBJECT_OWNER	Returns the owner of the object that is changed by the LCR
GET_SCN	Returns the system change number (SCN) of the LCR when it was committed at the source database.
GET_SOURCE_DATABASE_NAME	Returns the source database name.
GET_SOURCE_TIME	Returns the time when the LCR's change was generated in the redo log of the source database, or the time when a persistent LCR was created.
GET_TAG	Returns the LCR tag value
GET_TRANSACTION_ID	Returns the LCR transaction identifier
"IS_NULL_TAG	Returns LCR tag status. 'Y' if the tag is NULL, 'N' if the tag is not NULL

Tag usage

Avoid change cycling. We've seen how the default use of tags helps Capture processes determine if a change should be captured and how an Apply process avoids having its change captured. This method works well in a bi-directional, master-to-master configuration. The understanding here is that propagation only makes one "hop"; from the source to the destination, and then stops. We like to call this the "one hop prop" (when said with a rap rhythm, it's kinda catchy)!

We can take this logic one step further to a hub and spoke replicated environment. By setting the tag to a value specific to a site, we can tell a propagation job to send all changes from the master hub to a destination for all tag values except the tag value for the destination site. For instance: say you have a configuration with one "hub" (H1) and 3 (S1, S2, and S3) "spoke" masters. Changes can be made at any of the four master sites. H1 is responsible for receiving a change from one spoke master and passing it on to the other spokes.

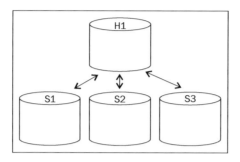

When the H1 master passes the change to the spokes, we want to avoid sending the change back to the spoke that originated it. This can be done using tags set to unique identifiers indicating where the change originated from (this is where those prior design activities we discussed in Chapter 2 come in really handy—you should already know how many unique tag values you will need, and which site will be assigned which value).

One way to accomplish this is to have the Apply process at the hub set the apply_tag value indicating where the change originated from and then have the Propagation process to each site check the tag value, sending only those that do not match the id assigned to the destination for that Propagation process.

In this case, we will assign the tag values of "A1", "A2", and "A3" to the changes originating from the spoke sites S1, S2, and S3 respectively. We will let the changes that originate at the Hub default to the null tag value.

Note: The following steps assume that the OE schema has already been instantiated in all 4 databases, the appropriate database links have been created, and the SCN has been set for each apply site at each site using the DBMS_APPLY_ADM.SET_SCHEMA_INSTANTIATION_SCN for the OE schema, and DBMS_APPLY_ADM.SET_TABLE_INSTANTIATION_SCN for each table in the OE scheme (both levels must be done). At this point no changes should be made to any of the objects at any of the sites until the Streams setup is completed.

Capture at the Hub

Prior to Oracle 11*g* and the introduction of Propagation Split and Merge, using the same capture queue for multiple destinations has the potential of impacting the performance of the overall Streaming if the connectivity to one or more destination sites is degraded. Thus, prior to 11*g*, we would want to create a separate outbound queue and Capture process for each spoke. This way, if the propagation to one spoke is slow or down, it will not impact propagation or queue management for the other spokes. In Oracle 11*g*, the Propagation Split and Merge feature can be implemented with a single capture queue to mitigate these potential issues. In our example, we are going to go ahead and use the "Separate Capture Queue Per Destination" to allow us to focus on Tag usage.

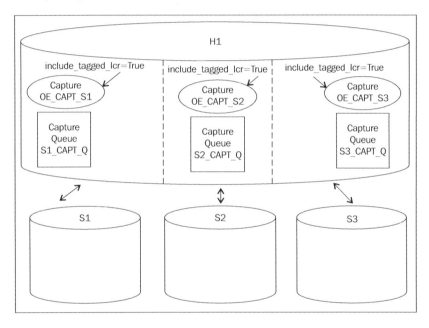

The following code creates the capture queues and processes, and can be found in the TAG_HubCapture.sql **code file.**

First we create the capture queues; one for each destination.

```
Begin
dbms_streams_adm.set_up_queue(
    queue_table => 'strm_admin.S1_CAPT_QT',
    storage_clause => NULL,
    queue_name => 'strm_admin.S1_CAPT_Q',
    queue_user => 'strm_admin');
End;
```

```
/
Begin
dbms_streams_adm.set_up_queue(
    queue_table => 'strm_admin.S2_CAPT_QT',
    storage_clause => NULL,
    queue_name => 'strm_admin.S2_CAPT_Q',
    queue_user => 'strm_admin');
End;
/
Begin
dbms_streams_adm.set_up_queue(
    queue_table => 'strm_admin.S3_CAPT_QT',
    storage_clause => NULL,
    queue_name => 'strm_admin.S3_CAPT_Q',
    queue_user => 'strm_admin');
End;
/
```

We then create Capture processes for each queue, making sure to include non-null tags. We want the AND_CONDITION to be NULL so we get all of the changes regardless of the tag value.

```
Begin
  dbms_streams_adm.add_schema_rules(
    schema_name => 'OE',
    streams_type => 'CAPTURE',
    streams_name => 'OE_CAPT_S1',
    queue_name => 'S1_CAPT_Q',
    include_dml => TRUE,
    include_ddl => TRUE,
    include_tagged_lcr => TRUE,     ---capture null and non-null tags
    source_database => 'H1.oracle.com',
    inclusion_rule => TRUE,
    and_condition => NULL);
End;
/

Begin
  dbms_streams_adm.add_schema_rules(
    schema_name => 'OE',
    streams_type => 'CAPTURE',
    streams_name => 'OE_CAPT_S2',
    queue_name => 'S2_CAPT_Q',
    include_dml => TRUE,
    include_ddl => TRUE,
```

```
      include_tagged_lcr => TRUE,      ---capture null and non-null tags
      source_database => 'H1.oracle.com',
      inclusion_rule => TRUE,
      and_condition => NULL);
End;
/

Begin
  dbms_streams_adm.add_schema_rules(
    schema_name => 'OE',
    streams_type => 'CAPTURE',
    streams_name => 'OE_CAPT_S3',
    queue_name => 'S3_CAPT_Q',
    include_dml => TRUE,
    include_ddl => TRUE,
    include_tagged_lcr => TRUE,      ---capture null and non-null tags
    source_database => 'H1.oracle.com',
    inclusion_rule => TRUE,
    and_condition => NULL);
End;
/
```

Capture, Propagate, and Apply at each spoke

At each spoke, we want to set up the basic capture and propagation to the Hub processes. We also want to create an Apply process that applies all changes sent to the spoke regardless of the tag value.

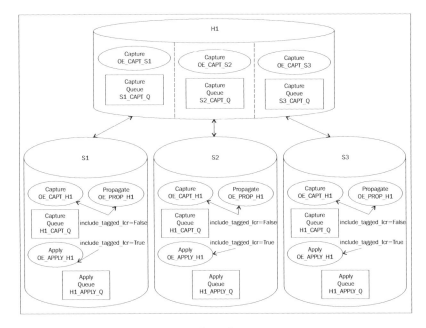

The following code creates the Capture and Apply queues, and the necessary Capture, Propagation, and Apply processes at each spoke. This code can be found in the `TAG_SpokeSQL.sql` code file.

First, we create the Capture and Apply queues.

```
Begin
dbms_streams_adm.set_up_queue(
    queue_table => 'strm_admin.H1_CAPT_QT',
    storage_clause => NULL,
    queue_name => 'strm_admin.H1_CAPT_Q',
    queue_user => 'strm_admin');
End;
/
Begin
dbms_streams_adm.set_up_queue(
    queue_table => 'strm_admin.H1_APPLY_QT',
    storage_clause => NULL,
    queue_name => 'strm_admin.H1_APPLY_Q',
    queue_user => 'strm_admin');
End;
/
```

Next, create the Capture rule, making sure to set the SOURCE_DATABASE with the appropriate spoke name, and only capture null tag changes. We do this because the spoke is only sending to one site, so we don't need to worry about tags here.

```
Begin
  dbms_streams_adm.add_schema_rules(
    schema_name => 'OE',
    streams_type => 'CAPTURE',
    streams_name => 'OE_CAPT_H1',
    queue_name => 'H1_CAPT_Q',
    include_dml => TRUE,
    include_ddl => TRUE,
    include_tagged_lcr => False,     ---capture just null tags -
changes made at this site
    source_database => 'S1.oracle.com',---substitute S2, S3 here
                                        ---for the other two spokes
    inclusion_rule => TRUE,
    and_condition => NULL);
End;
/
```

Create the Apply Rule to include non-null tags. We do this because we may be receiving changes from the hub that are forwarded from another spoke. These changes will have a non-null tag. If the change originated at the hub, the tag will be null. We do not need to evaluate the tag value past null or non-null. This would have already been done by the Propagation process for this destination at the hub. Setting the AND_CONDITION to NULL and the INCLUDE_TAGGED_LCR to TRUE, instructs the Apply process to apply any null and non-null tagged LCR's it receives.

```
BEGIN
  dbms_streams_adm.add_schema_rules(
    schema_name => 'OE',
    streams_type => 'APPLY',
    streams_name => 'OE_APPLY_H1',
    queue_name => 'strm_admin.H1_APPLY_Q',
    include_dml => TRUE,
    include_ddl => TRUE,
    include_tagged_lcr => TRUE,  --check null and non-null tags
    source_database => 'H1.oracle.com',
    inclusion_rule => TRUE,
    and_condition => NULL);
END;
/
```

Now create the propagation from the spoke to the Hub. As we want to send all of the changes originating at the spoke to the Hub, we don't need to worry about tags. We just need a basic null tag LCR propagation rule. Run the following at each spoke, substituting S1 with S2 and S3 for the respective spoke site. Because propagation is enabled when it is created, we will disable it immediately after creation to allow us to complete the configuration setup.

```
BEGIN
  dbms_streams_adm.add_schema_propagation_rules(
    schema_name => 'OE',
    streams_name => 'OE_PROP_H1',
    source_queue_name => 'H1_CAPT_Q',
    destination_queue_name => 'S1_APPLY_Q@H1.oracle.com',
    include_dml => TRUE,
    include_ddl => TRUE,
    include_tagged_lcr => FALSE, --send only null tags
    source_database => 'S1.oracle.com',
    inclusion_rule => TRUE,
    and_condition => NULL,
    queue_to_queue => TRUE);
```

```
--disable propagation until we are finished
BEGIN
   dbms_aqadm.disable_propagation_schedule(
      queue_name => 'H1_CAPT_Q',
      destination => ' H1.oracle.com ',
      destination_queue => 'S1_APPLY_Q@H1.oracle.com'
   );
EXCEPTION WHEN OTHERS THEN
   IF sqlcode = -24065 THEN NULL; -- propagation already disabled
   ELSE RAISE;
   END IF;
END;
END;
```

Apply at the Hub

We now want to create an inbound queue and Apply process for each spoke at the
Hub. This way, if one queue is slow or has errors, it will not hold up changes from
the other spokes. This also helps with maintenance. Should you need to drop and
recreate the queue, you are only impacting synchronization between the Hub and
the one spoke. You can use a single apply queue if you wish.

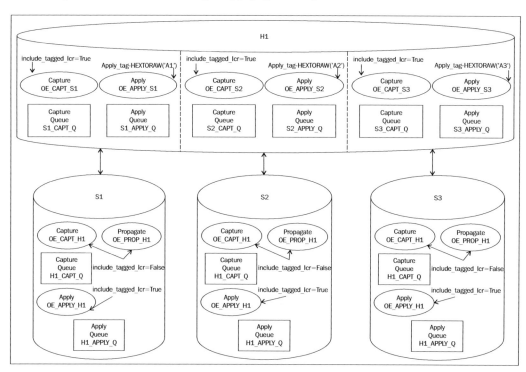

The following code creates the Apply queues and Apply processes at the Hub. This code can be found in the TAG_SpokeSQL.sql code file.

First we create the Apply queues; one for each source site.

```
Begin
dbms_streams_adm.set_up_queue(
    queue_table => 'strm_admin.S1_APPLY_QT',
    storage_clause => NULL,
    queue_name => 'strm_admin.S1_APPLY_Q',
    queue_user => 'strm_admin');
End;
/
Begin
dbms_streams_adm.set_up_queue(
    queue_table => 'strm_admin.S2_APPLY_QT',
    storage_clause => NULL,
    queue_name => 'strm_admin.S2__APPLY_Q',
    queue_user => 'strm_admin');
End;
/
Begin
dbms_streams_adm.set_up_queue(
    queue_table => 'strm_admin.S3_APPLY_QT',
    storage_clause => NULL,
    queue_name => 'strm_admin.S3__APPLY_Q',
    queue_user => 'strm_admin');
End;
/
```

We then configure an Apply process on H1 for each of the spoke sites, and set the apply_tag with that site's tag value.

```
Begin
  dbms_streams_adm.add_schema_rules(
    schema_name => 'OE',
    streams_type => 'APPLY',
    streams_name => 'OE_APPLY_S1',
    queue_name => 'S1_APPLY_Q',
    include_dml => TRUE,
    include_ddl => TRUE,
    include_tagged_lcr => TRUE,
    source_database => 'S1.oracle.com',
    inclusion_rule => TRUE,
    and_condition => NULL);
```

```
dbms_apply_adm.alter_apply(
apply_name           => 'OE_APPLY_S1',
apply_tag            => HEXTORAW('A1')   ---this is the key
  );
END;
/
Begin
  dbms_streams_adm.add_schema_rules(
    schema_name => 'OE',
    streams_type => 'APPLY',
    streams_name => 'OE_APPLY_S2',
    queue_name => 'S2_APPLY_Q',
    include_dml => TRUE,
    include_ddl => TRUE,
    include_tagged_lcr => TRUE,
    source_database => 'S2.oracle.com',
    inclusion_rule => TRUE,
    and_condition => NULL);
dbms_apply_adm.alter_apply(
apply_name           => 'OE_APPLY_S2',
apply_tag            => HEXTORAW('A2')   ---this is the key
  );
END;
/
Begin
  dbms_streams_adm.add_schema_rules(
    schema_name => 'OE',
    streams_type => 'APPLY',
    streams_name => 'OE_APPLY_S3',
    queue_name => 'S3_APPLY_Q',
    include_dml => TRUE,
    include_ddl => TRUE,
    include_tagged_lcr => TRUE,
    source_database => 'S3.oracle.com',
    inclusion_rule => TRUE,
    and_condition => NULL);
dbms_apply_adm.alter_apply(
apply_name           => 'OE_APPLY_S3',
apply_tag            => HEXTORAW('A3')   ---this is the key
  );
END;
/
```

Propagation at the Hub

Now we want to set up propagation from the Hub to each spoke. It is here where we evaluate the tag using the AND_CONDITION. As we want to send all changes, expect those originating from the destination spoke, it is easier to create a negative rule. Because propagation is enabled when it is created, we will disable it immediately after creation. As mentioned earlier, the AND_CONDITION is a string that is appended to system conditions created by the rule. Make sure to escape single quotes using PL/SQL syntax. Run the following at the hub for each spoke site, substituting S1 with S2 and S3 respectively, and A1 with A2 and A3 respectively.

The following code creates the Propagation processes at the Hub. This code can be found in the TAG_HUBProp.sql code file.

```
BEGIN
  dbms_streams_adm.add_schema_propagation_rules(
    schema_name => 'OE',
    streams_name => 'OE_PROP_S1',
    source_queue_name => 'S1_CAPT_Q',
    destination_queue_name => 'H1_APPLY_Q@S1.oracle.com',
    include_dml => TRUE,
    include_ddl => TRUE,
    include_tagged_lcr => TRUE,  --check null and non-null tags
    source_database => 'H1.oracle.com',
    inclusion_rule => FALSE,  --if condition is true, don't send
    and_condition => ':lcr.get_tag = HEXTORAW(''A1'')',
    queue_to_queue => TRUE);

  --disable propagation until we are finished
  BEGIN
    dbms_aqadm.disable_propagation_schedule(
      queue_name => 'S1_CAPT_Q',
      destination => ' S1.oracle.com ',
      destination_queue => 'H1_APPLY_Q@S1.oracle.com'
    );
  EXCEPTION WHEN OTHERS THEN
    IF sqlcode = -24065 THEN NULL;  -- propagation already disabled
    ELSE RAISE;
    END IF;
  END;
END;
/
```

Summary of what we have just done:

- We have created a Capture process at the Hub that looks for null and non-null tagged LCRs

- We have created a Capture process at each spoke that looks for null tag LCRs only

- We have created an Apply process at the hub, for each spoke site, that sets the LCR tag to a unique non-null value identifying where the change originated from

- We have created an Apply process at each spoke that applies all null and non-null tagged LCRs sent to it

- We have created a Propagation process from the hub, to each spoke site, that evaluates the LCR tag value, and sends all LCRs whose tag value is not equal to the destination spoke assigned identifier

- We have created a Propagation process from each spoke to the hub that sends any null tagged LCRs

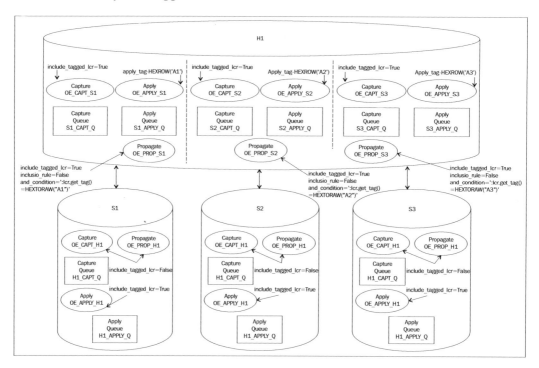

At this point you will need to set the Apply Instantiation SCN using the `DBMS_APPLY_ADM.SET_SCHEMA_INSTANITIATION_SCN` and then start each of the Apply processes using the `DBMS_APPLY_ADM.START_APPLY` procedure (see Chapters 4 and 5 for specifics). Enable the Propagation processes using the `DBMS_AQADM.ENABLE_PROPAGATION_SCHEUDLE` procedure. Then finally, start the Capture processes using the `DBMS_CAPTURE_ADM.START_CAPTURE` procedure.

Tags can also be used by Rules, such as Error handling, and Rule based transformations. These rules are configured to run specified PL/SQL packages in which the LCR properties can be evaluated and modified. In these cases, you would reference the `:dml`, or `:ddl` object type methods (similar to the `:lcr` object type referenced in the `AND_CONDITION`) to read or set the tag value as needed.

RULES—they're what we live by

Streams is all about the rules; literally. The action context that a Streams process takes is governed by the rule conditions. When you create a rule, Oracle generates system conditions, and evaluation contexts, that are used to evaluate each LCR to determine if the action context for the process should be accomplished. We have already addressed a number of these system conditions during our TAG discussion; for instance `INCLUDE_TAGGED_LCR=FALSE` generates a system evaluation for the `LCR$_ROW_RECORD_TYPE :dml.is_null_tag='Y'` subprogram.

 For more information on LCR Types, reference Oracle Database PL/SQL Packages and Types Reference manual.

You can control what system evaluations are included in the rule by the parameter values you specify, as well as add user-defined evaluations with the `AND_CONDITION` parameter.

There is a lot going on under the calm surface water of rules. Understanding how this activity flows together will help you become more advanced in creating rules to manipulate your Streams throughout your current environment. So, let's grab our snorkels and masks, and stick our heads under the surface and take a look.

Rule components

Rules have three components: conditions, evaluation context, and action context. These components coordinate with the "when", "what", and "how" of the LCR being processed. The conditions tell the Streams process "when" the LCR should be processed, the evaluation context defines "what" data/information the Streams process uses to process the LCR, and the action context tells the Streams process "how" to handle the LCR.

Rule conditions

The rule condition is essentially the "where clause". The conditions are evaluated against the properties of the LCR and return either TRUE or FALSE. The conditions can contain compound expressions and operators (**AND, OR, NOT,** and so on.). The final evaluation returned from the condition (TRUE or FALSE) is the final result of all the compound expressions. An example of a system-generated condition would be that of our good friend :dml.is_null_tag = 'Y' (generated by the INCLUDE_TAGGED_LCR=FALSE parameter of the DBMS_STREAMS_ADM.ADD_*_RULE procedures). On rule creation, the condition is passed in as a string (so make sure to escape any single quotes within the string).

```
':dml.get_object_owner() = ''OE'' and :dml.get_tag() =
HEXTORAW(''22'')'
```

It is important to remember that you want to keep your rule conditions as simple as possible. Complex rule conditions can have a significant impact on performance. The rule condition created by our Sub-Setting example is an example of a complex rule as it includes a PL/SQL call to a function. Also, rule conditions that contain NOT, or != can also impact performance.

Rule evaluation context

The rule evaluation context defines data external to the LCR properties that can be referenced in the rule conditions. This is comparable to the SQL statement from clause. This reference is a database object that contains the external data. The evaluation context provides the rule conditions with the necessary information for interpreting and evaluating the conditions that reference external data. If the evaluation context references objects, the rule owner must have the proper privileges to reference the object (select and execute) as the rule condition is evaluated in the schema of the evaluation context owner. Information contained in an Evaluation Context might include table aliases used in the condition, variable names and types, and/or a function to use to evaluate the rules to which the evaluation context is assigned.

Evaluation Context structure can get a bit confusing. To get a better feel of it, you may want to start by looking at the following database views:

- `DBA/ALL/USER_EVALUATION_CONTEXT_TABLES`: table alias used

- `DBA/ALL/USER_EVALUATION_CONTEXT_VARS`: variable types used

- `DBA/ALL/USER_EVALUATION_CONTEXTS`: functions used

Streams system created rules (created using `DBMS_STREAMS_ADM`) will create rules using the standard Oracle-supplied `SYS.STREAMS$_EVALUATION_CONTEXT` rule evaluation context. This evaluation context is composed of a `variable_types` list for the `:dml` and `:ddl` variables, and the evaluation function `SYS.DBMS_STREAMS_INTERNAL.EVALUATION_CONTEXT_FUNCTION` as seen in the previous DBA views.

You can create your own evaluation context using the `DBMS_RULE_ADM.CREATE_EVALUATION_CONTEXT` procedure:

```
DBMS_RULE_ADM.CREATE_EVALUATION_CONTEXT(
   evaluation_context_name IN  VARCHAR2,
   table_aliases           IN  SYS.RE$TABLE_ALIAS_LIST   DEFAULT NULL,
   variable_types          IN  SYS.RE$VARIABLE_TYPE_LIST DEFAULT NULL,
   evaluation_function     IN  VARCHAR2                  DEFAULT NULL,
   evaluation_context_comment IN  VARCHAR2               DEFAULT NULL
   );
```

If you create a custom Evaluation Context that uses the `SYS.DBMS_STREAMS_INTERNAL.EVALUATION_CONTEXT_FUNCTION`, it must include the same variables and types as in the `SYS.STREAMS$_EVALUATION_CONTEXT` (a.k.a. `:dml` and `:ddl`).

`Variable_types` can be defined using `SYS.RE$VARIABLE_TYPE_LIST`, which in turn accepts individual variable types defined using `SYS.RE$VARIABLE_TYPE`.

Similarly, if you create a custom function to use as the evaluation function, it must have the following signature:

```
FUNCTION evaluation_function_name(
   rule_set_name       IN  VARCHAR2,
   evaluation_context  IN  VARCHAR2,
   event_context       IN  SYS.RE$NV_LIST              DEFAULT NULL,
   table_values        IN  SYS.RE$TABLE_VALUE_LIST     DEFAULT NULL,
   column_values       IN  SYS.RE$COLUMN_VALUE_LIST    DEFAULT NULL,
   variable_values     IN  SYS.RE$VARIABLE_VALUE_LIST  DEFAULT NULL,
   attribute_values    IN  SYS.RE$ATTRIBUTE_VALUE_LIST DEFAULT NULL,
```

```
        stop_on_first_hit    IN    BOOLEAN                    DEFAULT FALSE,
        simple_rules_only    IN    BOOLEAN                    DEFAULT FALSE,
        true_rules           OUT   SYS.RE$RULE_HIT_LIST,
        maybe_rules          OUT   SYS.RE$RULE_HIT_LIST);
    RETURN BINARY_INTEGER;
```

Where the returned BINARY_INTEGER value must be one of the following:

```
DBMS_RULE_ADM.EVALUATION_SUCCESS
DBMS_RULE_ADM.EVALUATION_CONTINUE
DBMS_RULE_ADM.EVALUATION_FAILURE
```

> For more information on creating custom Evaluation Contexts and evaluation functions and Rule Types, refer to the Oracle Database PL/SQL Packages and Types Reference manual, and The Oracle Streams Extended Examples manual.

Once an Evaluation Context is created it can be assigned to a rule or a rule set using the evaluation_context parameter of the appropriate DBMS_RULE_ADM procedure.

The Evaluation Context for a Rule can be different than the Evaluation Context for a Rule Set to which the Rule might be assigned. The bottom line is that a Rule must be able to associate itself with an Evaluation Context at some level. We will revisit this concept as we discuss Rule Creation a little later on this section.

Action context

The rule action context is just that, the action information that the rule evaluation engine returns to the client application, to be acted upon by the client application, when the rule evaluates to true. This is not the action itself, but values to be used by the action code that are specific to the rule. The action context is of the SYS.RE$NV_LIST type, which contains an array of name-value pairs and is associated to a rule condition. A rule condition can only have one action context. The action context itself is optional and can contain zero to many name-value pairs.

The SYS.RE$NV_LIST has the following construct:

```
TYPE SYS.RE$NV_LIST AS OBJECT(
    actx_list  SYS.RE$NV_ARRAY);
```

Subprograms are:

```
ADD_PAIR (name    IN   VARCHAR2,
          value   IN   ANYDATA);
GET_ALL_NAMES ()
  RETURN SYS.RE$NAME_ARRAY;
```

```
GET_VALUE (name  IN  VARCHAR2)
  RETURN ANYDATA;
REMOVE_PAIR (name  IN  VARCHAR2);
```

> For more information on creating and populating Action Contexts types, refer to the Oracle Database PL/SQL Packages and Types Reference manual.
>
> For more information on Rule components refer to the Oracle Streams Concepts and Administration manual.

Creating your own rules

In some cases, we may need more complex rules than what the DBMS_STREAMS_ADM package creates. For instance, a rule condition that uses NOT to exclude a subset of LCRs from the overall inclusion evaluation. Or perhaps to only look for a specific combination of conditions other than those normally generated. Actually, a complex rule is defined as a rule that cannot be created with the DBMS_STREAMS_ADM package. In these cases, we can create our own rules and evaluation contexts using the DBMS_RULES_ADM package. Both packages create rule conditions evaluation contexts. However, you should avoid using them interchangeably with the same rule. This is because the DBMS_STREAMS_ADM package is an Oracle specialized package for setting up Streams rules to a specific design. It has a set functionality and tight controls on the variables so the generation and clean-up of associated metadata is more precise. Giving us users the DBMS_RULES_ADM package opens up a world of opportunities for us to exploit the power of these procedures and function, but also has the potential for generating unexpected or not generating expected metadata. Thus, the DBMS_RULES_ADM metadata management may differ in areas from that of the DBMS_STREAMS_ADM package. So it is best to use the same package to manage and remove the rules that you had used to create them.

Rule creation

To create a RULE, you use the DBMS_RULE_ADM.CREATE_RULE procedure.

```
DBMS_RULE_ADM.CREATE_RULE(
  rule_name           IN  VARCHAR2,
  condition           IN  VARCHAR2,
  evaluation_context  IN  VARCHAR2        DEFAULT NULL,
  action_context      IN  SYS.RE$NV_LIST  DEFAULT NULL,
  rule_comment        IN  VARCHAR2        DEFAULT NULL);
```

If you do not specify an evaluation_context here, it will default to that of the rule set to which the rule is added. If the evaluation_context is set here, it takes precedence over all other evaluation_context assignments.

Rule Sets

No rebel Rules allowed! Each Rule must belong to a Rule Set to be accessed by the Rules engine. A Rule Set can have one or more Rules assigned to it. First you create the Rule Set, and then add the Rule. When you do this, pay particular attention to where the evaluation context assignments are made in the process. This dictates which one is used in the case of multiple evaluation_context assignments.

To create a Rule Set, you use the DBMS_RULE_ADM.CREATE_RULE_SET procedure.

```
DBMS_RULE_ADM.CREATE_RULE_SET(
    rule_set_name       IN   VARCHAR2,
    evaluation_context  IN   VARCHAR2   DEFAULT NULL,
    rule_set_comment    IN   VARCHAR2   DEFAULT NULL);
```

If you set the evaluation_context here, it is only used by the Rule if the Rule has not already been assigned an evaluation_context when it was created or when it is added to the Rule Set.

To add the Rule to the Rule Set, you use the DBMS_RULE_ADM.ADD_RULE procedure.

```
DBMS_RULE_ADM.ADD_RULE(
    rule_name           IN   VARCHAR2,
    rule_set_name       IN   VARCHAR2,
    evaluation_context  IN   VARCHAR2   DEFAULT NULL,
    rule_comment        IN   VARCHAR2   DEFAULT NULL);
```

If you set the evaluation_context here when you add the Rule to the Rule Set this evaluation_context takes precedence over the evaluation_context that was set when the Rule Set was created. However, if you had already set the evaluation_context when you created the Rule, this evaluation_context is ignored.

It is possible to have different Rules in the Rule Set that have different evaluation_context assignments. Be careful when doing this as it may yield unexpected results when the Rule Set is used for evaluation (see Event Context below).

The evaluation_context has to be assigned at some point. If the evaluation_context has not been assigned at any point; Rule creation, Rule Set creation, or adding the Rule to the Rule Set, an error is raised when you attempt to add the Rule to the Rule Set.

Information on Rule Sets and Rules can be found in the following views:

- DBA_RULES
- DBA_RULE_SETS
- DBA_RULE_SET_RULES

- V$RULE

- V$RULE_SET

- V$RULE_SET_AGGREGATE_S

Event context

When a client application submits a payload to the Rules engine, it is called an "event". The client application submits the payload as an event context using the DBMS_RULE.EVALUATION procedure. This procedure accepts a SYS.RE$NV_LIST datatype containing the name-value pairs identifying the event, as well as the name of the Rule Set to be used for the evaluation, and other information. Notice the evaluation_context is required here. This tells the Rules engine to look only for Rules in the Rule Set that have been assigned this evaluation_context and use them to evaluate the payload. Be careful here as it could yield unexpected results if the wrong evaluation_context is specified inadvertently.

```
DBMS_RULE.EVALUATE(
  rule_set_name        IN   VARCHAR2,
  evaluation_context   IN   VARCHAR2,
  event_context        IN   SYS.RE$NV_LIST                DEFAULT NULL,
  table_values         IN   SYS.RE$TABLE_VALUE_LIST       DEFAULT NULL,
  column_values        IN   SYS.RE$COLUMN_VALUE_LIST      DEFAULT NULL,
  variable_values      IN   SYS.RE$VARIABLE_VALUE_LIST    DEFAULT NULL,
  attribute_values     IN   SYS.RE$ATTRIBUTE_VALUE_LIST   DEFAULT NULL,
  stop_on_first_hit    IN   BOOLEAN                        DEFAULT FALSE,
  simple_rules_only    IN   BOOLEAN                        DEFAULT FALSE,
  true_rules           OUT  SYS.RE$RULE_HIT_LIST,
  maybe_rules          OUT  SYS.RE$RULE_HIT_LIST);
DBMS_RULE.EVALUATE(
  rule_set_name        IN   VARCHAR2,
  evaluation_context   IN   VARCHAR2,
  event_context        IN   SYS.RE$NV_LIST                DEFAULT NULL,
  table_values         IN   SYS.RE$TABLE_VALUE_LIST       DEFAULT NULL,
  column_values        IN   SYS.RE$COLUMN_VALUE_LIST      DEFAULT NULL,
  variable_values      IN   SYS.RE$VARIABLE_VALUE_LIST    DEFAULT NULL,
  attribute_values     IN   SYS.RE$ATTRIBUTE_VALUE_LIST   DEFAULT NULL,
```

```
    simple_rules_only     IN    BOOLEAN                      DEFAULT
FALSE,
    true_rules_iterator   OUT   BINARY_INTEGER,
    maybe_rules_iterator  OUT   BINARY_INTEGER);
```

Also note that the procedure is overloaded. The `stop_on_first_hit` is only available in the first version. The out `paramaters` `true_rules` and `true_rules_iterator` are mutually exclusive, as are `maybe_rules` and `maybe_rules_iterator`.

> For more information on evaluation events, refer to the Oracle Streams Concepts and Administration manual.
>
> For more information on the `DBMS_RULE.EVALUATE` procedure, refer to the Oracle Database PL/SQL Packages and Types Reference manual.

How it all comes together

So, now that you have created all your Rules and assigned them to Rule Sets and Evaluation Contexts, how does it all work?

1. The client application generates an event and sends it to the Rules Engine via the `DBMS_RULE.EVALUATE` procedure.

2. The Rules Engine evaluates the event using the Rule Conditions for the Rules in the Rule Set whose `evaluation_context` match the `evaluation_context` in the `DBMS_RULE.EVALUATE` procedure call.

3. The results of the evaluation (TRUE, FALSE, or UNKNOWN) are returned to the Rules Engine.

4. The Rules Engine then returns those Rules that evaluated to TRUE back to the client application along with any Action Context associated with the Rule(s). The Client application then performs actions based on the results and using any action context returned by the Rule Engine.

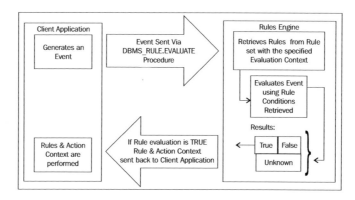

Rule based transformation—eat your heart out transformers!

As with all good rules, some are made to be broken; or maybe changed. In some circumstances we need to have rules that govern change. In Advance Replication, a number one rule is that a replicated table must have the same structure at all master sites. The column names and data types have to be identical or the "apply" of a deferred transaction will fail. With Streams, we can now break this rule by adding a new rule that allows the LCR to "morph" to a new structure. We call this ability Rule Based Transformation; and it is done via complex rules and action context.

When you plan your Rule Based Transformation design (remember Chapter 2?), you want to remember that Rule Based Transformation rules are only evaluated with positive Rule Sets. If the Rule Set is negative, the Rule Based Transformation is ignored.

Declarative versus User Created

In the real world, there are many ways to accomplish the same thing; just as there are many ways to model data. You may run into a situation where the table structure in one master database may be different from the structure of the table in another master database but data must be replicated between them. It could be that a table column at one master is a VARCHAR2, but is a DATE at another master site. Or perhaps the column does not exist at all. Rule Based Transformation provides the ability to capture the LCR and convert it to the necessary structure needed to apply it at the destination site. This is not to be confused with transformations accomplished via the DBMS_TRANSFORMATION package. That is a different fish (and doesn't swim in this stream).

A special note concerning SUBSET Rules and transformations. A SUBSET Rule has an internal row_migration transformation assigned to it when it is created. This internal transformation will always be the first one executed before any other transformations.

Another thing to keep in mind is the amount of "transformation" that will be applied to the LCR. If extensive transformations need to be made to the LCR, you may wish to consider using a custom DML handler instead to take advantage of the apply parallel capabilities.

The remainder of this section is going to use the premise that we have an LCR that we need to change a column name for, before we send it out from the source site. The LCR is generated on a table which has a different column name than the corresponding table at all the other sites. This being the case, we are going to create the transformation at the Capture process. There are two ways to accomplish this; either by using a declarative transformation or a user created transformation. We will review each, and then apply the method to our LCR that needs a column name change.

Depending on the Transformation type, you can use one of the following views to find information concerning the transformation:

- Declarative: DBA_STREAMS_TRANSFORMATIONS
- User Created: DBA_STREAMS_TRANSFORM_FUNCTION

Declarative transformation

As of 10*g*, Oracle provides commonly used transformations in the DBMS_STREAMS_ADM package. These transformations are referred to as declarative transformations.

Declarative transformations only work with row LCR's (aka DML LCR's). The row LCR can be a Streams captured LCR (basic or synchronous), or a user created message.

The procedures allow you to add transformation rules to do the following:

- Add a column (DBMS_STREAMS_ADM.ADD_COLUMN)
- Delete a column (DBMS_STREAMS_ADM.DELETE_COLUMN)
- Rename a column (DBMS_STREAMS_ADM.RENAME_COLUMN)
- Rename a table (DBMS_STREAMS_ADM.RENAME_TABLE)
- Rename a schema (DBMS_STREAMS_ADM.RENAME_SCHEMA)

Special considerations when DBMS_STREAMS_ADM.ADD_COLUMN

Be aware that the DBMS_STREAMS_ADM.ADD_COLUMN procedure does not support a number of data types. These include:

- LOBS (BLOB, CLOB, NCLOB, BFILE, and so on)
- LONG, LONG RAW, and so on
- ROWID

- User-defined types (including object types, REFs, varrays, nested tables, and so on)

- Oracle-supplied types (including ANY types, XML types, spatial types, and media types)

 For more information on DBMS_STREAMS_ADM Declarative Transformation subprograms, please refer to the Oracle Database PL/SQL Packages and Types Reference.

For our purposes, we want to use the DBMS_STREAMS_ADM.RENAME_COLUMN to create a declarative transformation. In our example, we will work with the JOB_HISTORY table from the Oracle Example HR Schema. We will assume that at our source database the HR.JOB_HISTORY table has a column named DEPARTMENT_ID, and at the destination database the corresponding column in the HR.JOB_HISTORY is DEPT_ID. Declarative Transformations can only be added to an existing rule. If the rules specified do not exist, an error is raised. Also, the transformation will be owned by STRM_ADMIN so make sure you have explicitly granted all privileges on HR.JOB_HISTORY to STRM_ADMIN.

First we find the rule to which we wish to add the declarative transformation, logged in as STRM_ADMIN we can look at the USER_RULES view:

```
SQL> select * from user_rules;
RULE_NAME
------------------------------
RULE_CONDITION
--------------------------------------
RULE_EVALUATION_CONTEXT_OWNER   RULE_EVALUATION_CONTEXT_NAME
------------------------------- -------------------------------
RULE_ACTION_CONTEXT(ACTX_LIST(NVN_NAME, NVN_VALUE()))
------------------------------------------------------------
RULE_COMMENT
------------------------------------------------------------
HR1
((:dml.get_object_owner() = 'HR') and :dml.get_source_database_name()
= 'STRM1'
)
SYS                             STREAMS$_EVALUATION_CONTEXT

HR2
((:ddl.get_object_owner() = 'HR' or :ddl.get_base_table_owner() =
'HR') and :ddl
.get_source_database_name() = 'STRM1' )
SYS                             STREAMS$_EVALUATION_CONTEXT
```

HR1 is our Row LCR (:dml) rule, so we will add

To create our declarative transformation Rule, we issue the following command:

```
begin
DBMS_STREAMS_ADM.RENAME_COLUMN(
    rule_name         => 'strm_admin.HR1',
    table_name        => 'HR.JOB_HISTORY',
    from_column_name  => 'DEPARTMENT_ID',
    to_column_name    => 'DEPT_ID',
    value_type        => '*',        -- default
    step_number       => 0,           --default
    operation         => 'ADD'        --default
);
end;
/
```

We can now check the rule in the USER_RULES view:

```
SQL> select * from user_rules where rule_name = 'HR1';
RULE_NAME
-------------------------------
RULE_CONDITION
------------------------------------------------------------
RULE_EVALUATION_CONTEXT_OWNER   RULE_EVALUATION_CONTEXT_NAME
-------------------------------  -------------------------------
RULE_ACTION_CONTEXT(ACTX_LIST(NVN_NAME, NVN_VALUE()))
------------------------------------------------------------
RULE_COMMENT
------------------------------------------------------------
HR1
((:dml.get_object_owner() = 'HR') and :dml.get_source_database_name()
= 'STRM1'
)
SYS                            STREAMS$_EVALUATION_CONTEXT
RE$NV_LIST(RE$NV_ARRAY(RE$NV_NODE('STREAMS$_INTERNAL_TRANS',
ANYDATA())))
```

Notice that the RULE_COMMENT now has an entry indicating the inclusion of the transformation rule.

We can also look at the DBA_STREAMS_TRANSFORMATION view:

```
SQL> select rule_owner, rule_name, transform_type,
  2  from_column_name, to_column_name, value_type,
  3  declarative_type, precedence, step_number
```

```
  4  from dba_streams_transformations;
RULE_OWNER
------------------------------
RULE_NAME                        TRANSFORM_TYPE
------------------------------ -------------------------
FROM_COLUMN_NAME     TO_COLUMN_NAME      VAL
------------------- ------------------- ---
DECLARATIVE_TYPE     PRECEDENCE STEP_NUMBER
------------------- ---------- -----------
STRM_ADMIN
HR1                             DECLARATIVE TRANSFORMATION
DEPARTMENT_ID       DEPT_ID              *
RENAME COLUMN                    2        0
```

To remove the declarative transformation from the rule, we use the same procedure we used to create the transformation, but set the operation parameter to REMOVE:

```
begin
DBMS_STREAMS_ADM.RENAME_COLUMN(
    rule_name           => 'strm_admin.HR1',
    table_name          => 'HR.JOB_HISTORY',
    from_column_name    => 'DEPARTMENT_ID',
    to_column_name      => 'DEPT_ID',
    operation           => 'REMOVE'         --default
);
end;
/
```

> Note: Removing the declarative transformation does not clear the RULE_COMMENT we see in the USER_RULES view. However, it does clear the entry from the DBA_STREAMS_TRANSFORMATION view.
>
> For more detailed information on using the DBMS_STREAMS_ADM.RENAME_COLUMN, and other declarative transformation procedures, please refer to the Oracle PL/SQL Packages and Types Reference, and the Oracle Streams Concepts and Administration Guide.

User created Rule Based Transformations (UCRBT)

You can also create your own Rule Based Transformations. These transformations are referred to as user-created transformations (imagine that).

The steps for creating a UCRBT are pretty basic.

Create the PL/SQL function that performs the transformation.

- The function should receive the LCR as a `SYS.ANYDATA IN` parameter
- The function should return either an LCR a `SYS.ANYDATA` or `STREAMS$_ANYDATA_ARRAY`
- If the function returns a `STREAMS$_ANYDATA_ARRAY`, it can only be associated with a capture rule

Grant the `EXECUTE` privilege on the function to the appropriate user as necessary.

Create or locate the rules for which the transformation will be used.

Set the custom rule-based transformation for each rule by running the `SET_RULE_TRANSFORM_FUNCTION` procedure.

In this example, we will setup a UCRBT that makes the same transformation as the previous declarative transformation. The UCRBT is going to be owned by `STRM_ADMIN` so make sure you have explicitly granted all privileges on `HR.JOB_HISTORY` to `STRM_ADMIN`.

The code for this example can be found in the `UCRBT.sql` code file.

First we create the PL/SQL function to accomplish the transformation; `STRM_ADMIN` will be the function owner, so make sure you are logged in as `STRM_ADMIN` in this example:

```
CREATE OR REPLACE FUNCTION DEPT_COLNAME_CHANGE (evt IN SYS.AnyData)
RETURN SYS.AnyData IS
 lcr SYS.LCR$_ROW_RECORD;
 obj_name VARCHAR2(30);
 rc   NUMBER;
BEGIN
 IF evt.GetTypeName='SYS.LCR$_ROW_RECORD' THEN
   rc := evt.getObject(lcr);
   obj_name := lcr.GET_OBJECT_NAME();
   IF obj_name = 'JOB_HISTORY' THEN
     lcr.RENAME_COLUMN('DEPARTMENT_ID','DEPT_ID','*');
     RETURN SYS.ANYDATA.ConvertObject(lcr);

   END IF;
 END IF;
 RETURN evt;
END;
/
```

Because STRM_ADMIN is the function owner, we do not need to grant EXECUTE on the function. If the function was created in a different schema, then we would want to explicitly grant execute on the function to STRM_ADMIN.

Next we determine which rule to which to add the transformation function. You can either create a new rule at this point, or use an existing rule. We will use our HR1 rule from above (we can do this because we removed the Declarative RENAME_COLUMN transformation from the rule in our last step of the Declarative Transformation example).

```
select * from dba_rules;
```

Then, we use the DBMS_STREAMS_ADM.SET_RULE_TRANSFORM_FUNCTION procedure to add the transformation function to the desired rule:

```
BEGIN
 DBMS_STREAMS_ADM.SET_RULE_TRANSFORM_FUNCTION(
   rule_name         => 'HR1',
   transform_function => 'strm_admin.DEPT_COLNAME_CHANGE');
END;
/
```

We will now see the transformation in the DBA/ALL_STREAMS_TRANSFORM_FUNCTION view:

```
SQL>  select * from all_streams_transform_function;

RULE_OWNER
------------------------------

RULE_NAME                        VALUE_TYPE
------------------------------ --------------------

TRANSFORM_FUNCTION_NAME           CUSTOM_TYPE
------------------------------------ -----------

STRM_ADMIN
HR1                              SYS.VARCHAR2
"STRM_ADMIN"."DEPT_COLNAME_CHANGE"  ONE TO ONE
```

> For more detailed information on UCRBT, please reference the Usage Notes for the DBMS_STREAMS_ADM.SET_RULE_TRANSFORM_FUNCTION procedure in the *Oracle PL/SQL Packages and Types Reference*, and the *Oracle Streams Concepts and Administration Guide*.

Transformation order of execution

It is possible to have a combination of declarative and user defined transformations assigned to a single rule. This being the case, how do you know which ones get executed when? Especially, if you have not assigned step numbers. There is a default order of execution for transformation that help keep the rule from running amuck.

- If the rule is a Subset rule, then Row Migration is always executed first
- Next are Declarative Rule based transformations

These are further ordered by the step number specified for each transformation if they have been assigned. If the step numbers are not assigned, the transformations are executed in the following order:

- `Delete_Column`
- `Rename_Column`
- `Add_Column`
- `Rename_Table`
- `Rename_Schema`
- Last (but not the least), the User Created Rule-Based Transformation is executed.

How the transformation is processed

The Streams process to which you assign the Rule Based Transformation determines when the transformation is applied to the LCR. The transformation is only applied if the rule belongs to a positive rule set and the LCR evaluates to true for the rule (if it belonged to a negative rule then evaluating to TRUE would mean that we don't send the change—so why transform it?).

At the Capture (basic and synchronous)

1. The Capture process creates the LCR from the redo log change
2. The transformation is applied (if the rule evaluates to TRUE)
3. The transformed LCR is stored in the Capture Queue

At the Propagation

1. The Propagation process begins the dequeue of the LCR
2. The transformation is applied to the LCR (if the rule evaluates to TRUE)
3. The Propagation process completes the dequeue of the LCR
4. The transformed LCR is sent to the destination queue

At the Apply

1. The Apply process begins the dequeue of the LCR
2. The transformation is applied to the LCR (if the rule evaluates to TRUE)
3. The Apply process completes the dequeue of the LCR
4. The transformed LCR is applied at the destination

Transformation errors

If the transformation errors, it has significant ramifications on the overall Streams processes. To protect data integrity between the source and destination databases, stringent rules are put in place. In most cases, the Streams process that is performing the transformation is disabled if there is an error. This means that all Streams configurations dependent on that process come to a halt until the error is addressed. The rule of thumb here is to make sure you have very thorough exception handling in your transformation PL/SQL packages.

At the Capture (basic and synchronous)

If the transformation is declarative and the error can be ignored (like removing a column that does not exist), the error is ignored and the process continues.

If the transformation is declarative and the error cannot be ignored, or if the transformation is user created; the LCR is not captured, the error is raised to the Capture process, and the Capture process is disabled.

At the Propagation

The LCR is not dequeued or propagated, and the error is raised to the Propagation process.

At the Apply

The LCR is not dequeued or applied, the error is raised to the Apply process, and the Apply process is disabled.

If some of the messages in the LCR were successfully transformed, the LCR is placed in the Apply Error queue. Those transformations that were completed are retained in the LCR when it is moved to the Apply Error queue. Attempts to execute the error with the DBMS_APPLY_ADM.EXECUTE_ERROR procedure will only process the LCR as-is and not attempt to execute further transformation.

To mitigate a transformation failure and re-enable any disabled Streams processes, you must either fix the problem in the PL/SQL function or remove the Rule Based Transformation.

Things to remember when working with Rules

If you wish to modify a rule created using `DBMS_RULE_ADM.CREATE_RULE`, it can be modified with `DBMS_RULE_ADM.ALTER_RULE` procedure.

If you wish to modify a rule created by `DBMS_STREAMS_ADM.ADD_*_RULE`, you may wish to drop the existing rule and create a new rule with the new parameters to ensure that the rule metadata is updated as expected.

`DBMS_RULE_ADM.ALTER_RULE` can support rules created using the `DBMS_STREAMS_ADM` package, but certain metadata may not be updated as expected.

It is recommended that you do not use the `DBMS_RULE_ADM.DROP_RULE` to drop a rule created using `DBMS_STREAMS_ADM` as it may not remove all the metadata for the rule. Instead, use the `DBMS_STREAMS_ADM.REMOVE_RULE` procedure.

In general, a good rule of thumb is to use the same package to modify, remove or drop a rule that was used to create the rule.

If you are creating your own Rules and Rule Sets, make sure to coordinate the evaluation_context assignments with the client application event generation specified evaluation_context. Otherwise you may receive unexpected results if the wrong evaluation_context is inadvertently used.

Downstream Capture—avoid white water at the source

In Chapter 1, we briefly mention **Downstream Capture (DSC)** and how it can be used to offload the Capture and Propagation processes off a Production/Source Server. In this section, we will take a deeper dive into DSC and cover:

- What is DSC?
- When to use DSC?
- How to set up DSC?

By covering the above with the example provided, you should have the information needed to understand and properly use DSC.

DSC is a configuration of Streams that has the Capture and Propagation Process on a different server from where the data is processed. Recall the first image that was seen in Chapter 1 of DSC.

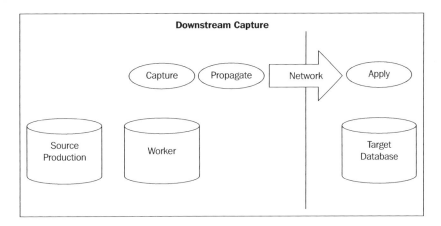

The Source Production database is where all the transactions are run against. The Worker database receives redo logs from the Source Production database and then the normal Streams process (Capture, Propagate) happens on the Worker database (flowing from left to right in the image) and then the Apply process is at the Target Database. Notice that we wrote that the Worker Database receives the redo logs.

The components of DSC are a mixture of concepts from Oracle Data Guard and Oracle Streams. The Oracle Streams processes we know about already. As for Oracle Data Guard components, the redo transport service is used in DSC. It is this redo transport service that is used in DSC to move logs from a Source Production database to a Worker Database. Also note that a Worker Database can be the end Target Database as seen in the following image:

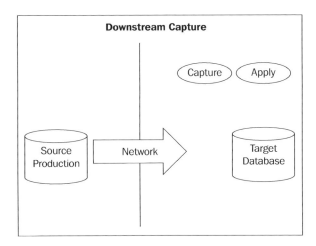

From the previous image, we can see that the **Target Database** has both the Capture and Apply processes. As all the processing is on the **Target Database** there is no need to have a Propagate process. To get a better understanding, let us start with one of the differences in DSC as compared to a "regular" Streams configuration—the parameter **LOG_ARCHIVE_DEST_n**.

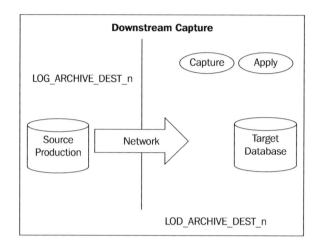

LOG_ARCHIVE_DEST_n is a parameter that is used on both the source and target sides. Setting this parameter will control how the redo logs are sent and received at the source and target side. We will configure the parameter, **LOG_ARCHIVE_DEST_2** on both source and target, as a part of the example used in this section.

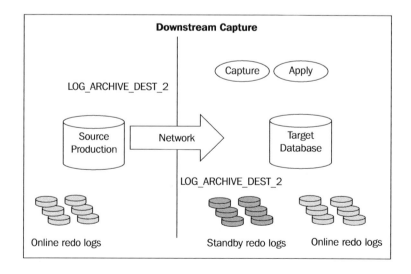

Evolving the diagram, we now show the local **Online redo logs** for each of the respective databases. Also, **Standby redo logs** have been added on the **Target Database** side. The Oracle recommendation for Standby redo logs is to have at least one more group than the number of online redo log file groups on the source. The properly configured Capture process will scan the Standby redo logs that came across the network. The Standby redo logs will cross the network as a result of configuring the parameter **LOG_ARCHIVE_DEST_2** on both source and target sides.

Up to this point we have covered a little of the what and how of DSC. Shifting focus to the when of DSC, we answer the question, when should you use DSC? DSC is most often used to "offload" the Capture and Propagation processes off of the host machine of your Source Production (Database).

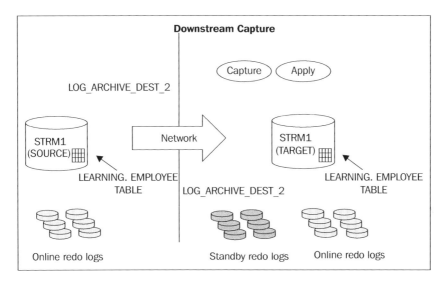

Now back to the how. We are going to take the image above and fully work through the scenario from ground zero. The scenario and assumptions are:

- We have a Production Level OLTP database, STRM1, and due to the policy and performance demand only required and necessary processing can be done on the host server.

- A replicated database is needed where activities that are not "required and necessary" can be done. The replicated database will be STRM2.

- Network and Storage resources have been properly scoped and allocated.

- Both databases are configured in archive log mode.

- The necessary supplemental logging and pre-work for Streams configuration has been completed and this includes setting up a Streams Administrator. We will use STRM_ADMIN as the Streams Administrator for this chapter. Please refer to Chapter 3 for details on the pre-work for Streams.

- The schema in this example is LEARNING.

We will be going over the set up of DSC with the following steps:

1. Setting up the redo log transport.

2. Configuring the Streams part of DSC.

Setting up the redo log transport

1. The SYS password needs to be the same on the source and target. Run the following command on source and target to make sure that the sys password is the same. Replace <password> with a password that meets your security policy requirement.

   ```
   alter user sys identified by <password>;
   ```

2. A DBLINK between STRM2 and STRM1 will also be used. Create this as Streams Administrator.

   ```
   -- run on STRM2.US.APGTECH.COM
   conn STRM_ADMIN/STRM_ADMIN
   -- create dblink
   create database link STRM2.US.APGTECH.COM connect to STRM_ADMIN
   identified by STRM_ADMIN using 'STRM2';
   -- test it
   select * from STRM2.US.APGTECH.COM;
   ```

3. The configuration of LOG_ARCHIVE_DEST_2 on STRM2 should be:

   ```
   ALTER SYSTEM SET LOG_ARCHIVE_DEST_STATE_2=ENABLE SCOPE=SPFILE;
   ALTER SYSTEM SET LOG_ARCHIVE_DEST_2='LOCATION=/u07/STRM2/standby-
   archives/
   VALID_FOR=(STANDBY_LOGFILE,PRIMARY_ROLE)'
   SCOPE=SPFILE;
   ```

4. Set the parameter LOG_ARCHIVE_CONFIG to enable the sending and receiving of redo logs between STRM1 and STRM2

   ```
   -- run on STRM2.US.APGTECH.COM
   ALTER SYSTEM SET LOG_ARCHIVE_CONFIG='DG_CONFIG=(STRM1,STRM2)'
   SCOPE=SPFILE;
   ```

5. Now for creating the Standby redo logs on STRM2. This example is for a single instance database. We will cover RAC at the end of this example. Let's "Keep It Simple" for right now.

- ° Determine the size of the redo log on source (STRM1)

```
SELECT L.THREAD#,
       L.GROUP#,
       L.BYTES / 1024 / 1024 MB,
       LF.MEMBER LOCATION
  FROM V$LOG L, V$LOGFILE LF
 WHERE L.GROUP# = LF.GROUP#;
```

- ° The result should be similar to below (shown in table format for clarity):

THREAD#	GROUP#	MB	LOCATION
1	1	50	/u04/oracle/STRM1/archives/
1	2	50	/u05/oracle/STRM1/archives/
1	3	50	/u06/oracle/STRM1/archives/

- ° Once the size of the redo logs is determined from Source we can create the Standby redo log on STRM2. Remember to create an additional group as recommended by Oracle.

```
-- run on STRM2.US.APGTECH.COM
conn /as sysdba
ALTER DATABASE ADD STANDBY LOGFILE GROUP 4
(/u07/STRM2/standby-archives/slog4.rdo') SIZE 50M;
ALTER DATABASE ADD STANDBY LOGFILE GROUP 5
(/u07/STRM2/standby-archives/slog5.rdo') SIZE 50M;
ALTER DATABASE ADD STANDBY LOGFILE GROUP 6
(/u07/STRM2/standby-archives/slog6.rdo') SIZE 50M;
ALTER DATABASE ADD STANDBY LOGFILE GROUP 7
(/u07/STRM2/standby-archives/slog7.rdo') SIZE 50M;
```

- ° Confirm that standby redo logs were created successfully:

```
-- run on STRM2.US.APGTECH.COM
conn /as sysdba
SELECT GROUP#, THREAD#, SEQUENCE#, ARCHIVED, STATUS
FROM V$STANDBY_LOG;
```

Now to configure redo transport service for the STRM1 side

6. The configuration of `LOG_ARCHIVE_DEST_2` on `STRM1` should be:

```
ALTER SYSTEM SET LOG_ARCHIVE_DEST_STATE_2=ENABLE SCOPE=SPFILE;
ALTER SYSTEM SET LOG_ARCHIVE_DEST_2='SERVICE=STRM2 LGWR SYNC
NOREGISTER
VALID_FOR=(ONLINE_LOGFILES,PRIMARY_ROLE)
DB_UNIQUE_NAME=ORCL102D'
SCOPE=SPFILE;
```

Note that we are using SYNC parameter for real-time downstream Capture process. Otherwise use SYNC.

7. Set the parameter `LOG_ARCHIVE_CONFIG` to enable the sending and receiving of redo logs between `STRM1` and `STRM2`

```
-- run on STRM1.US.APGTECH.COM
ALTER SYSTEM SET LOG_ARCHIVE_CONFIG='DG_CONFIG=(STRM1,STRM2)'
SCOPE=SPFILE;
```

Now we have the redo transport service configured for real-time downstream capture. Our next step is to configure.

Configuring the Streams part of DSC

If you have not already done so, create the schema LEARNING with a couple of tables on `STRM1` and `STRM2`. You can modify (see notes at the beginning of script) and use the supplied script, `Create_LEARNING.sql` to quickly create a tablespace, user, and the table EMPLOYEE with data.

From this point forward, the setting up of DSC should be fairly familiar with some slight important. The steps involved are all on `STRM2`. The following scripts are all run on `STRM2.US.APGTECH.COM`.

1. Create a single Queue to be used by both Capture and Apply process.

```
conn STRM_ADMIN/STRM_ADMIN
BEGIN
DBMS_STREAMS_ADM.SET_UP_QUEUE(
queue_table => 'STRM_ADMIN.DOWNSTREAM_Q_TABLE',
queue_name => 'STRM_ADMIN.DOWNSTREAM_Q',
queue_user => 'STRM_ADMIN');
END;
/
```

2. Create the Apply process.

```
conn STRM_ADMIN/STRM_ADMIN
BEGIN
DBMS_APPLY_ADM.CREATE_APPLY(
```

```
queue_name => 'STRM_ADMIN.DOWNSTREAM_Q',
apply_name => 'DOWNSTREAM_APPLY',
apply_captured => TRUE
);
END;
/
```

3. Create the Capture process.

```
conn STRM_ADMIN/STRM_ADMIN
BEGIN
DBMS_CAPTURE_ADM.CREATE_CAPTURE(
queue_name => 'STRM_ADMIN.DOWNSTREAM_Q',
capture_name => 'DOWNSTREAM_CAPTURE',
rule_set_name => NULL,
start_scn => NULL,
source_database => 'STRM1.US.APGTECH.COM',
use_database_link => true,
first_scn => NULL,
logfile_assignment => 'implicit'); -- Refer to Note below.
END;
/
```

It is at this point that we specifically focus on the logfile_assignment parameter. We set this parameter to 'implicit' to instruct the CAPTURE process to scan all redo log files added by redo transport services or manually from the source database to the downstream database.

4. Alter the Capture process for real-time capturing

Once the Capture process is created; this command will alter it so that real-time capturing can occur. Real-time Capture, captures changes in the online redologs from Source.

```
conn STRM_ADMIN/STRM_ADMIN
BEGIN
DBMS_CAPTURE_ADM.SET_PARAMETER(
capture_name => 'DOWNSTREAM_CAPTURE',
parameter => 'downstream_real_time_mine',
value => 'y');
END;
```

You will also need to archive the current redo log on the Source with this command:

```
ALTER SYSTEM ARCHIVE LOG CURRENT;
```

5. **Add the rule to the Capture process**

```
conn STRM_ADMIN/STRM_ADMIN
BEGIN
DBMS_STREAMS_ADM.ADD_SCHEMA_RULES(
schema_name => 'LEARNING',
streams_type => 'capture',
streams_name => 'downstream_capture',
queue_name => 'STRM_ADMIN.downstream_q',
include_dml => true,
include_ddl => true,
include_tagged_lcr => false,
source_database => 'STRM1.US.APGTECH.COM',
inclusion_rule => TRUE);
END;
/
```

6. **Instantiate the schema**

```
conn STRM_ADMIN/STRM_ADMIN
DECLARE
-- Variable to hold instantiation SCN value
iscn NUMBER;
BEGIN
-- Get current SCN from Source
iscn := DBMS_FLASHBACK.GET_SYSTEM_CHANGE_NUMBER@STRM1.US.APGTECH.COM;
DBMS_APPLY_ADM.SET_SCHEMA_INSTANTIATION_SCN(
source_schema_name => 'LEARNING',
source_database_name => 'STRM1.US.APGTECH.COM',
instantiation_scn => iscn,
recursive => TRUE);
END;
/
```

7. **Start up the Apply and Capture process**

```
Start the Apply process:
==================
conn STRM_ADMIN/STRM_ADMIN

exec DBMS_APPLY_ADM.START_APPLY(apply_name => 'DOWNSTREAM_APPLY');
select apply_name, status from dba_apply;

Start the Capture process:
==================
conn STRM_ADMIN/STRM_ADMIN

exec DBMS_CAPTURE_ADM.START_CAPTURE(capture_name =>
                                    'DOWNSTREAM_CAPTURE');
select capture_name, status from dba_capture;
```

8. Test and Celebrate

Now on `STRM1.US.APGTECH.COM` add some additional data and confirm Streaming.

```
Insert into LEARNING.EMPLOYEES (EMPLOYEE_ID, FIRST_NAME, LAST_
NAME, TIME) Values (5, 'Larry', 'Jonson', NULL);
Insert into LEARNING.EMPLOYEES (EMPLOYEE_ID, FIRST_NAME, LAST_
NAME, TIME) Values (6, 'Karen', 'Kim', NULL);
```

So, DSC, is just another configuration of Oracle Streams with a little bit of help from redo transport services. If you are in a situation where policy or performance reason dictates that "only ("pure") OLTP process can run on Production" then DSC is a possible solution.

Streams change tables—just tracking the "Facts" Ma'am

Streams Change Tables provide us with the ability to capture and replicate "data change audit information" that is often required to meet Regulatory Standards such as SOX, and FISMA. The Streams Change Tables are new in 11gR2 and are created and maintained using the `DBMS_STREAMS_ADM.MAINTAIN_CHANGE_TABLE` procedure. As discussed in Chapter 1, this procedure configures a separate change audit table for a Streamed table, and creates all the components necessary to capture, send, and record data change information to the change table. This procedure can also be used to create one-way replication of a table along with the change capture from a source to a destination database. Change tables can be implemented for local or downstream capture, and local or remote apply configurations.

Before configuring Change tables you will want to have made the following decisions:

- The type of environment to configure
- The source table columns to track
- If/what metadata to record
- The Values to Track for Update Operations (old, new)
- Whether to Configure a `KEEP_COLUMNS` Transformation
- Whether to Specify CREATE TABLE Options for the Change Table
- Whether to Perform the Configuration Actions Directly or With a Script
- Whether to Replicate the Source Table as well

For our purposes, we will make the following decisions:

- Type of environment Single-Source Master
- Table columns and values to track: all old and new
- Metadata: username and time
- No additional "create table" options
- We will keep all columns
- We will Replicate the source table as well

Based on this, we make the following call to DBMS_STREAMS_ADM.MAINTAIN_CHANGE_TABLE:

```
begin
DBMS_STREAMS_ADM.MAINTAIN_CHANGE_TABLE(
   change_table_name    => 'HR.EMPLOYEES_CHANGES',
   source_table_name    => 'HR.EMPLOYEES',
   column_type_list     => 'EMPLOYEE_ID NUMBER(6), FIRST_NAME
VARCHAR2(20),
                            LAST_NAME VARCHAR2(25), EMAIL VARCHAR2(25),
                            PHONE_NUMBER VARCHAR2(20), HIRE_DATE DATE,
                            JOB_ID VARCHAR2(10), SALARY NUMBER(8,2),
                            COMMISSION_PCT NUMBER(2,2),
                            MANAGER_ID NUMBER(6),
                            DEPARTMENT_ID NUMBER(4)',
   extra_column_list    => 'username,source_time',
   capture_values       => '*',
   options_string       => NULL,
   script_name          => 'changetable_employees.sql',
   script_directory_object => 'SCRIPT_DIR',
   perform_actions      => TRUE,
   capture_name         =>'HR_CAPT_EMP',
   propagation_name     => 'HR_PROP_EMP',
   apply_name           => 'HR_APPLY_EMP',
   source_database      => 'STRM1',
   destination_database    => 'STRM2',
   keep_change_columns_only => TRUE,
   execute_lcr          => TRUE);
end;
/
```

Note: At the time of writing, the Authors have experienced potential SQL parsing issues with the DBMS_STREAMS_ADM.MAINTAIN_CHANGE_ TABLE procedure on Linux. The Authors are working with Oracle to determine if the issues are related to parameter syntax/datatype or with internal processing. When the cause of the issues have been determined and resolved, this section will be updated to include additional information for the functionality of this new feature.

Some things to keep in mind when running the script:

- The Change table is created at the database specified for the destination_database parameter.

- There cannot be a table with the name specified for the change_table_name parameter at the database specified for the destination_database parameter.

- The apply_name parameter can only be null if there are no Apply processes at the destination database.

- If an apply_name is specified, no messaging client with the same name can exist at the destination database.

- If specified capture, propagation, and/or Apply processes already exists, the procedures adds the rules to the positive rule set of the process. If the process does not exist, it will create the process.

- If you specify the same database for the source_database and the destination_database, then you probably don't want to specify execute_lcr = TRUE as it could end up attempting to apply the same change back to the source table.

- As with the other DBMS_STREAMS_ADM.MAINTAIN_* procedures, and with a new functionality, we highly recommend that you first run the procedure with perform_actions = FALSE, and have it generate a script that you can then review to fully understand what the procedure is going to do before it does it. You can then either run the script as-is from SQLPlus as the Streams Administrator, or modify the script as you see necessary.

For more detailed information on Streams Change Tables and the DBMS_STREAMS_ADM.MAINTAIN_CHANGE_TABLE procedure, please reference the Oracle Streams Concepts and Administration Guide, and the Oracle PL/SQL Packages and Types Reference.

Automatic propagation split and merge—redirecting the current

Prior to Oracle 11g, maintaining a single capture queue for multiple destinations was not highly recommended due to performance impacts to the overall Streaming, and as a result, substandard propagation performance from the source to one or more destinations. As for Oracle 11g, Propagation Split and Merge not only allows the DBA to separate a sub-performant destination from a single capture queue on the fly, but also automates the remerging of the destination to the original capture queue, if and when the destination propagation performance reaches an acceptable level. Chapter 1 covers the theory of the Propagation Split and Merge feature, here we will review how to implement the feature.

The Propagation Split and Merge is managed using the following procedures:

- `DBMS_STREAMS_ADM.SPLIT_STREAMS`
- `DBMS_STREAM_ADM.MERGE_STREAMS_JOB`
- `DBMS_STREAM_ADM.MERGE_STREAMS`
- `DBMS_PROPAGATION_ADM.CREATE_PROPAGATION`

specifically the auto_merge_threshold parameter to automate the remerge of the Propagation process once propagation performance to the destination site reaches an acceptable level.

For our example, we have a Single-Source one Hub and two (2) Spoke environment (One master database, H1, and two secondary databases, S1 and S2). The Master Hub has a single capture queue and process, and two Propagation processes; one to each Spoke Site. Each Spoke has an Apply queue and process for changes received from H1.

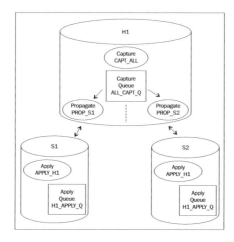

If propagation to S2 becomes degraded, the DBA can Split the propagation from the capture queue using the DBMS_STREAMS_ADM.SPLIT_STREAMS procedure as such:

```
declare
sched_name varchar2(50);
mergejob_name varchar2(50);
begin
DBMS_STREAMS_ADM.SPLIT_STREAMS(
    propagation_name           =>'PROP_S2',
    cloned_propagation_name    =>'CLONE_PROP_S2',
    cloned_queue_name          =>'CLONE_CAPT_S2_Q',
    cloned_capture_name        =>'CLONE_CAPT_S2',
    perform_actions            => TRUE,
    script_name                => 'Split_S2_Stream.sql',
    script_directory_object    => 'SCRIPT_DIR',
    auto_merge_threshold       => 6,
    schedule_name              =>sched_name,
    merge_job_name             =>mergejob_name);
end;
/
```

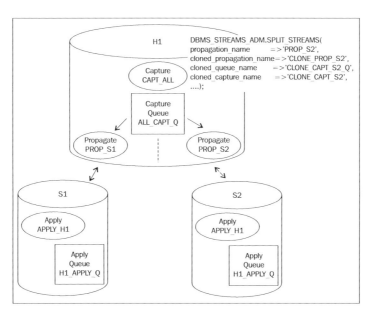

The result of this procedure is the creation of a new capture queue,
CLONE_CAPT_S2_Q, and process CLONE_CAPT_S2; and a new Propagation process
CLONE_PROP_S2 from the CLONE_CAPT_S2_Q to the APPLY_H1_Q at the S2 site. Also,
the original Propagation process PROP_S2 is removed all together.

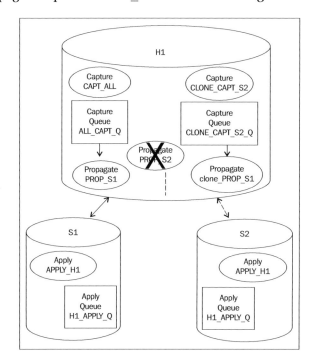

Notice we specified six seconds for the auto_merge_threshold. This means that a
scheduler job will be created to monitor the latency of the CLONE_CAPT_S2 Capture
process. We can access the scheduler name and merge job name via out parameters.
You can also view the job information in the DBMS_SCHEDULER_JOB view. The
scheduler job runs the DBMS_STREAMS_ADM.MERGE_STREAMS_JOB procedure based
on its schedule.

The DBMS_STREAMS_ADM.MERGE_STREAMS_JOB procedure is actually responsible for
comparing the latency of the cloned capture with the orignal capture and merging
the cloned processes back into the original processes if the difference falls at or
below the specified auto_merge_threshold.

If the latency for the new CLONE_CAPT_S2 process falls below a difference of six
seconds from the latency of the original CAPT_ALL Capture process, the job will
merge the cloned stream back into the original stream.

This latency is determined by comparing the `CAPTURE_MESSAGE_CREATE_TIME` for the original Capture process and the cloned Capture process in the `GV$STREAMS_CAPTURE` view.

If we had specified NULL or zero (0) for the `auto_merge_threshold`, a schedule job would not be created to automate the merge. We would need to accomplish this manually using the `DBMS_STREAM_ADM.MERGE_STREAM` procedure.

```
begin
DBMS_STREAMS_ADM.MERGE_STREAMS(
    cloned_propagation_name   => 'Clone_PROP_S2',
    propagation_name          => 'PROP_S2',
    queue_name                => 'CAPT_ALL_Q',
    perform_actions           => TRUE,
    script_name               => 'Merge_S2_Stream.sql',
    script_directory_object   => 'SCRIPT_DIR');
end;
/
```

The result of the merge is the deletion of the cloned queue, `CLONE_CAPT_S2_Q`, the cloned Capture process, `CLONE_CAPT_S2`, and the cloned Propagation process, `CLONE_PROP_S2`. A new Propagation process, `PROP_S2` is created from the original `CAPT_ALL_Q` at `H1` to the `APPLY_H1_Q` at `S2`. Essentially, returning the Stream back to its original configuration.

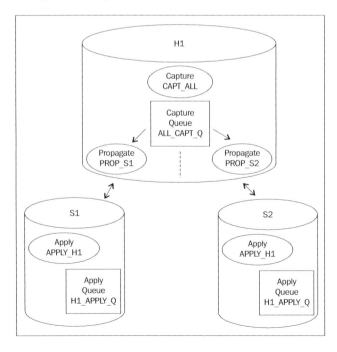

You can view information concerning Split/Merge operation in the
DBA_STREAMS_SPLIT_MERGE view.

 For more detailed information on Propagation Split and Merge, and associated packages, please reference the Oracle Streams Concepts and Administration Guide, and the Oracle PL/SQL Packages and Types Reference.

Basic Heterogeneous Configuration

Not all is Oracle (sorry Larry). In many situations, the need to share data between different database platforms is unavoidable. For many versions now, Oracle has support cross-platform data sharing with Oracle Heterogeneous Services (HS) and Transparent Gateways (TG). Heterogeneous Services is a service that can be installed in an Oracle database that will translate Oracle SQL syntax to a specific "generic" syntax. Heterogeneous Services works in concert with Oracle Transparent Gateways. A Transparent Gateway client allows Oracle to make a connection to a Non-Oracle database via a database link. The Transparent Gateway can then accept the generic SQL syntax generated by Heterogeneous Services and translate it into the platform specific SQL syntax for its specific Non-Oracle database platform, and run the translated SQL at the Non-Oracle database. Heterogeneous Services handles generic translation for code that is common among the different Gateways. The Gateways handle translation for code that is specific to that particular Gateway Non-Oracle database platform (A list of the different Gateway platforms supported in 11*g* can be found in chapter 1). If the SQL returns data, the Gateway retrieves the data from the Non-Oracle database, and returns it to the Oracle session. Transparent Gateway connectivity is configured via Oracle Net (a.k.a SQLNet) as a database link.

The basic steps for Oracle to Non-Oracle communications is as follows:

1. A distributed/remote SQL statement is issued to the Oracle Server (the SQL contains at database link).

2. Oracle determines that the data is external by the database link.

3. Oracle passes the distributed portion of the SQL to the Heterogeneous Services for generic translation.

4. Heterogeneous Services performs the initial translation and the passes the generic SQL to the Gateway configured for the database link.

5. The Gateway performs any platform specific translations.

6. The Gateway executes the translated SQL at the Non-Oracle database.

7. If the translated SQL returns data, the Gateway retrieves the data from the Non-Oracle Database.

8. The Gateway then maps the Non-Oracle datatypes to Oracle datatypes.

9. The Gateway then returns the data to the waiting Oracle session processing the SQL.

Streams can be configured to use HS and TG to replicate data to and from an Oracle database to a Non-Oracle database. The Apply process must be created on the Oracle database (because its an Oracle specific process) using the DBMS_APPLY_ADM.CREATE_APPLY procedure. The DBMS_APPLY_ADM.CREATE_APPLY procedure allows us to specify an apply_database_link. This database link used for a Non-Oracle database would be configured for Transparent Gateway connectivity. When the Apply process dequeues and processes an LCR, it constructs the SQL statement to accomplish the transaction contained in the LCR (as we discussed Chapter 1). This SQL statement is then passed through the HS and executed at the Non-Oracle database via the TG database link.

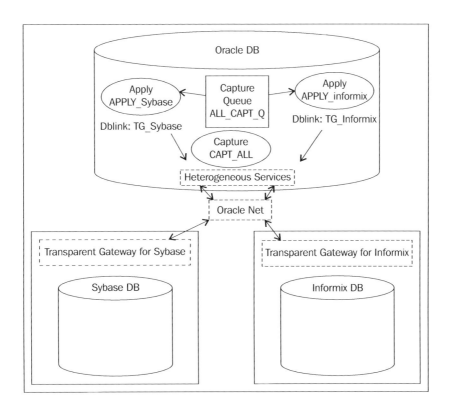

You can not alter an Apply process to add or remove an `apply_database_link`. It can only be added at Apply process creation, and only with the `DBMS_APPLY_ADM.` `CREATE_APPLY` procedure.

Capture and Propagation are created as normal. If the Capture is on the same database as the Apply process, propagation need not be configured. In this case, the Apply process can be configured to use the same queue as the resident Capture process.

Configuring a Heterogeneous Apply process

The following code for setting up a Heterogeneous Apply process can be found in the `HeterogeneousApply.sql` code file.

1. First, Configure Heterogeneous Services and the Appropriate Transparent Gateway to the Non-Oracle database.

   Refer to the Oracle Database Heterogeneous Connectivity User's Guide and the Oracle Database Gateway for [platform] User's Guide for information on this step.

2. Configure Oracle Net (listener.ora and tnsnames.ora) to use HS.

   Reference the "Configuring Oracle Net Services for Oracle Heterogeneous Services" section of Chapter 13 in the Oracle Database Net Services Administrator's Guide.

   listener.ora

```
SID_LIST_LISTENER=
  (SID_LIST=
   (SID_DESC=
    (SID_NAME=sybasegw)
    (ORACLE_HOME=/oracle11g)
    (PROGRAM=tg4sybs)))
```

   tnsnames.ora alias

```
TG_Sybase=
  (DESCRIPTION=
   (ADDRESS=(PROTOCOL=tcp)(HOST=sybase-server)(PORT=1521))
   (CONNECT_DATA=
     (SERVICE_NAME=sybasegw)
   )
     (HS=ok)))
  )
```

3. Create the database link (dblink) for the Non-Oracle Gateway.

   Note: for the USING clause, you can specify the gateway tnsalias in your tnsnames.ora or the "description" syntax for the alias. Also, make sure to specify a user that is configured at the Non-Oracle database that has the necessary DML privileges on target tables.

```
CREATE DATABASE LINK TG_SYBASE.oracle.com CONNECT TO "<sybase_user>"
    IDENTIFIED BY "&password" USING 'TG_Sybase';
      or
CREATE DATABASE LINK TG_SYBASE.oracle.com CONNECT TO "<sybase_user>"
    IDENTIFIED BY "&password"
    USING '(DESCRIPTION=
            (ADDRESS=(PROTOCOL=tcp)(HOST=sybase-server)(PORT=1521))
            (CONNECT_DATA=
              (SERVICE_NAME=sybasegw)
            )
              (HS=ok)))
          )';
```

4. Test the link by running a basic select statement using the dblink

```
select ... from "tablename"@tg_sybase.oracle.com;
```

5. Create the Apply process using the DBMS_APPLY_ADM.CREATE_APPLY procedure setting

```
BEGIN
  DBMS_APPLY_ADM.CREATE_APPLY(
    queue_name          => 'strmadmin.CAPT_ALL',
    apply_name          => 'APPLY_Sybase',
    apply_database_link => 'TG_SYBASE.oracle.com',
    apply_captured      => TRUE);
END;
/
```

6. Add an Apply Rule to the Apply process

```
BEGIN
  DBMS_STREAMS_ADM.ADD_TABLE_RULES(
    table_name     => 'hr.jobs',
    streams_type   => 'apply',
    streams_name   => 'APPLY_Sybase',
    queue_name     => 'strmadmin.streams_queue',
    include_dml    => TRUE,
    include_ddl    => FALSE,
```

```
        source_database => 'Oracle_DB.oracle.com',
        inclusion_rule   => TRUE);
    END;
    /
```

7. **Set any Apply Process parameters you wish**

```
BEGIN
  DBMS_APPLY_ADM.SET_PARAMETER(
    apply_name  => 'APPLY_Sybase',
    parameter   => 'disable_on_error',
    value       => 'N');
END;
/
```

8. **Prepare the table for instantiation and set the Apply process SCN**

```
DECLARE
  iscn  NUMBER;
BEGIN
  iscn := DBMS_FLASHBACK.GET_SYSTEM_CHANGE_NUMBER();
  DBMS_APPLY_ADM.SET_TABLE_INSTANTIATION_SCN(
    source_object_name    => 'hr.jobs',
    source_database_name  => 'Oracle_DB.oracle.com',
    instantiation_scn     => iscn);
  DBMS_APPLY_ADM.SET_TABLE_INSTANTIATION_SCN(
    source_object_name    => 'hr.jobs',
    source_database_name  => 'Oracle_DB.oracle.com',
    instantiation_scn     => iscn,
    apply_database_link   => 'TG_SYBASE.oracle.com');
END;
/
```

9. **Start the Apply Process**

```
BEGIN
  DBMS_APPLY_ADM.START_APPLY(
    apply_name  => 'APPLY_Sybase');
END;
/
```

For more information on setting up Heterogeneous Replication, please reference the Oracle Streams Concepts and Administration Guide, and the Oracle Streams Extended Examples manual.

Some basic rules to remember when configuring an Apply process for a Non-Oracle database.

- The Apply process and queue are configured at the Oracle database
- No queue is created on the non-Oracle database
- The replicated Oracle tables must be prepared for instantiation and the apply SCN set for the Apply process
- The tables at the Non-Oracle database must be created and populated with the necessary data manually
- To avoid data convergence, the Non-Oracle tables should have the same or "equivalent" data as their Oracle table counter-part
- Only basic DML operations are supported
- Captured DDL changes cannot be applied on the non-Oracle database
- Error handlers and conflict handlers are not supported
- Conflict detection is supported

Data Transfer via Queue Messaging

If you wish to populate Oracle tables from Non-Oracle databases, you must create a client application that retrieves the data from the Non-Oracle database and inserts it into the appropriate Oracle tables. The client application can be coded to retrieve the data directly from the Non-Oracle database, or from an Oracle session using HS and TG database links.

You can also use client applications that are coded to use advanced queue messaging and LCR datatypes to enqueue data into a Streams queue to which an Apply process is assigned.

Basic XSTREAMS Configuration

As discussed in Chapter 1, GoldenGate XSTREAMS is new in 11gR2 and provides an alternative to the above traditional Heterogeneous methods. XSTREAMS technology can be used to build LCRs from Non-Oracle database log files, that can then be enqueued into an Oracle Streams queue. While much of the XSTREAM OCI and Java API usage is beyond the scope of this book, we briefly discuss the Oracle database configuration and Specialized Server processes that support XSTREAMS OCI and Java API.

The following views provide XSTREAMS configuration and performance information:

- DBA/ALL_XSTREAM_OUTBOUND
- DBA/ALL_XSTREAM_OUTBOUND_PROGRESS
- DBA/ALL_XSTREAM_INBOUND
- DBA/ALL_XSTREAM_INBOUND_PROGRESS
- DBA/ALL_XSTREAM_RULES
- V$STREAMS_APPLY_READER
- V$STREAMS_APPLY_SERVER
- V$STREAMS_CAPTURE
- V$STREAMS_MESSAGE_TRACKING
- V$STREAMS_TRANSACTION

XSTREAMS Servers

First, let's look at configuring the Specialized Server processes that support XSTREAMS. There are two: XSTREAM Out and XSTREAM In.

The XSTREAM Out process is an Outbound Server that supports XSTREAM access to dequeue LCRs from a Streams Capture queue. The XSTREAMS In process is an Inbound server that supports XSTREAM access to enqueue LCR's and messages to a Streams apply queue.

You can configure multiple Outbound and Inbound Servers; just remember to increase your PROCESSES initialization parameter as necessary to accommodate the added processes. As with regular Streams client processes, an XSTREAMS Server process can only be assigned to a single queue. However, multiple Servers can be assigned to the same queue.

Configuring the Database

Before creating the XSTREAM Server processes, make sure that your Oracle Streams and database is configured to support the normal Streams clients and queues (capture, apply): this includes, database parameter, Streams Pool and Streams Administrator configuration, database link configuration, archive logging, etc (see Chapter 3 for configuring your database to support Streams). Once you have Oracle Streams configured, you can tap into the Stream using XSTREAMS.

The XSTREAMS Server processes are configured using the DBMS_XSTREAM_ADM package.

Configuring XSTREAMS Out

An XSTREAMS Out server can either be created with its own capture queue and process, or can be created to an existing capture queue and process. To create an Out server that uses its own capture queue and process, you use the DBMS_XSTREAMS_ADM. CREATE_OUTBOUND procedure. To create an Out Server that uses an existing capture queue and process, you use the DBMS_XSTREAMS_ADM.ADD_OUTBOUND procedure.

The DBMS_XSTREAMS_ADM.CREATE_OUTBOUND procedure accomplishes the following:

- Configures supplemental logging for the specified table objects if not already done
- Creates a Capture queue with a system-generated name used by the Outbound Server
- Creates and starts a Capture process with a system-generated name with appropriate capture rule sets
- Creates and starts an Outbound server with appropriate Apply rule sets
- Sets the current user as the connect user for the outbound server

Ideally, the current user is the Oracle Streams Administrator.

> Note: If you wish to specify names for the Capture queue and Process, you will need to create the Capture queue and process manually, and then use the DBMS_XSTREAMS_ADM.ADD_OUTBOUND procedure to add the Outbound Server rules to the Capture process.

The DBMS_XSTREAMS_ADM.ADD_OUTBOUND procedure accomplishes the following:

- Creates and starts an Outbound server with appropriate Apply rule sets
- Sets the current user as the connect user for the outbound server

Ideally, the current user is the Oracle Streams Administrator.

The CREATE_OUTBOUND and ADD_OUTBOUND procedures can be used to add Table, Schema, and Global level rules. The procedures have a table_names parameter and a schema_names parameter that accept either a DBMS_UTILITY.UNCL_ARRAY datatype (for multiple names), or a VARCHAR2 string (for single name). You can specify both parameters in the same call, just avoid specifying tables in the table_names parameter that will be included in the schema objects of the schemas specified in the schema_names parameter. If you want to generate Global Level Rules, Set both table_name and schema_name parameters to NULL.

An Outbound Server is essentially a specialized Apply process, and can be managed with the DBMS_APPLY_ADM procedures. However, not all DBMS_APPLY_ADM procedures can be used. The following lists which DBMS_APPLY_ADM procedures can be used to manage an XSTREAMS Outbound Server process:

- ALTER_APPLY Procedure
- DROP_APPLY Procedure
- SET_GLOBAL_INSTANTIATION_SCN Procedure
- SET_PARAMETER Procedure
- SET_SCHEMA_INSTANTIATION_SCN Procedure
- SET_TABLE_INSTANTIATION_SCN Procedure
- START_APPLY Procedure
- STOP_APPLY Procedure

Steps for configuring an XSTREAMS Outbound Server

The following code examples can be found in the XStreams.sql code file.

1. Create the Outbound Server:

   If the Capture queue and Process exist, use
   DBMS_XSTREAMS_ADM.ADD_OUTBOUND

   In this example we will assume that we have a Capture queue, HROE_CAPT_Q, and a Capture process, HROE_CAPT, that captures Schema level changes for the HR and OE schemas already configured. Here we want the Outbound Server to access all HR schema changes and table level changes for the OE.ORDERS and OE_ORDER_ITEMS tables.

```
DECLARE
   ob_tables   DBMS_UTILITY.UNCL_ARRAY;
   ob_schemas DBMS_UTILITY.UNCL_ARRAY;
BEGIN
     tables(1)   := 'OE.ORDERS';
     tables(2)   := 'OE.ORDER_ITEMS';
     schemas(1) := 'HR';
   DBMS_XSTREAM_ADM.ADD_OUTBOUND(
     server_name      => 'HROE_Out',
     queue_name       => 'STRM_ADMIN.HROE_CAPT_Q',
     source_database => 'STRM1',
     table_names      => ob_tables,
     schema_names     => ob_schemas);
END;
/
```

OR

To create a capture queue and process with the Outbound Server, use
`DBMS_XSTREAMS_ADM.CREATE_OUTBOUND`.

```
DECLARE
   ob_tables  DBMS_UTILITY.UNCL_ARRAY;
   ob_schemas DBMS_UTILITY.UNCL_ARRAY;
BEGIN
    tables(1)   := 'OE.ORDERS';
    tables(2)   := 'OE.ORDER_ITEMS';
    schemas(1) := 'HR';
  DBMS_XSTREAM_ADM.CREATE_OUTBOUND(
    server_name      =>  'HROE_Out',
    table_names      =>  ob_tables,
    schema_names     =>  ob_schemas);
END;
/
```

2. Create the Client Application that will use the Outbound Server process.

3. The client application must connect to the database as the user schema that created the XSTREAM Outbound Server to interact with that Server process.

 For an example client application, please reference the "Sample XSTREAM Client Application" Section of Chapter 3 — Configuring XStream in the Oracle Database XStream Guide.

4. Add Additional Outbound Servers as needed.

5. Start the Outbound Server

```
exec DBMS_APPLY_ADM.START_APPLY('HROE_Out');
```

6. To remove an Outbound Server configuration, use the `DBMS_XSTREAM_ADM.DROP_OUTBOUND` procedure

```
BEGIN
  DBMS_XSTREAM_ADM.DROP_OUTBOUND('HROE_Out');
END;
/
```

Subsetting Rules for an Outbound Server

You can also add Subsetting rules to an existing Outbound server

The `DBMS_XSTREAMS_ADM.ADD_SUBSET_OUTBOUND_RULES` adds subsetting rules, much like the `DBMS_STREAMS_ADM.ADD_SUBSET_RULES` procedure.

The `ADD_SUBSET_OUTBOUND_RULES` condition parameter equates to the `ADD_SUBSET_RULES` dml_condition parameter. The `ADD_SUBSET_OUTBOUND_RULES` keep parameter equates the `ADD_SUBSET` include_rule parameter (If `TRUE`, include the LCRs that meet the condition. If `FALSE`, ignore the LCRs that meet the condition).

```
DECLARE
   col_list DBMS_UTILITY.LNAME_ARRAY;
   x number := 0;
BEGIN
   select column_name from dba_tab_cols where owner = 'HR'
                                          and table_name = 'EMPLOYEES';
   for arec in (select column_name from dba_tab_cols
               where owner = 'HR' and table_name = 'EMPLOYEES')
   loop
     x := x+1;
     col_list(x) := arec.column_name;
   end loop;
   --last position in the array must be set to NULL
   If x >0 then
     x := x+1;
     col_list(x) := NULL;
   end if;
   DBMS_XSTREAM_ADM.ADD_SUBSET_OUTBOUND_RULES(
     server_name => 'HROE_Out',
     table_name  => 'HR.EMPLOYEES',
     condition   => 'department_id = 50',
     column_list => col_list,
     keep        => TRUE);
END;
/
```

To remove a Subsetting rule from an Outbound Server, first determine the Subset Rule names:

```
SELECT STREAMS_NAME, STREAMS_TYPE, STREAMS_RULE_TYPE,
      RULE_OWNER, SUBSETTING_OPERATION, RULE_NAME
   FROM DBA_XSTREAM_RULES
   WHERE SUBSETTING_OPERATION IS NOT NULL;
```

Then use the `DBMS_XSTREAM_ADM.REMOVE_SUBSET_OUTBOUND_RULES` procedure to remove the rules

```
DBMS_XSTREAM_ADM.REMOVE_SUBSET_OUTBOUND_RULES(
     server_name      IN VARCHAR2,
     insert_rule_name IN VARCHAR2,
     update_rule_name IN VARCHAR2,
     delete_rule_name IN VARCHAR2);
```

Configuring XSTREAMS In

XSTREAM Inbound Servers can receive DML and DDL changes, configured as an LCR, from a client application. These changes can be applied to Oracle database objects, or can be handled by customized processing via apply handlers. The client application can use the XSTREAMS OCI or Java API interface to generate and pass the LCR to the Inbound Server process.

As with the Outbound Server process, the Inbound Server process is a specialized Apply process. One big difference with an Inbound Server Apply process is that it only uses its assigned queue to store erred LCRs. Another difference is that, by default, the Inbound server does not use rules or rule sets. However, rules and rule sets can be added to an Inbound Server process using the DBMS_STREAMS_ADM or DBMS_RULE_ADM packages once the Inbound Server process is created.

An Inbound Server process is created using the DBMS_XSTREAMS_ADM.CREATE_INBOUND procedure.

The DBMS_XSTREAMS_ADM.CREATE_OUTBOUND procedure accomplishes the following:

- Creates an Inbound server process
- Assigns the specified queue to the Inbound Server process as its error queue
- If the queue does not exist, the procedure creates it
- Sets the current user as the Apply user for the Inbound Server process if the apply_user parameter is null

Steps for configuring an XSTREAMS inbound server

The following code examples can be found in the XStreams.sql code file.

1. Create the Inbound Server:

```
BEGIN
  DBMS_XSTREAM_ADM.CREATE_INBOUND(
     server_name => 'XSTRM_IN',
     queue_name  => 'XSTRM_IN_ERR_Q',
     apply_user => 'STRM_ADMIN'
     );
END;
/
```

2. Create the Client Application that will use the Inbound Server process.

   The client application must connect to the database as the apply_user for the XSTREAM Inbound Server to interact with that Server process.

For an example client application, please reference the "Sample XSTREAM Client Application" section of Chapter 3 — *Configuring XStream in the Oracle Database XStream Guide.*

4. Add Apply Handler to the Inbound Server as needed.
5. This can be done using the DBMS_APPLY_ADM package.
6. Start the Inbound Server

```
exec DBMS_APPLY_ADM.START_APPLY('XSTRM_IN');
```

Subsetting is not supported with XSTREAMS Inbound Server processes.

To remove an Inbound Server configuration, use the DBMS_XSTREAM_ADM.DROP_INBOUND procedure

```
BEGIN
  DBMS_XSTREAM_ADM.DROP_OUTBOUND('XSTRM_IN');
END;
/
```

 For more information on configuring XSTREAMS Server processes and using the DBMS_XSTREAMS_ADM package, please reference the Oracle Database XSTREAMS Guide.

Summary

In this chapter we looked at ways to implement advanced Streams features and configurations using specialized parameters, procedures, and techniques.

We covered how to replicate a subset of rows from a table to a destination site.

We addressed Tags; what they are, and how they can be used to fine-tune how capture, propagate, and Apply processes handle each individual LCR.

We looked at Rules, which are the framework of Streams, and their evaluation criteria and action context. We also investigated how to extend these components to meet special needs via Rule Based Transformation, and User-Created Rules and Evaluation Contexts. We also discussed how to manage rules created using the different packages available, and some does and don'ts along the way.

Plus, we presented examples of how to configure advanced Streamed environments such as Synchronous and Down-Stream Capture, Streams Change Tables, Propagation Split and Merge, and Heterogeneous Streaming using the traditional Heterogeneous Services and Transparent Gateways, and the new XSTREAMS.

In the next chapter we will address a necessary evil that almost every developer-techno-geek avoids like the plague…Documentation! It's a dirty job, but will make your life easier in the long run. No really, it will…Promise!

7
Document What You Have and How It Is Working

One of the things I joke about is the cliché and concern of losing a key member of any team. Try this joke with your client or manager and see their face of concern when you tell them that you are going to the local bus station to play chicken with the buses!

Even if you work with a team of DBAs, often the responsibility of a particular feature or functionality will be on the shoulders of the specialist within the team. This chapter will address some of the concerns about losing a key member of any team by creating and maintaining proper documentation. Yes, your co-workers will miss you. However, follow the suggestions in this chapter and they will sing your praises when you leave.

This chapter covers the following:

- How to create a map of your Streams environment
- Taking a look at some of the basic Streams Views
- How to use `UTL_SPADV` to automate collections of Streams performance statistics

Mapping the Stream

Being able to hand over documentation that fully describes your Oracle Streams environment is the goal we are trying to achieve. Getting to the goal in the most efficient manner is the goal of this chapter. As you are probably the person that set up Streams, you are the lucky winner who will do the documentation. If you are the person handed the "opportunity" to learn Streams earlier today, then reviewing, confirming, and building documentation will be part of your task when you take over administration responsibilities.

Like Chapter 5 on *N-Way Replication*, this chapter will focus on using the Oracle supplied packages. Oracle made substantial improvements to help the Streams Administrator: set up, document, and monitor Streams all through supplied packages. Knowing Streams down to the supplied packages level also allows for creative usages to build custom monitoring beyond Database Control and/or Grid Control.

The Stream without a map

In order to learn how to document, we have to start with the basic questions of "What should we document?" We want to document everything that we have set up and determine if Streams is working correctly or within acceptable baselines.

The documentation plan is to have a high level of current Streams environment. Then drive down to the detail components and baseline performance level. Fortunately, as you have probably set up the Streams environment, you can quickly sketch out the environment in a quick picture. If you are the lucky "winner" who inherited the Streams environment then you will need to derive this picture from the techniques covered in this chapter.

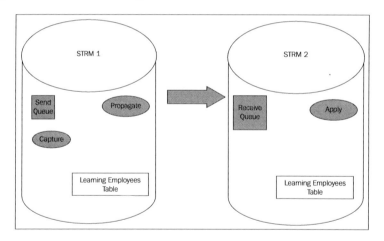

Oracle has supplied about two hundred and fifty or so supplied packages with Oracle 11*g*R2. Out of those, we will focus on two of them. They are as follows:

- DBMS_STREAMS_ADVISOR_ADM
- UTL_SPADV

These two supplied packages and a little creativity will build all your documentation. The documentation will be easily updated and maintained once you understand how to use these two key packages.

DBMS_STREAMS_ADVISOR_ADM

DBMS_STREAMS_ADVISOR_ADM has only one package and it is ANALYZE_CURRENT_
PERFORMANCE. Using DBMS_STREAMS_ADVISOR_ADM is conceptually similar to using
DBMS_WORKLOAD_REPOSITORY PACKAGE. You create snapshots to gather data into
data dictionary views. Then you can either query the related views directly or use
other packages to produce a report.

> Run all the scripts in the chapter as Streams Administrator. The Streams
> Administrator must have been granted all the necessary rights and
> permissions with DBMS_STREAMS_AUTH.GRANT_ADMIN_PRIVILEGE.
> We also set line size 200; or you can use the glogin.sql given in
> Chapter 5.

In Streams they did not call the gathering of data snapshots; that would be too easy.
Instead, the Streams Administrator gathers data by asking Oracle to ANALYZE CURRENT
PERFORMANCE for Streams. This is done by executing the following command:

```
exec DBMS_STREAMS_ADVISOR_ADM.ANALYZE_CURRENT_PERFORMANCE;
```

-- wait for some time period and then

```
exec DBMS_STREAMS_ADVISOR_ADM.ANALYZE_CURRENT_PERFORMANCE;
```

The commands above gather data related to the components and performance of your
Streams environment. Waiting between ANALYZE CURRENT PERFORMANCE commands
allows changes to be gathered. Essentially what happens is data is gathered from the
first execution of ANALYZE CURRENT PERFORMANCE, waits for some time to pass, and
executes ANALYZE CURRENT PERFORMANCE again. The difference between the first and
second run is what is in the views that are mentioned as follows:

View Name	Answer the question of	Life of Data
DBA_STREAMS_TP_COMPONENT	What are the parts of the Streams environment?	Permanent
DBA_STREAMS_TP_COMPONENT_LINK	How do the parts relate to each other?	Permanent
DBA_STREAMS_TP_DATABASE	What databases are involved in the Stream?	Permanent
DBA_STREAMS_TP_COMPONENT_STAT	How are the parts doing?	Temporary
DBA_STREAMS_TP_PATH_STAT	How is the path doing?	Temporary
DBA_STREAMS_TP_PATH_BOTTLENECK	What might be causing a slow down?	Temporary

The image following is another way to understand what data is permanent or temporary in which view.

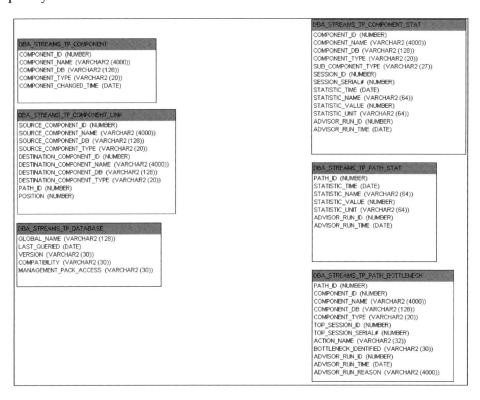

The data in the views on the left are permanent while the data in the views on the right are temporary. Taking a closer look at the tables reveals that the tables on the left relate to the "parts" of Streams, while the tables to the right are "performance" oriented. When you end your session that is performing queries above, then data related to performance is lost.

If you wish to persist this data in the temporary views, you can select it into a permanent table. For instance:

create table my_streams_tp_path_bottleneck as select * from dba_streams_tp_path_bottleneck

Making the map

The process of mapping out and gathering data about your Streams environment should be done in one session with the following steps:

1. Collect the data needed into the tables mentioned previously with

   `exec DBMS_STREAMS_ADVISOR_ADM.ANALYZE_CURRENT_PERFORMANCE;`

   -- wait for some time and

   `exec DBMS_STREAMS_ADVISOR_ADM.ANALYZE_CURRENT_PERFORMANCE;`

   At a minimum, run two `ANALYZE_CURRENT_PERFORMANCE`.

2. Querying the respective views in the previous figure. The following table has a listing of the supplied queries for this chapter. These queries are a modification of those supplied by Oracle.

Query Name	Purpose
`ListDBs.sql`	List out the databases that are part of the Streams environment
`ListParts.sql`	List out the parts of the Streams environment
`ListPaths.sql`	List the Path of the Streams environment
`ListARs.sql`	List out Advisor Runs that have been collected
`ListBNs.sql`	List out the Bottlenecks using the latest Advisor Run
	(The views used in this query require Oracle Diagnostic Pack)
`ListPerfParts.sql`	List the performance of the parts of the Streams environment using the latest Advisor Run
`ListPerfFlows.sql`	List the flow and/or waits for the Streams environment the latest Advisor Run
`ListPerfS2E.sql`	List the performance from start to end of the Stream using the latest Advisor Run

Learn by doing. Just having these queries mean nothing unless you take the time and try them in your environment. So, here is the framework for using these queries. You need to create the Streams environment for this chapter. Setting up Streams multiple times is good practice and by now you should be comfortable with the process. To make things easier for you the scripts to build the environment pictured in the first figure are included.

- `0000_CleanHouse.sql`
- `0025_Create_STRMADMIN_Both_Sides.sql`
- `0050_Create_Learning_Both_Sides.sql`
- `0100_Source_Grant_All.sql`

- 0200_Both_DB_Link.sql
- 0300_Source_Setup.sql
- 0400_Instantiate_Schema_Setup.sql
- 0500_Destination_Setup.sql
- 0600_Destination_Startup.sql
- 0700_Source_Startup.sql

If you have a Streams Administer already created, you can use 0000_CleanHouse.sql and skip 0025_Create_STRMADMIN_Both_Sides.sql then run the remainder of the scripts in numeric order. The comments and instructions are in each script.

If you are starting from scratch, start with 0025_Create_STRMADMIN_Both_Sides.sql and *do not* use 0000_CleanHouse.sql. Then, run the remainder of the scripts, comments, and instructions in each script in numeric order.

Now that your environment is up and running, here are some suggestions on mapping your environment and learning its particular performance characteristics. Make sure to use the glogin.sql of Chapter 5 to configure your SQLPlus session display.

Build your Streams map by running these scripts in the order presented as follows:

1. ListDBs.sql
2. ListParts.sql
3. ListPaths.sql

Take time to study the results of each query. The result from ListDBs.sql is easy to read and understand. As for ListParts.sql and ListPaths.sql, take some time and notice the order of the data. You should be able to build the Streams map from the result of running ListDBs.sql and ListParts.sql.

To cause a bottleneck, run BN_Exercise.sql. Use three separate SQL*Plus sessions connecting as follows:

1. SYS on STRM2
2. STRM_ADMIN on STRM1
3. STRM_ADMIN on STRM2

The LOCK TABLE command is used to cause the bottleneck. Full instructions and comments are in the BN_Exercise.sql script.

To obtain an understanding of the following, you will need to use `loop.sql` to cause some load.

1. `ListPerfParts.sql`
2. `ListPerfFlows.sql`
3. `ListPerfS2E.sql`

The `loop.sql` inserts records into `LEARNING.EMPLOYEES` at a rate of one record every half second for five minutes. While the load is running, run `advise.sql` a couple of times. Then run each of the `ListPerf*.sql`. Get a feel for each of the queries and what it provides. Note that each of the `ListPerf*.sql` will use the latest Advisor Run.

For a high-level view of how Streams is performing, run `ListPerfS2E.sql`. If performance is not what you expect then dig down using `ListPerfParts.sql` or `ListPerfFlows.sql`.

Basic Streams views

There are times when you already know or suspect where a problem may be in the Streams environment. So, having a handful of queries related to the main processes is useful. Here are some of the queries we keep in our toolbox and the reasoning on when to use each. The queries listed below are in `Handy.sql`. The scripts are from source side to destination side.

-- CHECK ON THE STATUS AND IF THERE ARE

-- ANY ERRORS WITH CAPTURE PROCESS

```
SELECT CAPTURE_USER, CAPTURE_NAME, QUEUE_OWNER, QUEUE_NAME,
STATUS,STATUS_CHANGE_TIME, ERROR_NUMBER, ERROR_MESSAGE
FROM DBA_CAPTURE;
```

-- TO CHECK ON THE BUFFER QUEUE PROPAGATION SCHEDULES ON THE

--SENDING (SOURCE) SIDE

```
SELECT QUEUE_ID, QUEUE_SCHEMA, QUEUE_NAME, STARTUP_TIME,
PROPAGATION_NAME, DBLINK, STATE
FROM V$PROPAGATION_SENDER;
```

-- CHECK ON THE PROPAGATION

```
SELECT PROPAGATION_NAME, SOURCE_QUEUE_OWNER, SOURCE_QUEUE_NAME,
DESTINATION_QUEUE_OWNER, DESTINATION_QUEUE_NAME, DESTINATION_DBLINK,
STATUS, ERROR_MESSAGE, ERROR_DATE
FROM DBA_PROPAGATION;
```

-- CHECK ON THE BUFFER QUEUE PROPAGATION SCHEDULES ON THE SENDING (DESTINATION) SIDE

```
SELECT SRC_QUEUE_SCHEMA, SRC_QUEUE_NAME, SRC_DBNAME,
DST_QUEUE_SCHEMA, DST_QUEUE_NAME, PROPAGATION_NAME, STATE
FROM V$PROPAGATION_RECEIVER;
```

-- CHECK ON THE STATUS OF APPLY

```
SELECT APPLY_NAME, STATUS, STATUS_CHANGE_TIME,
ERROR_NUMBER, ERROR_MESSAGE
FROM DBA_APPLY;
```

-- CHECKING THE PROGRESS OF THE APPLY PROCESS

```
SELECT APPLY_NAME, SOURCE_DATABASE,
APPLY_TIME-APPLIED_MESSAGE_CREATE_TIME AS LAG,
SPILL_MESSAGE_NUMBER
FROM DBA_APPLY_PROGRESS;
```

UTL_SPADV

The DBA's time is precious. So, automate and stop wasting it on mundane and tedious tasks. That is what UTL_SPADV does; it automates the collection of statistics related to Streams performance. UTL_SPADV is simple to use and once configured, you can forget about it. Then take it to the next level and automated custom reports against the data collected.

UTL_SPADV has six subprograms. Following are their names along with their definitions:

- UTL_SPADV.COLLECT_STATS

```
UTL_SPADV.COLLECT_STATS(
interval                      IN NUMBER DEFAULT 60,
num_runs                      IN NUMBER DEFAULT 10,
comp_stat_table               IN VARCHAR2 DEFAULT
                              'STREAMS$_ADVISOR_COMP_STAT',
path_stat_table               IN VARCHAR2 DEFAULT
                              'STREAMS$_ADVISOR_PATH_STAT',
top_event_threshold           IN NUMBER DEFAULT 15,
bottleneck_idle_threshold     IN NUMBER DEFAULT 50,
bottleneck_flowctrl_threshold IN NUMBER DEFAULT 50);
```

- UTL_SPADV.START_MONITORING

  UTL_SPADV.START_MONITORING(
  job_name   IN VARCHAR2 DEFAULT
                                   'STREAMS$_MONITORING_JOB',
  client_name   IN VARCHAR2 DEFAULT NULL,
  query_user_name   IN VARCHAR2 DEFAULT NULL,
  interval   IN NUMBER DEFAULT 60,
  top_event_threshold   IN NUMBER DEFAULT 15,
  bottleneck_idle_threshold   IN NUMBER DEFAULT 50,
  bottleneck_flowctrl_threshold   IN NUMBER DEFAULT 50,
  retention_time   IN NUMBER DEFAULT 24);

- UTL_SPADV.IS_MONITORING

  UTL_SPADV.IS_MONITORING(
  job_name   IN VARCHAR2 DEFAULT
                                   'STREAMS$_MONITORING_JOB',
  client_name   IN VARCHAR2 DEFAULT NULL)
  RETURN BOOLEAN;

- UTL_SPADV.SHOW_STATS

  UTL_SPADV.SHOW_STATS(
  path_stat_table   IN VARCHAR2 DEFAULT
                                   'STREAMS$_ADVISOR_PATH_STAT',
  path_id   IN NUMBER DEFAULT NULL,
  bgn_run_id   IN NUMBER DEFAULT -1,
  end_run_id   IN NUMBER DEFAULT -10,
  show_path_id   IN BOOLEAN DEFAULT TRUE,
  show_run_id   IN BOOLEAN DEFAULT TRUE,
  show_run_time   IN BOOLEAN DEFAULT TRUE,
  show_optimization   IN BOOLEAN DEFAULT TRUE,
  show_setting   IN BOOLEAN DEFAULT FALSE,
  show_stat   IN BOOLEAN DEFAULT TRUE,
  show_sess   IN BOOLEAN DEFAULT FALSE,
  show_legend   IN BOOLEAN DEFAULT TRUE);

- UTL_SPADV.ALTER_MONITORING

  UTL_SPADV.ALTER_MONITORING(
  interval   IN NUMBER DEFAULT NULL,
  top_event_threshold   IN NUMBER DEFAULT NULL,
  bottleneck_idle_threshold   IN NUMBER DEFAULT NULL,
  bottleneck_flowctrl_threshold   IN NUMBER DEFAULT NULL,
  retention_time   IN NUMBER DEFAULT NULL);

- UTL_SPADV.STOP_MONITORING(

  purge   IN BOOLEAN DEFAULT FALSE);

Automating the collection of Streams performance data

Using the Streams setup of STRM1 to STRM2 at the beginning of this chapter we will do the following:

1. Configure UTL_SPADV using defaults settings.
2. Configure and confirm automated collection of data.
3. Place load on STRM1 to be STREAMed to STRM2.
4. Analyze the data.
5. Change UTL_SPADV to more aggressive collection schedule.
6. Use UTL_SPADV to stop collection of data.

The above should be done as STRM_ADMIN@STRM1.US.APGTECH.COM, except where noted in Step 1.

1. Configure UTL_SPADV using defaults settings

   For some unknown reason Oracle decided not to include the package UTL_SPADV as a default install. So, we have to do some additional work before using it.

   - As SYSDBA

     ```
     GRANT EXECUTE ON sys.dbms_lock TO STRM_ADMIN;
     ```

   - As STRM_ADMIN
     - Locate and run the utlspadv.sql script.
     - It can be found in ORACLE_HOME/ rdbms/admin directory
     - @utlspadv.sql

Use UTL_SPADV.COLLECT_STATS to start things all off. Think of it as a manual collection of Advisor Runs for a small period. It also creates the STREAMS$_ADVISOR_COMP_STAT and STREAMS$_ADVISOR_PATH_STAT tables.

```
exec UTL_SPADV.COLLECT_STATS
```

By default, this runs for 10 minutes creating Advice Runs (think snapshots) every 60 seconds. We would suggest running it with the following, just to get the tables created and so we can move on to setting up the automated version:

```
exec UTL_SPADV.COLLECT_STATS( interval => 30,
                              num_runs => 2);
```

2. Configure and confirm automated collection of data.

    You first start of by using:

    ```
    exec UTL_SPADV.START_MONITORING
    ```

    The Advice Runs are taken every 60 seconds and retained for 24 hours. We
    will modify this to be more aggressive and retain data for a longer period
    in a moment. It continues collecting until we stop it.

    To confirm that the Advice Runs are being collected, use:

    ```
    SET SERVEROUTPUT ON
    DECLARE
    this_collecting BOOLEAN;
    BEGIN
        this_collecting := UTL_SPADV.IS_MONITORING(
    job_name => 'STREAMS$_MONITORING_JOB');
    IF this_collecting=TRUE THEN
    DBMS_OUTPUT.PUT_LINE('Good job collecting of advice is
    automatic.');
    ELSE
    DBMS_OUTPUT.PUT_LINE('Nothing is being collected.');
    END IF;
    END;
    /
    ```

3. Place load on STRM1 to be STREAMed to STRM2

    Just simply run the included script on STRM1, loop_50.sql to create inserts
    for the next 25 minutes.

    ```
    declare
      n_numb number := 1;
    begin
        loop
          Insert into LEARNING.EMPLOYEES  (EMPLOYEE_ID, FIRST_NAME,
    LAST_NAME, TIME) Values (n_numb, 'Hello' || n_numb , 'You', NULL);
          COMMIT;
          n_numb := n_numb + 1;
          DBMS_LOCK.SLEEP(.25);   -- quarter second pause
          exit when n_numb >= 6000; -- about 25 minutes
        end loop;
    end;
    /
    ```

4. Analyze the data

```
-- run this if you used UTL_SPADV.COLLECT_STATS
spool run1.txt
SET SERVEROUTPUT ON SIZE 50000
BEGIN
UTL_SPADV.SHOW_STATS();
END;
/
spool off;
```

Once automatic collection of Advisor Runs is set up, use the following:

```
-- run this if you used UTL_SPADV.START_MONITORING
spool run2.txt
SET SERVEROUTPUT ON SIZE 50000
BEGIN
UTL_SPADV.SHOW_STATS(path_stat_table => 'STREAMS$_PA_SHOW_PATH_
STAT');
END;
/
spool off;
```

5. Change `UTL_SPADV` to more aggressive collection schedule

Changing the collections of Advisor Runs is accomplished with the following:

```
-- more aggressive monitoring every 30 seconds
-- retain for 48 hours
BEGIN
UTL_SPADV.ALTER_MONITORING(
interval => 30,
retention_time => 48);
END;
/
```

6. Use `UTL_SPADV` to stop collection of data.

```
exec UTL_SPADV.STOP_MONITORING
```

The collection of data from the previous gathering of Advisor Runs will still be retained.

It is easy to use `UTL_SPADV` packages. There are some minor "issues".

- You need to `GRANT EXECUTE ON sys.dbms_lock TO STRM_ADMIN`.

- You have to install the package with `@utlspadv.sql`. It is not installed by default.

- Format of output from `UTL_SPADV.SHOW_STATS` should be much easier to read.(I honestly think that Oracle support must have some kind of PERL script that makes the output of `UTL_SPADV.SHOW_STATS` more readable.)

But even with these minor "issues", the use of `UTL_SPADV` packages is similar to the use and evolution of `DBMS_WORKLOAD_REPOSITORY PACKAGE`. The `UTL_SPADV` packages will mature as more people use and ask for enhancements. Until then, the decision to use the `UTL_SPADV.SHOW_STATS` or to query the tables created by `utlspadv.sql` will be the choice of the Streams Administrator. The twelve core tables created are listed at the end of this chapter.

- `STREAMS$_PA_COMPONENT`
- `STREAMS$_PA_COMPONENT_LINK`
- `STREAMS$_PA_COMPONENT_PROP`
- `STREAMS$_PA_COMPONENT_STAT`
- `STREAMS$_PA_CONTROL`
- `STREAMS$_PA_DATABASE`
- `STREAMS$_PA_DATABASE_PROP`
- `STREAMS$_PA_MONITORING`
- `STREAMS$_PA_PATH_BOTTLENECK`
- `STREAMS$_PA_PATH_STAT`
- `STREAMS$_PA_SHOW_COMP_STAT`
- `STREAMS$_PA_SHOW_PATH_STAT`

 The `DBA_STREAMS_TP_*` and the `STREAMS$_PA_*` are very similar. They do not exactly match. But a good starting point is modifying the scripts supplied after the summary.

Summary

From being lost without a map to using `DBMS_STREAMS_ADVISOR_ADM` and `UTL_SPADV` to map out the Streams environment, this was a quick ride on how to be a cartographer for your Streams environment.

We used `DBMS_STREAMS_ADVISOR_ADM` for mapping out Streams and immediate troubleshooting. Then we moved on to setting up `UTL_SPADV` for the automated collection of Advisor Runs. Some of the minor concerns relating to `UTL_SPADV` were also covered. Those issues will most likely go away with the usage and maturity of `UTL_SPADV`.

8

Dealing with the Ever Constant Tides of Change

It *WAS* Working!

Number 1 claim when things stop working: Nothing Changed!

Number 1 reason when things stop working: Something Changed.

Change within a Streamed environment often has a far reaching impact. Changes come in two types: expected, and unexpected. Even the simplest of changes can bring the distributed environment to a halt; and unexpected changes can be the most detrimental. In the first section of this chapter, we will look at the impacts of, and dealing with, expectedly changing your existing Streamed environment. The focus will be on planning expected changes and knowing what to do to minimize their impact. The second section will address what to look for when things "stop working" due to unexpected changes . It will take you through techniques for identifying and troubleshooting issues with Streams that could result from such changes. Finally, the third section will give you some out-of-the-mainstream tips and tricks, and a brief introduction to additional tools.

In this chapter, we paddle through:

- Change Planning
- Troubleshooting unexpected changes and errors
- Helpful troubleshooting Tools
- And couple of tricks and tips

Affecting expected change effectively

The most consistent thing in life is change. Eventually, you will need to modify your Streamed environment or something in it. Big or small, the modification must be planned (back to that old design thing again) and the ramifications identified. Some changes may be external to the database but still impact on your Streamed environment (for instance IT notifies you that the allocated networking bandwidth between your databases will be reduced by 25% to accommodate a new application being added to the environment). Other changes may be required to support new and improved features for a distributed application (adding or modifying database object structures such as tables, view definitions, PL/SQL code, and so on), or an additional site (to accommodate a new region). And then of course, there are always the Oracle upgrades. As you become more familiar with the inner workings of Streams, you develop the ability to foresee how certain changes will impact on the overall Streamed environment as well as each component within the environment. And, most importantly, how these changes impact other components that do not change.

Changing States: Starting and stopping processes

One rule of thumb for affecting changes to the Streams processes is to configure and start and stop the processes in a specific order. You want to make sure your receiving processes are up and ready when you start the process that sends to it; a comparison that could be drawn is not throwing the ball to the home plate before the catcher gets there. This will help avoid the possible loss of events as mentioned in Chapter 4, *Single-Source Configuration*.

Start the processes in the following order:

- Apply
- Propagation
- Capture

Stop the processes in the follow order:

- Capture
- Propagation
- Apply

Another rule of thumb is to avoid collecting and sending changes for an object that is in the process of being configured for replication. This too can result in a loss of events. If you are adding a rule to an existing process, stop the process cleanly first. Once the rule has been successfully added, start the process and it will pick up where it left off. For Capture processes, this does require that all redo/archive from the Capture process `REQUIRED_CHECKPOINT_SCN` (or `FIRST_SCN`, if `REQUIRED_CHECKPOINT_SCN` is 0) be available to LogMiner.

Database changes

The key to affecting database changes is to ensure that everything is kept synchronized between the Streamed sites. The Streams Capture, Propagation, and Apply processes can be configured to handle DDL propagation as well as DML propagation, so DDL changes can be made at a primary master site and propagated via normal Streams processing. However, it may be necessary to coordinate the changes via other means.

Structure changes to existing objects

If DDL changes are necessary, make sure the Streams processes are configured to include DDL changes. If they are not, the DDL change must be manually made at each site at which the object is streamed.

If you intend to make object structure changes only at certain sites in your Streamed environment and not others, you must remember that by not applying a DDL change to all Streamed sites, the object behavior in the system will differ between the sites. Make sure this is well documented, so that when troubleshooting you are expecting the correct behavior from the object at any one site.

For tables, if a DDL change is not affected at all streamed sites hosting the table, the Apply processes where the DDL change is not made will break, and potentially, existing conflict resolution. You must make sure you put rule based transformation in place to accommodate a structure change not made at that site, as well as update any conflict resolution that may be affected by the structure change.

Data changes—beware the bulk load!

Bulk loads can generate massive amounts of redo that, when in a distributed environment, may bring the system to its knees. To avoid this, many choose to bypass Streams and run the bulk load at each site. To do this, make sure FORCE LOGGING is disabled on the databases to be loaded. You can then use the UNRECOVERABLE option in SQL*LOADER, or specify NO LOGGING for your load operation. This keeps the load from recording entries in the redo. If the entries are not in the redo, the Capture processes will not pick up the changes. Note that if you have synchronous capture configured, either remove the synchronous capture, or disable the capture triggers. Once the load is complete, remember to re-enable FORCE LOGGING on the database, and rebuild/re-enable your synchronous capture triggers. These methods are fine as long as the following precautions are taken:

- No changes are made at any site in the Streamed environment that must receive the load once the loading begins

- The bulk load is accomplished in the exact same manner at all master sites

- Any errors that occur during the bulk load at each site are rectified before Streaming is re-enabled

- All data is identical between master tables once the loading is complete; the number of records, and data values for each record are the same, and so on.

- In the event that some secondary master sites may have only subsets of the data loaded at a primary master, ensure that the secondary site data subset is complete when compared to the primary master site(s)

Otherwise, the data will not be synchronized and could result in erred or lost apply transactions (a.k.a the dreaded data divergence).

Expanding your Streamed environment

It often becomes necessary to expand an existing Streamed environment to accommodate new sites, or database objects. You pretty much use the same approach to expand, or add to a Streamed environment as you would for its initial creation. You want to make sure that you do not (or do) overwrite existing objects, and in some instances you may need to manually prepare objects at the capture site for reinstantiation.

As with your initial design, it helps to break down the changes needed into "single-master to single-destination views", using the Streams Site Matrix.

Let's look at two examples of expanding a Streamed environment. First, we will expand a Single-Source environment to include an additional Master site. Second, we will add a table to a Replicated Schema.

Example: Adding a Master Site

We start with our Streams Site Matrix that shows us what our current Streams environment looks like.

Streams Site Matrix for:	Replication Level:	Schema		Color Key:	Existing
	Name:	HR			Add/Remove
	Add/Remove:	Add	Comment:	Current Single Source	
				MS1 master to SS3 secondary	
		Destinations			
Source Sites		MS1	SS3		
MS1					
Capture	Process Name:	HR_CAPT			
	Queue Name:	HR_CAPT			
	DDL (Y/N):	Y			
	Transformations:				
Propagate	Process Name:		HR_PROP_SS3		
	From Queue Name:		HR_CAPT		
	To Queue Name:		HR_MS1_APPLY		
	DDL (Y/N):		Y		
	Transformations:				
Apply	Process Name:				
	Queue Name:				
	DDL (Y/N):				
	Transformations:				
	Conflict Resolution				
SS3					
Capture	Process Name:				
	Queue Name:				
	DDL (Y/N):				
	Transformations:				
Propagate	Process Name:				
	From Queue Name:				
	To Queue Name:				
	DDL (Y/N):				
	Transformations:				
Apply	Process Name:	HR_MS1_APPLY			
	Queue Name:	HR_MS1_APPLY			
	DDL (Y/N):	Y			
	Transformations:				
	Conflict Resolution	Site Priority - MS1			

Our current environment is Single-Source where MS1 is the master source site and SS3 is a secondary destination site. At MS1 we have a Capture process HR_CAPT, and a Propagation process HR_PROP_SS3 that propagates from the HR_CAPT queue to the HR_MS1_APPLY queue at SS3. At SS3, we have an Apply process HR_MS1_APPLY that has Site Priority conflict resolution defined where MS1 changes have priority over SS3 changes (just in case someone makes a change on SS3 that they really weren't supposed to make).

We want to add a master site MS2 that will have a Master-to-Master relationship with MS1, and a Master-to-Secondary relationship with SS3. We are going to choose to use the existing queues on MS1 and SS3 for MS2 stream processes (however, you do have the option to create a separate set of queues if you wish—just remember to add queue creation to your steps).

We are going to choose not to propagate DDL changes from MS2. This means that DDL changes can only be sent from MS1. By only propagating DDL changes from one master site, we are mimicking the old Master Definition Site architecture of Advanced Replication. If you choose to allow multiple masters to propagate DDL changes, you must implement conflict resolution to handle situations where DDL changes between masters conflict.

First, we will look at the "single source to single destination view" for MS1 to MS2.

MS1 already has a Capture process and queue for the HR schema, so no additions are needed there. One thing we need to consider is conflict resolution, since changes can be made at either MS1 or MS2. In this case, we will use Latest Timestamp (the latest change is applied if there is a conflict). This means that each of our tables in the HR schema must have a column that records the time the change was made (this opens up a whole new can of worms! BUT, because we sat down and worked out our design with the Streams Site Matrix, we are forewarned and thus forearmed). Time zone time differences need to be taken into account here. We need to either make sure the DB_TIMEZONE for all databases in the environment is the same, or we convert the time to equivalent time zone values when the record is created/modified, or during conflict resolution. We will also need to make sure that any application inserts/updates to the HR Schema tables update this new column. We can do this by creating a before trigger that sets the value of the column on insert/update to make the change transparent to any applications with code that manipulates data in the tables. Otherwise, application code must be modified to include the column in the DML operation. To configure Latest timestamp resolution, we would use the MAXIMUM resolution method referencing the time column.

To configure replication from MS1 to MS2, we will need to:

- Create the database on MS2 and configure for replication following the steps listed in Chapter 3
- Add timestamp columns and triggers to all HR tables at MS1
  - ° DDL propagation from MS1 to SS3 will automatically push these new columns to SS3
  - ° By adding the column and trigger to the tables before instantiating MS2, they are automatically picked up via the instantiation
- Capture MS2 SCN at this point to be used on MS1 and SS3 in later steps to avoid change loss should changes be made on MS2 before you complete
- Configure an Apply process at MS2 (HR_MS1_APPLY)
- Add conflict resolution at MS2 for the Apply process using the timestamp column as the resolution column

- Configure a Propagation process from MS1 to MS2
- Prepare the HR Schema on MS1 for instantiation
- Add/instantiate the HR Schema on MS2; including supplemental logging for the conflict resolution columns; privileges for the apply user and so on
- Set the MS1 instantiation SCN at MS2 if it was not accomplished via the above instantiation method
- Start the Apply process on MS2
- Start the Propagation process from MS1 to MS2
- Start the Capture process on MS1 (if stopped)

At this point our Streams Site Matrix looks like this:

Streams Site Matrix for:	Replication Level:	Schema		Color Key	Existing
	Name:	HR			Add/Remove
	Add/Remove:	Add	Comment:	Add MS2 to environment	
				Master-to-Master with MS1, Master-to-Secondary with SS3	
		Destinations			
Source Sites		MS1	SS3	MS2	
MS1					
Capture	Process Name:	HR_CAPT			
	Queue Name:	HR_CAPT			
	DDL (Y/N):	Y			
	Transformations:				
Propagate	Process Name:		HR_PROP_SS3	*HR_PROP_MS2*	
	From Queue Name:		HR_CAPT	*HR_CAPT*	
	To Queue Name:		HR_MS1_APPLY	*HR_APPLY*	
	DDL (Y/N):		Y	*Y*	
	Transformations:				
Apply	Process Name:				
	Queue Name:				
	DDL (Y/N):				
	Transformations:				
	Conflict Resolution				
SS3					
Capture	Process Name:				
	Queue Name:				
	DDL (Y/N):				
	Transformations:				
Propagate	Process Name:				
	From Queue Name:				
	To Queue Name:				
	DDL (Y/N):				
	Transformations:				
Apply	Process Name:	HR_MS1_APPLY			
	Queue Name:	HR_MS1_APPLY			
	DDL (Y/N):	Y			
	Transformations:				
	Conflict Resolution	Site Priority - MS1			
MS2					
Capture	Process Name:				
	Queue Name:				
	DDL (Y/N):				
	Transformations:				
Propagate	Process Name:				
	From Queue Name:				
	To Queue Name:				
	DDL (Y/N):				
	Transformations:				
Apply	Process Name:	*HR_MS1_APPLY*			
	Queue Name:	*HR_MS1_APPLY*			
	DDL (Y/N):	Y			
	Transformations:				
	Conflict Resolution	*Latest Time Stamp*			

Next we look at the "single source to single destination view" from MS2 to MS1 (the opposite path).

Because we have created the HR schema on MS2 as part of our set up from MS1 to MS2, we just need to handle changes going from MS2 to MS1.

To configure replication from MS2 to MS1 we will need to:

- Configure the Capture process on MS2 (it should not be started)
- Configure an Apply process on MS1 for MS2
- Add conflict resolution at MS1 for the Apply process using the timestamp column as the resolution column (for the DDL LCRs, you can use the DDL_HANDLER parameter of the Apply process to define a "conflict handler" for DDL changes)
- Configure a Propagation process from MS2 to MS1
- Prepare the HR Schema on MS2 for instantiation
- Instantiate the MS2 SCN on MS1
- Start the Apply process on MS1
- Start the Propagation process from MS2 to MS1
- Do not start the Capture process on MS2 yet (we still need to configure SS3)

We have now completed the design for the replication between MS1 and MS2. Our Streams Site Matrix now shows:

Streams Site Matrix for:	Replication Level:	Schema			Color Key:	Existing	
	Name:	HR				*Add/Remove*	
	Add/Remove:	Add		Comment:	Add MS2 to environment.		
					Master-to-Master with MS1, Master-to-Secondary with SS3		
		Destinations					
Source Sites		MS1	SS3		MS2		
MS1							
Capture	Process Name:	HR_CAPT					
	Queue Name:	HR_CAPT					
	DDL (Y/N):	Y					
	Transformations:						
Propagate	Process Name:		HR_PROP_SS3		*HR_PROP_MS2*		
	From Queue Name:		HR_CAPT		*HR_CAPT*		
	To Queue Name:		HR_MS1_APPLY		*HR_APPLY*		
	DDL (Y/N):		Y		*Y*		
	Transformations:						
Apply	Process Name:				*HR_MS2_APPLY*		
	Queue Name:				*HR_MS2_APPLY*		
	DDL (Y/N):						
	Transformations:						
	Conflict Resolution				*Latest Time Stamp*		
SS3							
Capture	Process Name:						
	Queue Name:						
	DDL (Y/N):						
	Transformations:						
Propagate	Process Name:						
	From Queue Name:						
	To Queue Name:						
	DDL (Y/N):						
	Transformations:						
Apply	Process Name:	HR_MS1_APPLY					
	Queue Name:	HR_MS1_APPLY					
	DDL (Y/N):	Y					
	Transformations:						
	Conflict Resolution	Site Priority - MS1					
MS2							
Capture	Process Name:				*HR_CAPT*		
	Queue Name:				*HR_CAPT*		
	DDL (Y/N):						
	Transformations:						
Propagate	Process Name:	*HR_PROP_MS1*					
	From Queue Name:	*HR_CAPT*					
	To Queue Name:	*HR_APPLY*					
	DDL (Y/N):						
	Transformations:						
Apply	Process Name:	*HR_MS1_APPLY*					
	Queue Name:	*HR_MS1_APPLY*					
	DDL (Y/N):	*Y*					
	Transformations:						
	Conflict Resolution	*Latest Time Stamp*					
		DDL - Conflict Resoltion					
		MS1 overwrites					

Let us turn our attention now to the "single source to single destination view" for MS2 to SS3.

SS3 only receives changes, it does not send them. This means we only need to create an Apply process for the changes coming from MS2. This is the easy part. Coordinating changes from two master sites is a little trickier.

If changes are made directly on SS3 in the As Is configuration, they are overwritten by changes from MS1 if a conflict occurs; easy enough. However, we now have to receive changes from MS2 as well. The expectation would be that if a change is made directly on SS3, it would be overwritten by an MS2 change if a conflict between the two occurred. However, what happens if the conflict arises as a result of a change on SS3 coming from MS1 that did not get toMS2 before the same row was changed at MS2 by another user and sent to SS3 (did that make your head hurt)? Should the MS2 change win on SS3, or should the old MS1 change win? In our master-to-master relationship between MS1 and MS2, we determined that the most recent change wins. So, not only do we need to implement Site priority conflict resolution to handle conflicts between direct SS3 changes and each master, we now need to also evaluate if the conflict is a result of a change from the other master. Take heart! There is actually a way to do this. User defined conflict resolution allows us to combine Site priority and Latest Timestamp evaluations to yield multiple levels of resolution. The user defined conflict resolution function first evaluates the site that created the change on SS3. The site value can be passed with the LCR via a tag or a column. If the originating site was SS3, then the record is overwritten by the master change. If the originating site was one of the masters, the change is evaluated for Latest Timestamp. The oldest change is discarded and the newest change is applied/kept. Keep in mind here that time zone differences need to be taken into consideration at this point. If the timestamps are for different time zones, they will need to be converted to equivalent times.

Believe it or not, this approach is pretty straight forward. But think of what it would be if you had more than 2 master sites sending changes and you had to apply multiple levels of conflict evaluation. The more masters, the more complicated and unmanageable conflict resolution becomes. That is why Oracle (and an architect that wishes to maintain his/her, and other's sanity) recommends keeping the number of master sites in a distributed environment to a minimum. It also helps to keep the number of conflict resolution evaluation levels used between master sites to a minimum as well.

So, to complete our addition of MS2 to our environment, we need to do the following on SS3:

- Configure an Apply process for MS2 changes
- Add user defined conflict resolution to the MS2 Apply process that evaluates first by Site Priority, and then by Latest Timestamp.
- Redefine the conflict resolution for the MS1 Apply process so that it evaluates first by Site Priority, and then by Latest Timestamp.
- Instantiate the MS2 SCN on SS3
- Start the MS2 Apply process on SS3
- Start the Propagation process from MS2 to SS3
- Start the Capture process on MS2

We now have a completed Streams Site Matrix from which we have gained great insight as to the more effective and efficient way to affect the change. You will notice that even though we are not changing replication from MS1 to SS3 (insert "but nothing changed between MS1 and SS3, so why did it break?" question here). However, we found out that we do indeed need to change components of the MS1 to SS3 replication to accommodate the new MS2 site. If we are focusing on only adding the new master site, the addition would end up causing a cascade of apply errors at SS3 which we do not see with just the MS1 master.

Streams Site Matrix for:	Replication Level:	Schema		Color Key:	Existing	
	Name:	HR			Add/Remove	
	Add/Remove:	Add	Comment:	Add MS2 to environment		
				Master-to-Master with MS1, Master-to-Secondary with SS3		
		Destinations				
Source Sites		MS1	SS3	MS2		
MS1						
Capture	Process Name:	HR_CAPT				
	Queue Name:	HR_CAPT				
	DDL (Y/N):	Y				
	Transformations:					
Propagate	Process Name:		HR_PROP_SS3	HR_PROP_MS2		
	From Queue Name:		HR_CAPT	HR_CAPT		
	To Queue Name:		HR_MS1_APPLY	HR_APPLY		
	DDL (Y/N):		Y	Y		
	Transformations:					
Apply	Process Name:			HR_MS2_APPLY		
	Queue Name			HR_MS2_APPLY		
	DDL (Y/N):					
	Transformations:					
	Conflict Resolution			Latest Time Stamp		
SS3						
Capture	Process Name:					
	Queue Name:					
	DDL (Y/N):					
	Transformations:					
Propagate	Process Name:					
	From Queue Name:					
	To Queue Name:					
	DDL (Y/N):					
	Transformations:					
Apply	Process Name:	HR_MS1_APPLY		HR_MS2_APPLY		
	Queue Name	HR_MS1_APPLY		HR_MS2_APPLY		
	DDL (Y/N):	Y				
	Transformations:					
	Conflict Resolution	Site Priority - MS1		Site Priority - MS2		
		Latest Time Stamp		Latest Time Stamp		
MS2						
Capture	Process Name:			HR_CAPT		
	Queue Name:			HR_CAPT		
	DDL (Y/N):					
	Transformations:					
Propagate	Process Name:	HR_PROP_MS1	HR_PROP_SS3			
	From Queue Name:	HR_CAPT	HR_CAPT			
	To Queue Name:	HR_APPLY	HR_MS2_APPLY			
	DDL (Y/N):					
	Transformations:					
Apply	Process Name:	HR_MS1_APPLY				
	Queue Name:	HR_MS1_APPLY				
	DDL (Y/N):	Y				
	Transformations:					
	Conflict Resolution	Latest Time Stamp				
		DDL - Conflict Resoltion				
		MS1 overwrites				

Time based values used for comparision and time zones.

One point came out of this example that bears additional discussion: time zones. It is this author's overwhelming desire to call a special meeting of the UN and have us all agree that life and the universe would be so much easier to deal with if we all just got on the same time. 8 o'clock am is 8 o'clock am regardless of where you are in the world. Think of all the brain power and sleep that is lost over keeping track of 24 different time zones that all change, at different intervals, on different dates depending on the year. Look at how many patches Oracle has had to put out just to keep up with them all. After all, if those wonderful planetary inhabitants South of the equator can celebrate Christmas in the middle of summer, surely those of us in the Western continents can handle going to work at noon (actually, many of us already do). So why not unite! One planet, one time, one people!

However, until this happens, we must accommodate for the ever changing time zones and the impact on time-based conflict resolution. As mentioned above, you will need to make sure the time values used for conflict resolution are equivalent by time zone. Your most efficient practice is going to be to store all of the time-based columns in the database at the same time zone. If needed, convert the time value via a trigger or code prior to inserting or updating the record. This way you only have to convert once, when you store, not every time you retrieve. In a distributed environment, it is highly recommended that you set the DBTIMEZONE on all databases to the same time zone. UTC/GMT is recommended (with no Daylight Savings time change). Then, incoming time-based values can be converted from its known time zone to the database time zone. For example, use the FROM_TZ/AT TIME ZONE statement:

```
FROM_TZ(CAST(<my_date_type_data>) AS TIMESTAMP),
('<my_time_zone_name>')) AT TIME ZONE (DBTIMEZONE)
```

Note: You must convert your time-based data type to a simple TIMESTAMP if it is not already one. This is done with the CAST (...) AS TIMESTAMP.

 For more information on working with time-based values and time zone conversions, please reference the Datetime Data Types and Time Zone Support Chapter in the Oracle Database Globalization Support Guide.

Example: Adding a table to a replicated schema

Our next challenge is to add a table to a replicated schema. Since our sites are not going to change, we can refer to our Streams Site Matrix to help us keep track of all the sites where we need to add the table and configure it for replication. We won't be making any changes to the matrix. In our previous example, we extended our streamed environment to include a second master site. We will use this extended environment as our base for adding a table to our HR schema.

The first step is to understand which commands can be issued once and propagated throughout the environment, and which commands must be issued at each site.

We know from our Streams Site Matrix that the HR Schema is hosted at MS1, MS2, and SS3.

We know that the create table command is DDL and when issued at MS1 will be propagated to MS2 and SS3. However, it would not be propagated if issued at MS2.

We know that `DBMS_STREAMS_ADM` procedures needed to configure the table replicaton are not DDL and therefore are not propagated.

The table must exist on the local database to be referenced in a `DBMS_STREAMS_ADM` procedure call.

Since this is a new table, we do not need to worry about data synchronization for this table between sites. However, we should take precautions to make sure no one adds data to the table at any site until we have added the capture rule to the Capture process for the table at each site.

From the above analysis of what we know, we can conclude:

- The DDL to create the new table (and associated indexes and triggers) can be issued at MS1 and propagated to MS2 and SS3
- Once the propagated DDL has been applied at MS2 and SS3, `DBMS_STREAMS_ADM` procedures must be issued at each site to configure the appropriate capture and Apply process rules for the table at each site
- To ensure the table is empty of data when the capture rule is added to the `HR_CAPT` Capture process, we can issue a truncate table command on the table just prior to adding the capture rule
- As soon as the capture rule is added to the `HR_CAPT` process, we want to get the SCN at the capture site to avoid losing any apply for changes made after the Capture process is created but before the table apply rule is instantiated

To accomplish adding the table to the replicated Schema, we can do the following:

- Issue the DDL to create the table and any associated indexes and triggers at MS1
- Allow the DDL to be propagate and applied at MS2 and SS3
- Stop `HR_CAPT` processes at MS1 and MS2
- Stop all Propagation processes
- Stop `HR_MS1_Apply` process at MS2 and SS3
- Stop `HR_MS2_Apply` process at MS1 and SS3
- Add apply table rule to all Apply processes

- Add the appropriate apply rule conflict resolution for the table to all Apply processes
- Add propagation table rule to the all Propagation processes
- Add capture table rule to all Capture processes
- Prepare the table for instantiation at MS1 and MS2 (this is done automatically if you used the DBMS_STREAMS_ADM package to add the rule to the Capture process)
- Instantiate MS1 SCN at MS2 for the table
- Instantiate MS1 SCN at SS3 for the table
- Instantiate MS2 SCN at MS1 for the table
- Instantiate MS2 SCN at SS3 for the table
- Start all Apply processes
- Start all Propagation processes
- Start all Capture processes

Shrinking the Streamed environment

Shrinking a Streamed environment is much less complicated than extending it. It is accomplished by simply removing the rules/rulesets that govern the capture, propagation, and Apply processes for the replication level and site.

Removing table, scheme, and tablespace level replication from Streams

DBMS_STREAMS_ADM.REMOVE_RULE or DBMS_RULE_ADM.DROP_RULE

As mentioned in Chapter 6, remember to use the same package to remove the rules as used to add them. Using a standard procedure for creating Streams rules will help with this. For example, you always use DBMS_STREAMS_ADM to configure replication capture, apply and propagation rules, rather than DBMS_RULE_ADM

Removing a site from a Streamed environment

There may be times when a site becomes so badly desynchronized within a Streamed environment, that it is more efficient to remove the site entirely and rebuild it. Or, it is no longer needed in the environment.

Use DBMS_PROPAGATION_ADM.DROP_PROPAGATION to remove Propagation processes to the database to be rebuilt/removed. It is more efficient to drop and recreate a Propagation process than it is attempt to resynchronize it with a capture and/or apply queue and process that has been dropped and recreated.

Use `DBMS_STREAM_ADM.REMOVE_STREAMS_CONFIGURATION` locally at the database that is to be removed. It leaves the database and the Streams users intact, but removes the objects created for Streams processes (queues, processes, rules, and so on).

Troubleshooting unexpected changes and resulting Streams errors

Expect the unexpected. Whether the failure occurs after the Streams environment has been up and running or occurs while you are attempting to implement the environment, your best defense is knowing the failure points in a Streamed environment, and the most likely causes for the failures. In this section, we will address this very thing, as well as present a methodical approach to troubleshooting errors. We will also discuss various COTS and custom tools that you may find helpful in monitoring and troubleshooting the environment.

Failure Points and Most Likely Causes (a.k.a. FPs and MLCs)

The following diagram shows the overall flow of DML/DDL change through the Streams processes from source to destination. Each transition constitutes a potential point of failure (notated by the circled number). We will start at the beginning and work our way through the flow describing the failure point and the most likely causes. The following section is not intended to be an "All Inclusive" list of every issue you may encounter. Rather, it provides some basic, well known issues at specific points that are intended to help you begin to associate where to look when issues are encountered.

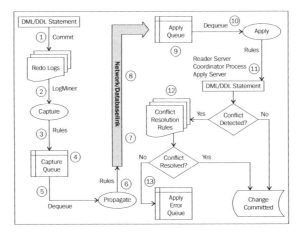

Failure Point 1: DML/DDL statement commit logging

At this FP, we want to make sure that committed changes are being recorded in the redo. If the changes are not in the redo, they cannot be captured.

Successful commit

Make sure the statement was successfully committed.

DML/DDL statements must execute and commit successfully to the redo to be eligible for capture. If the DML/DDL is not successfully executed and committed, it will not be captured. If you are using Synchronous Capture, make sure triggers are enabled and valid. Again, the DML/DDL must be successfully committed to "kick off" the Synchronous Capture triggering.

NOLOGGING option

Mitigate potential use of the NOLOGGING option on the session issuing DML/DDL statements with the NOLOGGING option will keep the change from being entered into the redo log completely. To avoid this, all capture databases should be configured with FORCED LOGGING. This ensures that DML/DDL changes are logged in the redo regardless of the use of the NOLOGGING option specification.

You can either create the database or tablespaces with the FORCE LOGGING option or use the alter database or alter tablespace commands to enable FORCE LOGGING.

Archive Log mode

Make sure the database is in Archive log mode and the Archive process is started (you may see **ORA-01001: Invalid Cursor ,ORA-01405:Fetched column value is NULL** errors).

Failure Point 2: LogMiner

At this FP, we want to make sure that LogMiner has the configuration and resources it needs.

Supplemental logging

Make sure supplemental logging has been configured for each table replicated.

- Check Supplemental Logging at the Database level:
  ```
  select supplemental_log_data_pk pk_logging,
  supplemental_log_data_ui ui_logging
  from v$database;
  ```

```
PK_LOGGING    UI_LOGGING
------------  ------------
NO            NO
```

- Check Supplemental Logging at the table level:

  ```
  select lg.log_group_name, lg.table_name, lg.always, lgc.column_
  name, lgc.position

  from dba_log_groups lg,

  dba_log_group_columns lgc

  where lg.log_group_name = lgc.log_group_name(+);
  ```

- To enable Database level Supplemental Logging issue the following command:

  ```
  ALTER DATABASE ADD SUPPLEMENTAL LOG DATA (PRIMARY KEY, UNIQUE
  INDEX) COLUMNS;
  ```

- To enable table level Supplemental Logging issue the following command:

  ```
  ALTER TABLE <table_name> ADD SUPPLEMENTAL LOG GOUP <log_group_
  name> (col1, col2) ALWAYS;
  ```

_LOG_PARALLELISM

This parameter sets the redo allocation concurrency level. If one or more Capture processes are run on the database, this parameter should be set to 1 (Note: this does not affect capture parallelism). Attempting to set the value greater than 1 could result in an **ORA-01374: Log_parallelism_max greater than 1 not supported in this release**.

LOGMNR_MAX_PERSISTENT_SESSIONS

Make sure this parameter is set as equal to, or more than, the number of Capture processes configured on the database (this could result in **ORA-01353: Exisiting LogMiner Session**).

Each Capture process requires its own persistent LogMiner mining session. If the number of Capture processes exceed the number of persistent sessions, then those Capture processes will not be able to start.

Failure Point 3: Capture process and rules

This FP focuses on making sure the Capture process has the resources, configuration, and proper rules in place to Capture changes. If you've confirmed the Capture process is up and running, and capturing changes, you will want to look at the rules defined for the process. On thing to keep in mind, it is possible that changes in data handling via applications can impact behavior of a Capture rule if unexpected or new values are not handled in rule conditions that use those values. If your Capture process starts "missing" changes, take a good hard look at the data values, and compare them to the rule conditions.

Memory allocation

Make sure Streams has adequate memory allocation. Either implement Automatic Memory Management (10g and higher), or increase the shared pool and streams pool by at least 10MB per Capture process. In the event you see an **ORA-01341: LogMiner out-of-memory**, you can increase LogMiner memory allocation by increasing the Capture process parameter `_sga_size`. The default for this memory allocation is 10MB. Note that if you increase the `_sga_size`, you will most likely want to make a corresponding increase the streams pool size as well to accommodate the additional memory allocation for the capture. The following command allocates 50 MB to LogMiner memory

```
exec dbms_capture_adm.set_parameter('STRMADMIN_CAPTURE','_SGA_
SIZE','50');
```

Capture process status

Make sure the Capture process (and queue) is enabled.

```
select capture_name, queue_name, status, error_number, error_ message
from dba_capture;
```

CAPTURE_NAME	QUEUE_NAME	STATUS	ERROR_NUMBER	ERROR_MESSAGE
SCHEMA_HR_CAPTURE	SCHEMA_HR_CAPTURE_Q	ENABLED		

If the Capture process has a status of DISABLED, attempt to start the process.

If the Capture process has a status of ABORTED, you should see accompanying errors. Address the errors and attempt to restart the process.

If the Capture process is ENABLED, but not capturing recent transactions, it may have fallen behind.

```
select to_char(enqueue_message_create_time,'DD-MON-YY HH24:MI:SS')
last_enqueue, to_char(sysdate,'DD-MON-YY HH24:MI:SS') cur_time

from v$streams_capture;
```

```
   LAST_ENQUEUE              CUR_TIME
                             23-AUG-09 20:09:12
```

Notice the lack of enqueued time. Even though our process is enabled, it is not capturing.

In this case, the next step is to check the state of the Capture process.select capture_name, startup_time, state from v$streams_capture;

```
   CAPTURE_NAME  STARTUP_TIME      STATE

   SCHEMA_HR_    Aug 22, 2009      WAITING FOR DICTIONARY REDO: FIRST SCN
   CAPTURE       4:01:00 PM        960867
```

In this case, the Capture process is expecting to find the archive log with the noted SCN to access the Data Dictionary info in the redo log to build the LogMiner Data Dictionary. However, the archive log has been deleted. If possible, restore the archive log with the FIRST_SCN to the archive log destination folder and re-register it with the Capture process.

```
   alter database register logfile <path\filename> for <capture_name>;
```

If the required archive log is not available, you will need to recreate the Capture process.

If a Capture process appears to be "stuck" in the INITIALIZING state, it could be a result of one of the following:

- Combined Capture and Apply is enabled and the Apply site is not available
- Downstream capture is configured and redo is still in transit or unavailable
- The START_SCN is significantly higher than the REQUIRED_CHECKPOINT_SCN/ FIRST_SCN and the process is still scanning the redo
- One or more required redo logs are not available
- Indoubt distributed transactions can keep capture checkpoints from advancing as expected

  Check for issues in the DBA_2PC_PENDING and DBA_2PC_NEIGHBORS views and also, reference the Viewing Information about Distributed Transactions chapter in the *Oracle Database Administrator's Guide 11g*

Capture queue designation

Verify that the Capture process is assigned to the correct queue.

```
select capture_name, queue_name, queue_owner
from dba_capture;

CAPTURE_NAME       QUEUE_NAME         QUEUE_OWNER
---------------    ---------------    -------------
HR_CAPTURE         HR_CAPTURE_Q       STRM_ADMIN
```

Capture Rules and Rule Sets

While most expectations are to capture changes, it is quite possible to not want to capture changes. Keep in mind that if any rule in a rule set evaluates to TRUE, the whole rule set evaluates to TRUE.

- Verify Capture Rules are configured properly for expected capture.

  The obvious verification is to make sure that the capture rule set contains rules (an empty rule set can throw an **ORA-01405: Fetched column value is null**). There should be at least one rule (DML) in the rule set, and an additional rule for DDL if `include_DDL` is set to true for the capture.

  If the rules were created with the DBMS_STREAMS_ADM, you can query the following views.
  ```
  Select * from dba_streams_<level>_rules;
  ```
  Where `<level>` is table, schema, or global. Add appropriate where clause to filter on the rules of interest.

  Otherwise, query `dba_rules`
  ```
  Select * from dba_rules;
  ```
  Add appropriate `where` clause to filter on the rules of interest.

- Verify if the values for `source_database`, and `:dml.get_source_database_name()` are the same as the capture database `global_name`. If the `global_name` has been changed, the Capture process will no longer capture changes.

- Verify the rule conditions are set as expected for the capture rules.

  Compare the rule evaluations to the values of the change that was not or was captured. Rules behave the opposite of rule sets. If one or more conditions evaluates to FALSE, the rule returns FALSE.

  Is it a negative rule set ()?—remember this is a double negative. If the negative rule evaluates to TRUE, the change is NOT captured.

  If the rules set has multiple rules, do one or more rules cancel each other out?

If the rule set has multiple rules defined, make sure they do not cancel each other out; especially if you mix positive and negative rules in the rule set.

 See the Tricks and Tips section below for an example of altering a Streams process rule.

- Check Tag settings

  Make sure you are, or are not including tags as expected. Verify the tag value in the rule to the tag value being set when the change is originated if possible (most of the time this is done via code, so you can do this. However, if a user manually set the tag you may or may not be able to determine the tag value used).

- Verify any transformations for the rules.

  ```
  select r.rule_name, rac.nvn_name ac_name, rac.nvn_value.
  accessvarchar2() ac_value
  from dba_rules r, table (r.rule_action_context.actx_list) rac;
  ```

  Add the appropriate `where` clause to filter on the rules of interest.

  Transformations can affect the capture of an event. If a transformation exists, verify the logic and outcome of the PL/SQL code. If the transformation fails the Capture process is aborted (see chapter 6).

- Check for Capture process errors in `alert.log`

  Also look for any tracefiles. Check EM for failed capture operations alerts.

Failure Point 4: Capture enqueue

This FP focuses on the ability of the Capture process to enqueue LCR's to its assigned Capture queue.

Capture user privileges

Make sure the capture user either owns the queue or has been granted enqueue privileges on the queue.

```
select capture_name, capture_user, queue_name, queue_owner
from dba_capture;
```

CAPTURE_NAME	CAPTURE_USER	QUEUE_NAME	QUEUE_OWNER
HR_CAPTURE	STRM_ADMIN	HR_CAPTURE_Q	STRM_ADMIN

Failure Point 5: Propagation dequeue from Capture queue

At this FP, we want to make sure the Propagation process is able to dequeue LCRs from the Capture queue.

Propagation Status

- Verify the Propagation process is started

    Set the date display to show time as well

```
alter session set nls_date_format='DD-MON-YY HH24:MI:SS';
select propagation_name, status, error_date, error_message
from dba_propagation;


PROPAGATION_NAME    STATUS    ERROR_DATE           ERROR_MESSAGE
------------------  --------  -------------------  ---------------
HR_PROPAGATION      ENABLED   25-AUG-09 15:47:58
```

You can also view information in the DBA_QUEUE_SCHEDULES view.

If you see an error date but not an error_message, check the propagation site alert log. If the destination site is down, you will see entries similar to the following:

****

Fatal NI connect error 12518, connecting to:

(DESCRIPTION=(ADDRESS_LIST=(ADDRESS=(PROTOCOL=TCP)(HOST=STRM2_HOST)(PORT=1521)))(CONNECT_DATA=(SID=STRM2)(server=DEDICATED)(CID=(PROGRAM=c:\oracle\11gr2\product\11.2.0\db_1\bin\ORACLE.EXE)(HOST=STM2_HOST)(USER=SYSTEM))))

VERSION INFORMATION:

　　　　TNS for 32-bit Windows: Version 11.2.0.0.1 - Beta

　　　　Windows NT TCP/IP NT Protocol Adapter for 32-bit Windows: Version 11.2.0.0.1

Time: 25-AUG-2009 17:29:49

Tracing not turned on.

Tns error struct:

  ns main err code: 12564

TNS-12564: TNS:connection refused

  ns secondary err code: 0

  nt main err code: 0

  nt secondary err code: 0

  nt OS err code: 0

Propagation source configuration

- Verify if the Propagation process is pointed to the correct capture queue
- Verify if the propagation user either owns the capture queue or has been granted dequeue privileges on the capture queue

```
select propagation_name, rule_set_owner, source_queue_owner srcq_owner,
source_queue_name srcq_name from dba_propagation;
```

```
PROPAGATION_NAME    RULE_SET_OWNER          SRCQ_OWNER    SRCQ_NAME

-----------------   --------------------    ----------    -------------

HR_PROPAGATION      STRM_ADMIN              STRM_ADMIN    HR_CAPTURE_Q
```

Propagation Job

Verify that the propagation job is running and does not have errors.

```
Select * from dba_propagation;
```

Failure Point 6: Propagation Rules

These are pretty much the same as for Capture Rules (See Failure Point 3 for more detail on rules). You just want to focus on the propagation rule types (via filter).

- Verify Propagation Rules are configured properly for expected Propagation process.

  If the rules were created with the DBMS_STREAMS_ADM, you can query the following views.

  ```
  Select * from dba_streams_<level>_rules;
  ```

  Where <level> is table, schema, or global. Add appropriate where clause to filter on the rules of interest.

  Otherwise, query DBA_RULES

  ```
  Select * from dba_rules;
  ```

  Add appropriate where clause to filter on the rules of interest.

- Verify the value for source_database, and :dml.get_source_database_name() are the same as the capture database global_name
- Verify the rule conditions are set as expected for the propagation rules
- Check Tag settings
- Verify any Transformations for the rules

- Check propagation errors in the `alert.log`

  Also check Propagation process trace files. Check EM for failed propagation operations alerts

Failure Point 7: Database link configuration

- Verify the database link named for process is correct
- Verify database link works

  The database link (dblink) name must be the same as `global_name` of the database to which it connects. If `global_name` of the destination database has been changed, the dblink will need to be dropped and recreated (You may see ORA-02082 or other associated errors indicate db global naming is not configured correctly).

  The user connection information is correct (the Propagation process will be aborted with invalid username/ password error).

  The "using" parameter is a valid sqlnet connection description: either a valid tnsalias or the full connection description string.

- Verify that the propagation user owns the dblink used by the Propagation process

Failure Point 8: Network connectivity and stability

- Verify `tnsnames.ora` configuration is correct/current and in the correct Oracle home.
- Check environment variables:

  `TNS_NAMES` and `PATH` settings can unexpectedly redirect the OracleNet connection to use a `tnsnames.ora` file that does not contain the tnsalias used in the db link "using clause". If you are in an environment where these may change, consider using the full connection description string in the database link "using" parameter rather than a tnsalias.

```
Create database link STRM2
connect to strm_admin identified by strm_admin
using '(DESCRIPTION =
    (ADDRESS = (PROTOCOL = TCP)(HOST = STRM2_HOST)
      (PORT = 1521)
    )
    (CONNECT_DATA =
      (SERVER = DEDICATED)
      (SERVICE_NAME = STRM2)
    )
  )';
```

- Verify Host value: Has the host name or IP address changed for the host? If host name is used, is the domain needed to locate the host in a different domain (recommended for multi-domain environments)?

- Verify Port value: Did the listener port for the destination database change?

- Verify Invited_Nodes: If set in the destination sqlnet.ora, is the source database in the list? If host name is used, is the domain needed (recommended for multi-domain environments)?

- Check for ORA-3113 on propagation job. ORA-03113: end-of-file on communication channel indicates that the network throughput was interrupted causing the propagation job to abort. Attempt to restart the Propagation process manually. In most cases the propagation should start back up. If you are on a network experiencing these types of comlink issues regularly, consider creating a scheduled job owned by the Propagation process owner that checks the propagation status on a regular basis and attempts to restart the process if it is not enabled. Example code for this can be found in the Tricks and Tips section below.

- TNS errors (ex: ORA-12505, ORA-12514; could not resolve sid/service name) indicate issues with connecting via alias's. Troubleshoot these errors for database links just as you would for a straight SQL*PLUS connection.

Failure Point 9: Propagation enqueue to the Apply queue

We need to make sure that the Propagation process is able to enqueue the LCR's to its assigned Apply queue.

Destination availability

Verify that the destination database is open and the destination listener is started.

> If a Capture process status is initializing, it could indicate that a destination database associated with the capture via a Propagation process is down. Check the source and destination database alert logs for any TNS connection refusal errors.

Propagation destination configuration

- Verify that the db link connect user either owns the apply queue or has enqueued privileges on the queue

- Verify that the Propagation process is pointed to the correct capture queue

```
select propagation_name, destination_dblink dst_dblink, username
connected_user,
destination_queue_owner dstq_owner,
destination_queue_name dstrcq_name
from dba_propagation,
     dba_db_links
where destination_dblink=db_link;
```

PROPAGATION_NAME DSTRCQ_NAME	DST_DBLINK	CONNECTED_USER	DSTQ_OWNER
HR_PROPAGATION HR_APPLY_Q	STRM2	STRM_ADMIN	STRM_ADMIN

Failure Point 10: Apply dequeue

Here, we want to make sure the Apply process is able to dequeue the LCRs from the Apply queue

Apply process status

- Verify the Apply process (and queue) is up and running.

  If the status id DISABLED, attempt to restart the process

  If the status is ABORTED, check the accompanying error information, address the errors, and attempt to restart the process.

- Verify the Apply process is configured to apply captured events

  If APPLY_CAPTURE is NO, the Apply process will only apply user enqueued events for the rule set.

```
select apply_name, status, apply_captured apply_capt,
error_number err_num, error_message err_msg
from dba_apply;
```

APPLY_NAME	STATUS	APPLY_CAPT	ERR_NUM	ERR_MSG
HR_APPLY	ENABLED	YES		

Apply user privileges

Make sure the Apply user either owns the Apply queue or has been granted dequeue privileges on the queue.

Failure Point 11: Apply Rules

These are pretty much the same as for Capture Rules (See Failure Point 3 for more detail on rules). You just want to focus on the Apply rule types (via filter).

- Verify Apply Rules are configured properly for expected Apply process.

  If the rules were created with the DBMS_STREAMS_ADM, you can query the following views.

  ```
  Select * from dba_streams_<level>_rules;
  ```

  Where `<level>` is table, schema, or global. Add appropriate where clause to filter on the rules of interest.

  Otherwise, query DBA_RULES.

  ```
  Select * from dba_rules;
  ```

  Add appropriate where clause to filter on the rules of interest.

- Verify the value for source_database, and :dml.get_source_database_name() are the same as the capture database global_name

- Verify that the rule conditions are set as expected for the capture rules

- Check Tag settings

- Verify any Transformations for the rules

- Check any existing Apply handlers

- Check for Apply process errors in alert.log

  Also look for any tracefiles. Check EM for failed Apply operations alerts

Apply latency

- Determine if the Apply process is keeping up with workload.

  ```
  select hwm_message_number message_id,
  hwm_message_create_time create_time,
  hwm_time apply_time,
  ((hwm_time-hwm_message_create_time) * 86400) apply_lag_secs
  from v$streams_apply_coordinator;
  ```

MESSAGE_ID	CREATE_TIME	APPLY_TIME	APPLY_LAG_SECS
3103329	25-AUG-09 13:01:46	25-AUG-09 13:01:56	10

If transactions are coming in faster than the Apply process can Apply them, try increasing the parallelism of the Apply processes. Or, consider adding an additional Apply queue and process, and splitting the inbound Propagation processes between them (this means that those Propagation processes that need to be redirected to the new queue must be recreated).

- Check for LARGE transactions.

The APPLY reader will keep dequeing the large transaction until it reaches the transaction end marker. During this time, the coordinator and APPLY slaves will be IDLE. To determine if there is a large transaction in progress, you can check the capture site alert log for large transaction messages and match it with the transaction id in the APPLY views.

- Check for Apply spill to disk.

If the number of messages in a transaction exceeds the `txn_lcr_spill_ threshold` the Apply process will begin to spill messages to disk. This can slow down the Apply process. Use the `DBA_APPLY_SPILL_TXN` view to see information on spilled messages.

Failure Point 12: Conflict detection and resolution rules

Oracle's conflict detection determines if old values or data structure in the event LCR do not match the existing data in the destination table. When this happens, it checks to see if there is any conflict resolution defined for the Apply ruleset. If none is found, the LCR is placed in the Apply Error Queue (this is a persistent queue which allows us to query it at will).

If conflict resolution methods are defined for the apply rule they are used to continue processing the LCR. If the conflict is still not resolved after applying all the conflict resolution methods to the LCR, the LCR is put in the Apply Error queue.

- Verify the conflict resolution method resolves the conflict as expected.

Conflict resolution methods are a type of transformation and they can change the data. Make sure the resolution and data change logic are correct and yield the expected result with the values of the LCR.

- Make sure supplemental logging has been configured for each table replicated.

- Verify that supplemental logging is configured for conflict resolution columns at both the capture and apply sites

    Check Supplemental Logging at the Database level:

    ```
    select supplemental_log_data_pk pk_logging,
    supplemental_log_data_ui ui_logging
    from v$database;
    ```

    ```
    PK_LOGGING    UI_LOGGING
    ------------  ------------
    NO            NO
    ```

    Check Supplemental Logging at the table level:

    ```
    select lg.log_group_name, lg.table_name, lg.always,
    lgc.column_name, lgc.position
    from dba_log_groups lg,
    dba_log_group_columns lgc
    where lg.log_group_name = lgc.log_group_name(+);
    ```

    To enable Database level Supplemental Logging issue the following command:

    ```
    ALTER DATABASE ADD SUPPLEMENTAL LOG DATA (PRIMARY KEY, UNIQUE
    INDEX) COLUMNS;
    ```

    To enable table level Supplemental Logging issue the following command:

    ```
    ALTER TABLE <table_name> ADD SUPPLEMENTAL LOG GOUP <log_group_
    name> (col1, col2) ALWAYS;
    ```

Failure Point 13: Apply Errors

If there are errors in the apply error queue, it means that a conflict was encountered that could not be resolved. These errors must be resolved manually. It may be helpful to extract the LCR of the event to determine the old and new values and change type for the change event. This can be done via Enterprise Manager DB Console/Grid Control Streams Apply Error drill down screens, or you can use scripts to extract the LCR like the one below in the Troubleshooting Tools section. One thing to understand at this failure point is that change transactions that reach the Apply Error queue have not been handled by the conflict resolution or transformation design and should not be "fixed and forgotten". The following tells you how to address errors quickly so that the Apply process can be fixed when these errors occur, allowing Streaming to function. However, a record of the errors and causes should be kept and reviewed with the appropriate parties so that appropriate change handling design modifications can be implemented to circumvent the cause of the errors and avoid them in the future.

It is extremely important to monitor the Apply Error queue. If an LCR fails, all subsequent LCR's with a direct or indirect dependency on that LCR will fail as well. This can quickly lead to the Apply site becoming totally out of sync with its master site(s).

When you address the events in the Apply Error queue, you will want to sort them so that you address the oldest error first.

```
select * from dba_apply_error
order by local_transaction_id;
```

Address the first error. Determine what the change was and what the original values of the row were by extracting the LCR. Compare these value to the existing row in the table at the Apply site.

If may be possible that changes from another master may have been applied after the erred change you are addressing failed. This being the case you may not wish to apply the change at all. If this is the case, you can delete the change using the DBMS_APPLY_ADM.DELETE_ERROR procedure. If you wish to attempt to reapply the change, update the existing row in the table to match the old values so the Apply process can "find" the old record and it can pass conflict detection (remember, conflict detection compares the old values of the LCR to the current values in the destination table). You can then reapply the change using the DBMS_APPLY_ADM. EXECUTE_ERROR. Verify that the change was applied as expected. Note: capitalization in text fields makes a difference.

You may wish to just manually update the existing data in the destination table to match the new values of the change. This is also acceptable.

If you choose to Apply the change to the destination table, and it has been successfully applied, you may want to run the DBMS_APPLY_ADM.EXECUTE_ALL_ ERRORS('APPLY'). The reason being that what may have kept the rest of the errors from being applied, was the first error. Now that you have fixed the first error, the Apply process can now reprocess the rest of the errors without issue. This could drastically reduce the size of your error queue and the number of errors you will need to manually address.

The same method can be accomplished via the EM Streams Management GUI if you prefer that to command line. See the next section for more on troubleshooting Tools.

Troubleshooting tools

The following section addresses some useful and recommended tools that will help you monitor and troubleshoot your Streamed environment.

Enterprise Manager: Streams management

Your new best friend! The following screenshots highlight the EM DBConsole/Grid Control UI's that allow you to monitor, troubleshoot, and administer the Streams processes in each database. If nothing else worked in EM, with exception of these UI's, this tool would still be worth its weight in gold. Keep in mind however, that as a DBA, you should always know what is going on under the buttons and links. Meaning, you should understand the database level commands that the UI issues to accomplish tasks and displays. If things do not work as expected from the UI, you will want to attempt the operation from command line (a.k.a SQLPlus) to determine if the problem is with the tool or the database. As you go through the screen shots, see what you recognize in the UI's from our previous failure point section.

To get to Streams Management, go to the **Database** tab. Click on the **Data Movement** link. Click on the **Management** link under the **Streams** section. This will bring you to the **Streams Overview** page.

Streams Overview

This page gives a summary view of Streams Capture, Propagate, Apply, and User Messaging. Notice we have an Error in our Apply Process.

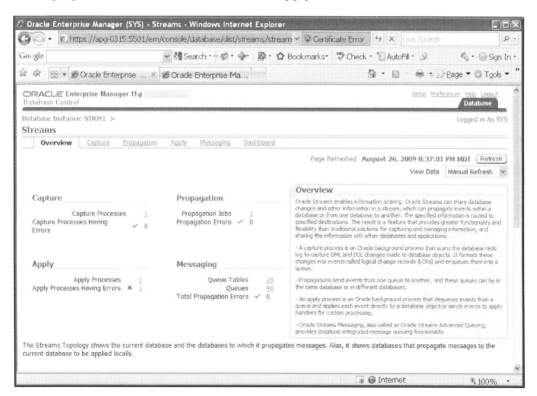

By clicking on the **Error** link we go to a summary page showing the error.

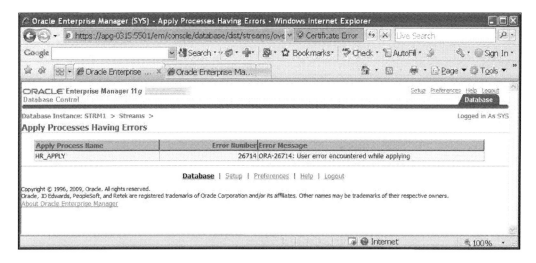

Or we can go directly to the Apply process home page by clicking on the **Apply** Tab.

The status of the Apply process shows **ABORTED**. This usually happens when the Apply process encounters an error and the DISABLE_ON_ERROR is set to Yes.

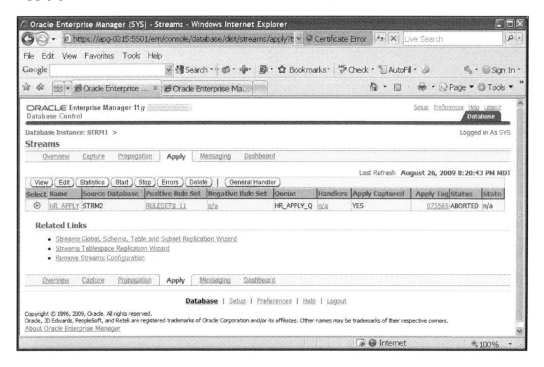

You can verify the Apply process configurations by clicking on the **View** and **Edit** buttons. To see the errors, click on the **Error** button.

You now see the records that are in the local `DBA_APPLY_ERROR` queue. You can drill down into the LCR by clicking on the icon in the **View Error LCRs** column.

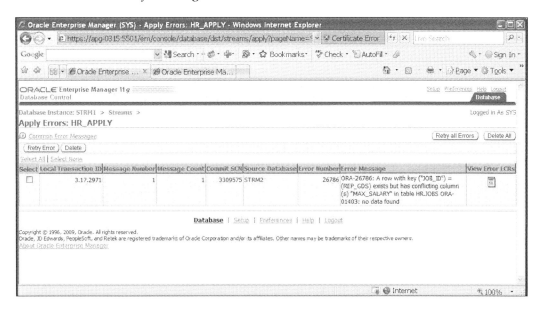

The LCR information lists all messages contained in the LCR.

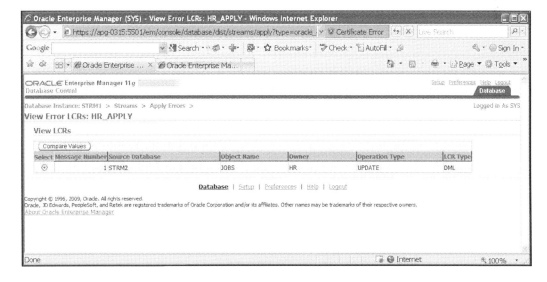

Select a message via its radio button and click on **Compare Values** to extract the LCR message and display the actual change values.

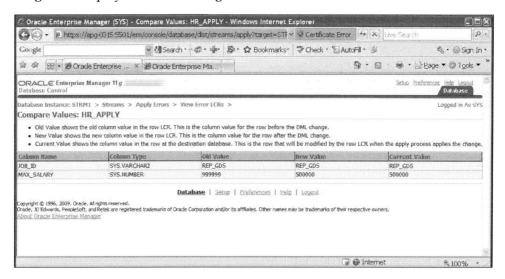

Return to the **Apply Errors** page, when you have resolved the issue that caused the LCR to fail, you can retry or delete the error by clicking on the appropriate buttons.

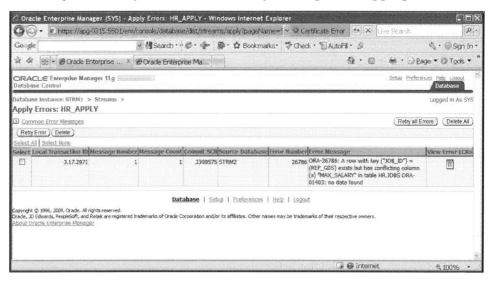

Now let's look at the Capture Process. Notice that even though the status is **ENABLED** the state is **n/a**. This is a good indication that one or more of the Apply sites associated to the Capture process (via propagation) is not available. When the Apply returns to operations, you should see the state of the Capture process go to **CAPTURING CHANGES**.

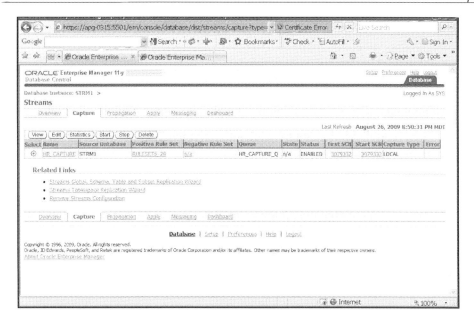

Our next stop is the propagation page (hey! stop, prop, one-hop prop—feeling a hit single coming on!).

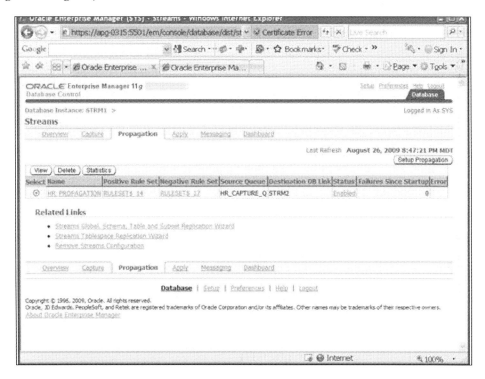

You can check statistics for any process by clicking on the **Stastics** button and view or edit process configuration by clicking on the **View** and **Edit** buttons respectively as you see on the **Propagation** screen.

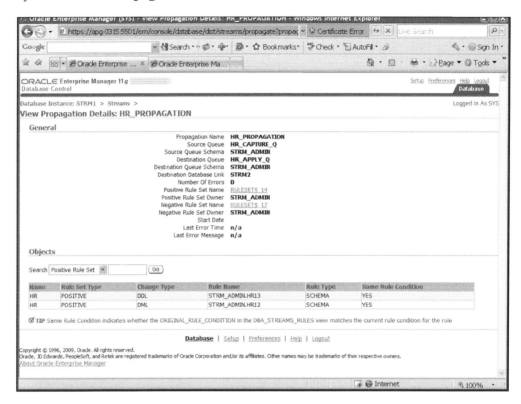

Command line packages and scripts

In the event that you do not have access to the EM console, you can still efficiently monitor your Streamed environment using a number of command line PL/SQL packages and scripts. This chapter provides a few examples that the authors have found most useful over the years. However, do not limit yourself. A number of Streams command line monitoring scripts can be found on Oracle Technical Network, Metalink, and the Internet. Play with them. Find out what works best for you. Keep in mind one rule of thumb that we've seen get even seasoned DBAs: Role level privileges and PL/SQL execution do not mix. The context user of the script (whomever the script runs as, by default is the owner of the script) must be explicitly (directly) granted privileges on certain objects and database packages, procedures, and functions to access them via PL/SQL script. Privilege assignment via a Role is not recognized by the PL/SQL execution engine by design.

If you encounter "object does not exist" errors when you know the object does exist, or "insufficient privilege" errors during PL/SQL execution, log on as a SYSDBA and grant the package owner privileges on the object directly.

Compare and Converge divergent data.

Depending on the circumstance, it may not be feasible to manually find and fix divergent data between sites. Oracle supplies a package to help us do just this. This package is the DBMS_COMPARISON package. This handy-dandy little package can be used to automate the comparison of the data between two objects (a lot faster than we can), and even converge (fix and synchronize) the data. The object itself must be table-based. Meaning, the object stores data in a record format, such as a table type, an index type, or a materialized view type.

Comparing data

You first must define what is to be compared; the schema and object, the dblink to the remote object (the object is assumed to be in the local database). You use the CREATE_COMPARISON procedure to do this. This procedure also allows you to compare objects that may be in a different schema or have a different name at the remote site, set a limit on when to stop comparing, replace null values with a specific value, just determine how many rows do not match, or show actual rows that do not match, to name a few.

Once you have created the "Comparison", use the DBMS_COMPARISON.COMPARE function to compare a shared object between two databases.

The function returns a boolean, but also has an out parameter (scan_info) that is of the COMPARISON_TYPE record type of which the SCAN_ID value can then be used to find scan results in the following views.

- DBA/USER_COMPARISON_SCAN
- DBA/USER _COMPARISON_SCAN_VALUES
- DBA/USER _COMPARISON_ROW_DIF

Each execution of the COMPARE function will generate a new SCAN_ID for the scan_info.

The COMPARISON_TYPE record has the following attributes:

- scan_id(number): The ID of the scan
- loc_rows_merged(number): The number of rows in the local database object that differ from matching rows in the remote database object

- `rmt_rows_merged`(number): The number of rows in the remote database object that differ from matching rows in the local database object

- `loc_rows_deleted`(number): The number of rows found in the remote database object not found in the local database object

- `rmt_rows_deleted`(number): The number of rows found in the local database object not found in the remote database object

The function returns TRUE is no differences are found, it returns FALSE if differences are found.

Once you determine if and what row differences there are, you can use the DBMS_COMPARISON.CONVERGE procedure to either make the remote site look like the local site, or the local site look like the remote site. This is specified via the CONVERGE_OPTIONS parameter. The converge option choices are either CMP_CONVERGE_LOCAL_WINS or CMP_CONVERGE_REMOTE_WINS.

Note: The option is all inclusive. It is an all or nothing, either/or. There is no "this one from the local and that one from the remote". If you need this level of granularity for a converge, you can run the compare, and then create a procedure to loop through the records in the DBA_COMPARISON_ROW_DIF view and handle each record separately as needed.

Once you have completed your compare and converge operations, you can recheck the compare (this only rechecks the differing rows for the identified compare scan_id), purge the scan information from the comparison views, and drop the compare definition as you wish.

For more information on using DBMS_COMPARISON please refer to the *Comparing and Converging Data* chapter in the *Oracle Streams Replication Administrators' Guide*, and the *Oracle Database PL/SQL Packages and Types Reference*.

Oracle HealthCheck

For each major release, Oracle provides a Streams HealthCheck script that you can download from Oracle Metalink. This script runs at a SQLPlus prompt, connected as a SYSDBA and queries various Streams views and tables to generate a compressive report detailing the Streams configuration in the instance and the health of the configuration. This script is exceedingly useful to Oracle Support if you require their assistance to resolve issues. To access these scripts, log on to Metalink and search on **Streams Health Check Scripts**.

Custom QuickCheck

If you just wish to run a quick check on your Streams processes the following script provides a basic report for all sites designated in the script. The script uses union all queries to pull information from multiple dblinked sites into the summary report. Of course the expectation here, is that you run the script from a database that has the dblinks to the sites you wish to monitor. To use the script, edit the union queries to include a select from each database link you wish to monitor (our example shows 3 sites). If you are handy with PL/SQL, you can even auto generate this script by creating a procedure that loops through the Stream Administrators database links and "builds" the union queries for each link. A quick hint if you do not already know. You can mimic a loopback database link on the site that you are running the script on by using the `global_name` of the local database as the dblink name. This causes the database to "connect" to itself and lets us standardize the query segment.

The script does the following:

- Shows the status of all the Capture Processes at all the specified database link sites, including the last SCN captured

- Shows the status of all the Apply Processes at all the specified database link sites, including the Last SCN applied, and the Last SCN dequeued

  - In most cases the last SCN applied and the last scn dequeued will be the same unless there is some lag time where the Apply process is still applying the last dequeued SCN.

  - You can compare your last applied SCN at the destination sites with the last captured SCN at the source site to quickly determine if your Streams is working and keeping up. You should see all values increment as LCR activity flows through the Streamed environment.

- Show any/all Erred transactions in DBA_APPLY_ERROR at the destination site

- Shows the status of all the Propagation Processes at all the specified database link sites inlcluding the last acknowledged SCN from the associated Apply process

  - Special note here: In the Oracle documentation the ACK_SCN is described as being the last "dequeued" SCN acknowledged by the Apply process. If the Apply queue is a buffered queue, then "dequeue" means both dequeued and successfully processed. This because if the buffered apply queue is flushed from memory, it needs to be reloaded from the source Capture process. To avoid potential event/LCR loss, the Apply process must not acknowledge the SCN until it has completed processing it.

We like to call this script `check_rep_status.sql`. It should be run as the stream admin user from SQLPlus and it goes like this:

```
--CHECK_REP_STATUS.sql
set echo off
set serveroutput on
set pagesize 150
set linesize 100

column capture_site format a45
column apply_site format a45
column propagation_site format a45
column error_message format a45

alter session set nls_date_format='DD-MON-YY HH24:MI:SS';
exec dbms_output.put_line('***********************************');
exec dbms_output.put_line('System Capture Progress');
exec dbms_output.put_line('***********************************');
select c.capture_site, c.capture_queue, c.last_captured_scn
from
(select source_database capture_site, queue_name capture_queue,
last_enqueued_scn last_captured_scn
from dba_capture@STRM1
union all
select source_database, queue_name, last_enqueued_scn
from dba_capture@STRM2
union all
select source_database, queue_name, last_enqueued_scn
from dba_capture@STRM3
) c
order by c.capture_site;

exec dbms_output.put_line('***********************************');
exec dbms_output.put_line('System Apply Progress');
exec dbms_output.put_line('***********************************');
select a.apply_site, a.apply_name, a.OLDEST_SCN_NUM, a.last_apply_scn
from (
select (select global_name from global_name@STRM1) apply_site,
apply_name, OLDEST_SCN_NUM ,DEQUEUED_MESSAGE_NUMBER last_apply_scn
from v$streams_apply_reader@STRM1
union all
select (select global_name from global_name@STRM2) db_name,
apply_name, OLDEST_SCN_NUM, DEQUEUED_MESSAGE_NUMBER
from v$streams_apply_reader@STRM2
union all
select (select global_name from global_name@STRM3) db_name,
apply_name, OLDEST_SCN_NUM, DEQUEUED_MESSAGE_NUMBER
```

```
from v$streams_apply_reader@STRM3
) a
order by a.apply_name, a.apply_site;

exec dbms_output.put_line('**********************************');
exec dbms_output.put_line('Apply Progress Errors');
exec dbms_output.put_line('**********************************');

select  c.apply_site, c.apply_name, c.source_commit_scn,
c.message_number, c.error_number, c.error_message,
c.error_creation_time
from (
select (select global_name from global_name@STRM1) apply_site,
apply_name, source_commit_scn, message_number, error_number,

error_message, error_creation_time from dba_apply_error@STRM1
union all
select (select global_name from global_name@STRM2) apply_site,
apply_name, source_commit_scn, message_number, error_number,

error_message, error_creation_time from dba_apply_error@STRM2
union all
select (select global_name from global_name@STRM3) apply_site,
apply_name, source_commit_scn, message_number, error_number,

error_message, error_creation_time from dba_apply_error@STRM3
) c
order by c.apply_site, c.apply_name;

exec dbms_output.put_line('**********************************');
exec dbms_output.put_line('System Propagation status');
exec dbms_output.put_line('**********************************');
select p.propagation_site, p.propagation_name, p.aked_scn
acknowledged_scn, p.status, p.error_message, p.error_date
from (select (select global_name from global_name@STRM1)
propagation_site, propagation_name, acked_scn, status,
error_message, error_date
from dba_propagation@STRM1
union all
select (select global_name from global_name@STRM2)
db_name,propagation_name, acked_scn, status, error_message, error_date
from dba_propagation@STRM2
union all
select (select global_name from global_name@STRM3) db_name,
propagation_name, acked_scn, status, error_message, error_date
from dba_propagation@STRM3
) p;
/
```

Extract LCRs.

While the UI in Enterprise Manager DB Console/Grid Control Streams Apply Error drill-down into the LCR values is the next best thing since sliced bread, there may be times when you only have command line access available to you, or you wish to extract an LCR to a spool file for analysis. Oracle supplies scripts (found in "Displaying Detailed Information about Apply Errors" section, in the Monitoring Oracle Streams Apply Processes chapter in *Oracle Streams Concepts and Administration Guide 11g*) to help you "unpack" an LCR associated with an erred transaction for analysis. We have provided a PL/SQL procedure below to create these scripts for you as well as added one or two enhancements (like the ability to print a specific erred transaction). You will need to make sure the schema used to build the scripts has explicit privileges on the necessary objects and procedures/functions referenced in the scripts (you'll quickly find out which ones you need the first time you execute the scripts). As you become familiar with how these scripts work, you can adjust the code to format the output and expand the functionality as you wish. As with the quick check scripts, it is recommended that you create these in the stream admin schema.

```
--LCR_EXTRACT.sql
SET heading OFF
--SET feedback OFF
--SET echo OFF
--SET verify OFF
SET pagesize 0
SET linesize 10000
SET serveroutput on
set echo ON
set feedback ON

exec dbms_output.put_line('create print_any');
-- ***************************************************************
-- Description: Print the contents of the sys.anydata payload
--
-- Input Parameters: Data, sys.anydata
--
-- Output/Returned Parameters:  NONE
--
-- Error Conditions Raised: NONE
--
-- Notes: This procudure is call by:
--          print_lcr
--          SET SERVEROUTPUT ON before calling the procedure
--
```

```
--  ****************************************************************
create or replace PROCEDURE print_any (DATA IN SYS.ANYDATA)
IS
  tn     VARCHAR2 (61);
  str    VARCHAR2 (4000);
  chr1   CHAR (255);
  num    NUMBER;
  dat    DATE;
  rw     RAW (4000);
  res    NUMBER;
BEGIN
  IF DATA IS NULL
  THEN
    dbms_output.put_line ('NULL value');
    RETURN;
  END IF;
  tn := DATA.gettypename ();

  IF tn = 'SYS.VARCHAR2'
  THEN
    res := DATA.getvarchar2 (str);
    dbms_output.put_line (str);
  ELSIF tn = 'SYS.CHAR'
  THEN
    res := DATA.getchar (chr1);
    dbms_output.put_line (chr1);
  ELSIF tn = 'SYS.VARCHAR'
  THEN
    res := DATA.getvarchar (chr1);
    dbms_output.put_line (chr1);
  ELSIF tn = 'SYS.NUMBER'
  THEN
    res := DATA.getnumber (num);
    dbms_output.put_line (num);
  ELSIF tn = 'SYS.DATE'
  THEN
    res := DATA.getdate (dat);
    dbms_output.put_line (dat);
  ELSIF tn = 'SYS.RAW'
  THEN
    res := DATA.getraw (rw);
    dbms_output.put_line (RAWTOHEX (rw));
  ELSE
    dbms_output.put_line ('typename is ' || tn);
  END IF;
END print_any;
```

```
/
show errors

exec dbms_output.put_line('create print_lcr');
-- ****************************************************************
-- Description: Print the contents of the sys.anydata payload
--
-- Input Parameters: lcr payload as sys.anydata
--
-- Output/Returned Parameters:  NONE
--
-- Error Conditions Raised: NONE
--
-- Notes: This procudure is call by:
--          print_errors
--          print_transaction
--        Set serveroutput on before running this procedure
--
-- ****************************************************************
create or replace PROCEDURE print_lcr (lcr IN SYS.ANYDATA)
IS
   typenm      VARCHAR2 (61);
   ddllcr      SYS.lcr$_ddl_record;
   proclcr     SYS.lcr$_procedure_record;
   rowlcr      SYS.lcr$_row_record;
   res         NUMBER;
   newlist     SYS.lcr$_row_list;
   oldlist     SYS.lcr$_row_list;
   ddl_text    CLOB;
BEGIN
   typenm := lcr.gettypename ();
   dbms_output.put_line ('type name: ' || typenm);
   IF (typenm = 'SYS.LCR$_DDL_RECORD')
   THEN
      res := lcr.getobject (ddllcr);
      dbms_output.put_line ('source database: ' ||
                            ddllcr.get_source_database_name);
      dbms_output.put_line ('owner: ' || ddllcr.get_object_owner);
      dbms_output.put_line ('object: ' || ddllcr.get_object_name);
      dbms_output.put_line ('is tag null: ' || ddllcr.is_null_tag);
      DBMS_LOB.createtemporary (ddl_text, TRUE);
      ddllcr.get_ddl_text (ddl_text);
      dbms_output.put_line ('ddl: ' || ddl_text);
      DBMS_LOB.freetemporary (ddl_text);
```

```
      ELSIF (typenm = 'SYS.LCR$_ROW_RECORD')
    THEN
      res  := lcr.getobject (rowlcr);
      dbms_output.put_line ('source database: ' ||
                                rowlcr.get_source_database_name);
      dbms_output.put_line ('owner: ' || rowlcr.get_object_owner);
      dbms_output.put_line ('object: ' || rowlcr.get_object_name);

      dbms_output.put_line ('is tag null: ' || rowlcr.is_null_tag);

      dbms_output.put_line ('command_type: ' ||
                                  rowlcr.get_command_type);
      oldlist := rowlcr.get_values ('OLD');
      FOR i IN 1 .. oldlist.COUNT
      LOOP
        IF oldlist (i) IS NOT NULL
        THEN
          dbms_output.put_line ( 'old(' || i || '): ' ||
                                    oldlist (i).column_name);
          print_any (oldlist (i).DATA);
        END IF;
      END LOOP;
      newlist := rowlcr.get_values ('NEW');
      FOR i IN 1 .. newlist.COUNT
      LOOP
        IF newlist (i) IS NOT NULL
        THEN
          dbms_output.put_line ( 'new(' || i || '): ' ||
                                    newlist (i).column_name);
          print_any (newlist (i).DATA);
        END IF;
      END LOOP;
    ELSE
      dbms_output.put_line ('Non-LCR Message with type ' || typenm);
    END IF;
END print_lcr;
/
show error

exec dbms_output.put_line('create print_errors');
-- ******************************************************************
-- Description: Print the contents of the DBA_APPLY_ERROR queue
--
-- Input Parameters: NONE
```

```
--
-- Output/Returned Parameters:  NONE
--
-- Error Conditions Raised: NONE
--
-- Notes: None
--
-- ********************************************************************

create or replace PROCEDURE print_errors
IS
  CURSOR c
  IS
    SELECT   local_transaction_id, source_database, message_count,
             error_number, error_message
    FROM     dba_apply_error
    ORDER BY source_database, source_commit_scn;
  i          NUMBER;
  txnid      VARCHAR2 (30);
  sourcedb   VARCHAR2 (128);
  msgcnt     NUMBER;
  errnum     NUMBER   := 0;
  errno      NUMBER;
  errmsg     VARCHAR2 (500);
  lcr        SYS.ANYDATA;
  r          NUMBER;
BEGIN
  FOR r IN c
  LOOP
    errnum     := errnum + 1;
    msgcnt     := r.message_count;
    txnid      := r.local_transaction_id;
    sourcedb   := r.source_database;
    errmsg     := r.error_message;
    errno      := r.error_number;
    dbms_output.put_line ('****************************************');
    dbms_output.put_line ('----- ERROR #; || errnum');
    dbms_output.put_line ('----- Local Transaction ID: ' || txnid);
    dbms_output.put_line ('----- Source Database: ' || sourcedb);
    dbms_output.put_line ('----Error Number: ' || errno);
    dbms_output.put_line ('----Message Text: ' || errmsg);
    FOR i IN 1 .. msgcnt
    LOOP
      dbms_output.put_line ('--message: ' || i);
```

```
      lcr := DBMS_APPLY_ADM.get_error_message (i, txnid);
      print_lcr (lcr);
    END LOOP;
  END LOOP;
END print_errors;
/
show error

exec dbms_output.put_line('create print_error_id');
-- *****************************************************************
-- Description: Print error infomation for a specific transaction id
--              in DBA_APPLY_ERROR
--
-- Input Parameters: Ltran_id:  the local transaction Id of
--                   the erred transaction
--
-- Output/Returned Parameters:  NONE
--
-- Error Conditions Raised: NONE
--
-- Notes: None
--
-- *****************************************************************
create or replace PROCEDURE print_error_id (ltran_id in varchar2)
IS
  CURSOR c
  IS
    SELECT   local_transaction_id, source_database, message_count,
             error_number, error_message
    FROM     dba_apply_error
    WHERE    local_transaction_id = ltran_id
    ORDER BY source_database, source_commit_scn;
  i          NUMBER;
  txnid      VARCHAR2 (30);
  sourcedb   VARCHAR2 (128);
  msgcnt     NUMBER;
  errnum     NUMBER := 0;
  errno      NUMBER;
  errmsg     VARCHAR2 (500);
  lcr        SYS.ANYDATA;
  r          NUMBER;
BEGIN
  FOR r IN c
  LOOP
```

```
      errnum        := errnum + 1;
      msgcnt        := r.message_count;
      txnid         := r.local_transaction_id;
      sourcedb      := r.source_database;
      errmsg        := r.error_message;
      errno         := r.error_number;
      dbms_output.put_line ('****************************************');
      dbms_output.put_line ('----- ERROR #; || errnum');
      dbms_output.put_line ('----- Local Transaction ID: ' || txnid);
      dbms_output.put_line ('----- Source Database: ' || sourcedb);
      dbms_output.put_line ('----Error Number: ' || errno);
      dbms_output.put_line ('----Message Text: ' || errmsg);
      FOR i IN 1 .. msgcnt
      LOOP
        dbms_output.put_line ('--message: ' || i);
        lcr := DBMS_APPLY_ADM.get_error_message (i, txnid);
        print_lcr (lcr);
      END LOOP;
    END LOOP;
END print_error_id;
/
show error

exec dbms_output.put_line('create print_transaction');
-- ****************************************************************
-- Description: Print the lcr transaction metadata for the local
--              transaction id passed in
-- Input Parameters: Ltxnid local transaction ID of the erred
-- transaction
--
-- Output/Returned Parameters:  NONE
--
-- Error Conditions Raised: NONE
--
-- Notes: None
--
-- ****************************************************************
create or replace PROCEDURE print_transaction (
  ltxnid                        IN        VARCHAR2)
IS
  i           NUMBER;
  txnid       VARCHAR2 (30);
  sourcedb    VARCHAR2 (128);
  msgcnt      NUMBER;
```

```
    errno       NUMBER;
    errmsg      VARCHAR2 (128);
    lcr         SYS.ANYDATA;
BEGIN
    SELECT local_transaction_id, source_database, message_count,
           error_number, error_message
    INTO   txnid, sourcedb, msgcnt, errno, errmsg
    FROM   dba_apply_error
    WHERE  local_transaction_id = ltxnid;
    dbms_output.put_line ('----- Local Transaction ID: ' || txnid);
    dbms_output.put_line ('----- Source Database: ' || sourcedb);
    dbms_output.put_line ('----Error Number: ' || errno);
    dbms_output.put_line ('----Message Text: ' || errmsg);
    FOR i IN 1 .. msgcnt
    LOOP
      dbms_output.put_line ('--message: ' || i);
      --gets the LCR
      lcr := DBMS_APPLY_ADM.get_error_message (i, txnid);
      print_lcr (lcr);
    END LOOP;
END print_transaction;
/
show error

spool off
/
```

Tricks and tips

In this section we offer some examples of how to "get around" a couple of troublesome situations. While we have been offering advice and best practice recommendations throughout this book, this section is dedicated to out-of-the-mainstream techniques. As this publication matures, we hope to expand this section to include tricks and tips suggested by our readers. We would love to see this section grow into its own chapter!

Keep propagation going on an unstable network

If your Propagation is plagued by constant network disconnection or interruption causing the process to disable or abort throughout the day, you can automate a job to check the status of the Propagation process and attempt to restart it if it finds it stopped. The following script does this on a 15 minute interval. It also creates an audit table that the job populates when it runs, to allow you to review the down history of the Propagation and associated errors.

```
--AUTOFIX_PROP.sql

set serveroutput on
spool c:\create_autofix_prop.txt
exec dbms_output.put_line('create table prop audit');
--********************************

create table strmadmin.propagation_audit (
PROPAGATION_NAME  VARCHAR2(30)
,SOURCE_QUEUE_NAME VARCHAR2(30)
,DESTINATION_QUEUE_NAME VARCHAR2(30)
,DESTINATION_DBLINK VARCHAR2(128)
,STATUS VARCHAR2(8)
,ERROR_MESSAGE VARCHAR2(4000)
,ERROR_DATE DATE
);
exec dbms_output.put_line('create ckprop proc');
-- ****************************************************************
-- Description: Query the status for all propagation jobs
--                 scheduled in dba_propagation.
--               Insert a record of the status for each job into
--                 the propagation_audit table.
--               If the job is disabled, attempt to enable it
--               If an error occurs on enable attempt it is logged
--                 in the propagation_audit table.
--
-- Input Parameters: None
--
-- Output/Returned Parameters:  NONE
--
-- Error Conditions Raised: NONE.  Errors are recorded in
--                                  propagation_audit table.
--
-- Notes: This procedure is called by a scheduled
--          job that runs every 15 mins
--
```

```
-- Author:        A. McKinnell
-- ******************************
create or replace procedure strmadmin.ckprop_enable
as
errnum number;
errmsg varchar2(4000);
cursor prop_status is select propagation_name, destination_dblink,
                             status, source_queue_name,
                             destination_queue_name,
                             error_message, error_date
                      from dba_propagation
                      where status != 'ENABLED';

begin

for rec in prop_status loop
    insert into propagation_audit
    values (rec.propagation_name, rec.source_queue_name,
            rec.destination_queue_name, rec.destination_dblink,
            rec.status, rec.error_message, rec.error_date);
    commit;

    begin
      dbms_aqadm.enable_propagation_schedule(rec.source_queue_name,
rec.destination_dblink);
    exception
      when others then
        errnum := SQLCODE;
        errmsg := SQLERRM;
        insert into propagation_audit
            values ('CKPROP_ENABLE', rec.source_queue_name,
                    're-enable propagation for',
                    rec.destination_dblink,
                    'ERROR', errnum ||': ' ||errmsg, sysdate);
        commit;
    end;
 end loop;

exception
      when others then
        errnum := SQLCODE;
        errmsg := SQLERRM;
        insert into propagation_audit
          values ('CKPROP_ENABLE', 'Exception handler', null, null,
```

```
                                   'ERROR', errnum ||': ' ||errmsg, sysdate);
           commit;

end ckprop_enable;
/
show error
-------------------------------
--Schedule a job to run every 15 mins to re-enable any disabled
  propagation.
-------------------------------
exec dbms_output.put_line('schedule chk prop job');
exec DBMS_SCHEDULER.CREATE_JOB (   -
    job_name => 'propagation_check', -
    job_type => 'STORED_PROCEDURE', -
    job_action => 'ckprop_enable', -
    number_of_arguments => 0, -
    start_date =>sysdate, -
    repeat_interval => 'FREQ=MINUTELY;INTERVAL=15', -
    end_date => null, -
    enabled => TRUE, -
    auto_drop=>FALSE, -
    comments => 'This job kicks off every 15 minutes and checks
dba_propagation for any disabled propagation schedules and attempts
to re-enable.  Audits of this job are captured in table strmadmin.
propagation_audit');
spool off
/
```

How to change a Streams process Rule

Based on what we reviewed in Chapter 6 on Rules, we can modify a rule condition directly. Use this power with caution. Changes made via this method may not be reflected in existing rule metadata. If you make a change, document it to avoid confusion down the road.

An Example: Enterprise Manager Streams Creation Wizard Created Process with INCLUDE_TAGGED_LCR = TRUE, but you want it to be FALSE.

As mentioned earlier, if you use the EM Streams Setup wizard to configure your Streams, be aware that it graciously sets all process INCLUDE_TAGGED_LCR to TRUE.

```
select streams_name, streams_type, include_tagged_lcr include_tag
 from dba_streams_rules;
```

```
STREAMS_NAME                    STREAMS_TYPE INCLUDE_TAGGED_LCR

----------------------------    ------------ ------------------

HR_APPLY                        APPLY        YES

HR_APPLY                        APPLY        YES

HR_PROPAGATION                  PROPAGATION  YES

HR_PROPAGATION                  PROPAGATION  YES

HR_PROPAGATION                  PROPAGATION  YES

HR_PROPAGATION                  PROPAGATION  YES

HR_CAPTURE                      CAPTURE      YES

HR_CAPTURE                      CAPTURE      YES


8 rows selected.
```

To change the behavior without dropping the Capture process and recreating it manually with the DBMS_STREAMS_ADM.ADD_SCHEMA_RULES setting INCLUDE_TAGGED_LCR => FALSE, you can alter the existing Rule for the capture.

Using SQLPlus:

First determine the Rule name and condition text for the Capture Rule.

```
set long 4000

select streams_type, streams_name, rule_owner, rule_name, rule_condition
from dba_streams_rules where streams_type = 'CAPTURE'
and streams_name = 'HR_CAPTURE';


STREAMS_TYPE STREAMS_NAME                      RULE_OWNER
------------ ----------------------------- -----------------------------
RULE_NAME
-----------------------------
RULE_CONDITION
---------------------------------------------------------------
CAPTURE      HR_CAPTURE                       STRM_ADMIN
HR19
(((((:ddl.get_object_owner() = 'HR' or :ddl.get_base_table_owner() = 'HR')
and :ddl.get_source_database_name() = 'STRM1' )) and
(:ddl.get_compatible() <= dbms_streams.compatible_11_1))


CAPTURE      HR_CAPTURE                       STRM_ADMIN
HR18
(((((:dml.get_object_owner() = 'HR') and :dml.get_source_database_name()
= 'STRM1 POSITIVE SCHEMA')) and (:dml.get_compatible() <=
dbms_streams.compatible_11_1))
```

You can also find the condition in the `dba_rules` table, as shown:

```
select rule_name, rule_condition from dba_rules where rule_name = 'HR18';
```

```
RULE_NAME
-----------------------------
RULE_CONDITION
------------------------------------------------------------------
HR18
(((( (:dml.get_object_owner() = 'HR') and :dml.get_source_database_name()
 = 'STRM1 POSITIVE SCHEMA')) and (:dml.get_compatible() <= dbms_streams.
compatible_11_1))
```

In our case we are only going to change the DML Rule. The Rule name is HR18. We copy and edit the text to include an evaluation for a null tag (the equivalent of setting `INCLUDE_TAGGED_LCR = FALSE` when adding Rules via `DBMS_STREAMS_ADM`).

```
((((( :dml.get_object_owner() = 'HR') and :dml.is_null_tag() = 'Y' and :
dml.get_source_database_name() = 'STRM1 POSITIVE SCHEMA')) and (:dml.get_
compatible() <= dbms_streams.compatible_11_1))
```

Next, alter the Rule to use the new condition (make sure to escape the single quotes in the condition string).

The syntax is `dbms_rule_adm.alter_rule('<rulename>','<condition>');`

```
    begin
    dbms_rule_adm.alter_rule('HR18',
    '(((((:dml.get_object_owner() = ''HR'') ' ||
    'and :dml.is_null_tag() = ''Y'' ' ||
    'and :dml.get_source_database_name() = ''STRM1 POSITIVE SCHEMA'')) ' ||
    'and (:dml.get_compatible() <= dbms_streams.compatible_11_1))');
    end;
    /
```

```
select streams_name, rule_name, rule_condition
from dba_streams_rules
where rule_name = 'HR18';
```

```
STREAMS_NAME                          RULE_NAME
-----------------------------         -------------------------------
RULE_CONDITION
------------------------------------------------------------------
HR_CAPTURE                            HR18
((((( :dml.get_object_owner() = 'HR') and :dml.is_null_tag() = 'Y' and
```

```
:dml.get_source_database_name()
 = 'STRM1 POSITIVE SCHEMA')) and (:dml.get_compatible() <= dbms_streams.
compatible_11_1))
```

One thing to be aware of when using this method is that changing the Rule condition itself to exclude tagged LCR's does not change the INCLUDE_TAGGED_LCR value. That is ok, it is the rule_condition that is used for the actual evaluation, not the INCLUDE_TAGGED_LCR value. You will also notice the columns original_rule_condition and same_rule_condition. These show the original Rule condition for the Streams name and whether it is the same as the current Rule condition (YES/NO) respectively. If the change does not work as expected you can use the original_rule value to quickly fall back to the original condition. In our example we see the original condition that we started with and NO that indicates the Rule condition for the capture has been changed.

```
select streams_name, rule_name,include_tagged_lcr,
original_rule_condition, same_rule_condition
from dba_streams_rules
where rule_name = 'HR18';


STREAMS_NAME            RULE_NAME      INCLUDE_TAGGED_LCR
-------------------- ------------ --------------------
ORIGINAL_RULE_CONDITION
----------------------------------------------------
SAME_RULE_CONDITION
------------------------------
HR_CAPTURE              HR18           YES
(((((:dml.get_object_owner() = 'HR') and
:dml.get_source_database_name() = 'STRM1' )) and
(:dml.get_compatible() <= dbms_streams.compatible_11_1))
NO
```

While the above method is directed at changing the Rule condition to not capture tagged LCRs, the same method can be used to add, change, or delete any condition in the Rule.

Summary

This chapter converges techniques we have covered throughout the book and demonstrates how they can be utilized to introduce known changes to your existing environment, as well as address ramifications of unknown changes.

We used the Streams Site Matrix to help us break down the Streamed environment architecture into manageable pieces and focus on how a change affects each piece. We saw that the same change requires different tasks at each piece, and may even require changes that may not be initially apparent.

We also dissected the Streams flow and identified failure points. We analyzed common causes for failures at these points and provided some suggested approaches to mitigating those failures.

We presented a brief discussion on tools available to help you monitor, and troubleshoot your environment, as well as a couple of Tricks and Tips on how to address a couple of common, yet potentially annoying problems.

9
Appendix and Glossary

Both the authors have put in many hours creating and rewriting this book. But, there are areas of Oracle Streams that fall outside the previous chapter. This chapter is the catch-all chapter dealing with subjects that did not quite fit in the previous chapters. Subjects that we wanted to mention to provoke thought are along the lines of the following:

- Alternative methods of monitoring Streams
- Streams and Oracle RAC
- Oracle GoldenGate

Read on and be creative. Use what you have learned in this book to come up with solutions to problems. Know what Streams should be used for and when Streams is NOT a good fit.

Oracle Streams Commander

Spend some time researching Oracle Streams on OTN or Google Oracle Streams and you will eventually come across **Oracle Streams Commander (OSC)**. OSC comes out of Oracle Deutschland GmbH. It is a standalone product that is separate from Grid Control. Personally, I think it is a solution that probably came out of the Oracle Deutschland GmbH Consulting group. OSC is a product that is constantly maturing and seems to be separate from the main development efforts of Oracle Headquarters.

As a tool, OSC is something I do not use because it is an Oracle Consulting solution and NOT an official Oracle product. But, you may like it for its ease of use and simple 'point and click' abilities. As the OSC matures more, I can envision it being an add-on "pack" to Grid Control. For more information on OSC, please visit the website
`http://www.oracle.com/global/de/community/platform/osc/index.html`.

Streams and Oracle RAC

Oracle **Real Application Cluster (RAC)** is one of the components used in Oracle **Maximum Available Architecture (MAA)**. As such, we are seeing more Oracle RAC configurations being deployed more often to support High Availability requirements. Oracle Streams does work in an Oracle RAC configuration.

Pre-planning must be done in order to fully utilize both Oracle Streams and Oracle RAC. There must be careful considerations related to the design, and implementation of: Capture, Queues, Propagation, and Apply processes. Oracle RAC must be configured so that all archive logs can be accessed by Capture process. As Capture process will follow the Queue if an instance goes down, the configuration of Capture and Queues should be planned accordingly.

The use of the procedure DBMS_AQADM.ALTER_QUEUE_TABLE is suggested to set up primary_instance and secondary_instance. This will help when determining where the Queue migrates, should an instance fail in a RAC environment. To determine the instance number, use:

```
SELECT INST_ID, INSTANCE_NAME, HOST_NAME
FROM GV$INSTANCE;

DBMS_AQADM.ALTER_QUEUE_TABLE (
queue_table          IN VARCHAR2,
comment              IN VARCHAR2 DEFAULT NULL,
primary_instance     IN BINARY_INTEGER DEFAULT NULL,
secondary_instance IN BINARY_INTEGER DEFAULT NULL);
```

Parameter	Description
queue_table	Name of a queue table to be created.
comment	Modifies the user-specified description of the queue table. This user comment is added to the queue catalog. The default value is NULL which means that the value will not be changed.
primary_instance	This is the primary owner of the queue table. Queue monitor scheduling and propagation for the queues in the queue table will be done in this instance. The default value is NULL, which means that the current value will not be changed.
secondary_instance	The queue table fails over to the secondary instance if the primary instance is not available. The default value is NULL, which means that the current value will not be changed.

Propagation needs to be configured to connect to the queue of the destination instance using the proper database link. The database link should refer to the tnsnames.ora entry that contain the **Virtual IPs (VIPs)**.

For instance, the entry below in `tnsnames.ora` is as follows:

```
db02.mycompany.com=
(description=
(address=(protocol=tcp)(host=node2-vip)(port=1521))
(address=(protocol=tcp)(host=node4-vip)(port=1521))
(connect_data=
(service_name=db02.mycompany.com)))
```

Then, building the database link:

```
create database link 'db02.mycompany.com' connect to <username>
identified by <password> using 'db02.mycompany.com';
```

For the Propagation, focus on the parameter `destination_queue_name` when adding the Propagation rule. The `destination_queue_name` should point to the queue name and database link mentioned previously.

The Apply process also follows the Queues, so careful creation of the related Queue is a must. Once the Queue is created, adjustments using `DBMS_AQADM.ALTER_QUEUE_TABLE` should be done.

Pulling it all together, we have the configuration as seen in the following figure:

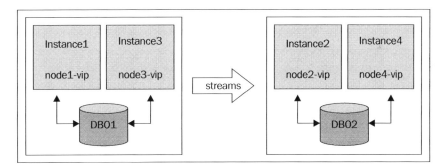

The following steps explain the configuration:

1. Database **DB01** with **Instance 1** and **Instance 3**.

2. Database **DB02** with **Instance 2** and **Instance 4**.

3. Capture, Queue, and Propagation is on **Instance 1**. Streaming to Queue, and Apply **Instance 2**.

4. Use of DBMS_AQADM.ALTER_QUEUE_TABLE to configure Capture, Queue, and Propagation to failover from **Instance 1** to **Instance 3**. Queue and Apply to failover from **Instance 4** to **Instance 4**.

5. Configuration of Propagation to use database link db02.mycompany.com which has the alias in tnsnames.ora as shown previously.

Oracle Support also provides the following as background to setting up Streams and RAC:

- In an RAC configuration, all Streams processes run from a single "owning" instance. The owning instance is identified in the DBA_QUEUE_TABLES view in the column OWNER_INSTANCE. If the instance that "owns" the queue goes down, ownership is switched to one of the surviving instances. All Streams processes automatically migrate and restart at the new "owning" instance.

- Instance ownership can be explicitly set for individual queue tables. Use the DBMS_AQADM.ALTER_QUEUE_TABLE procedure to specify the primary_instance and secondary_instance ownership for a particular queue table and its associated queues. The Streams processes will automatically start on the owning instance of the queue. If both the primary and secondary instance for a queue table containing a destination queue become unavailable, then queue ownership is transferred automatically to another instance in the cluster. In this case, if the primary or secondary instance becomes available again, then ownership is transferred back to one of them accordingly.

- When a queue is created, it also creates a service for the queue, which follows the queue. The NAME column in the DBA_SERVICES data dictionary view contains the service name for a queue. You can also determine the service_name for a particular queue from the NETWORK_NAME column of DBA_QUEUES. Use GV$ACTIVE_SERVICES to confirm that the queue service is available.

- A queue-to-queue propagation always has its own exclusive propagation job to propagate messages from the source queue to the destination queue. Because each propagation job has its own propagation schedule, the propagation schedule of each queue-to-queue propagation can be managed separately. Even when multiple queue-to-queue propagations use the same database link, you can enable, disable, or set the propagation schedule for each queue-to-queue propagation separately.

Oracle GoldenGate

Oracle has recently completed the acquisition of GoldenGate software during the writing of this book. The acquisition brings an exciting and interesting time to Oracle's line-up of Data Integration and Replication technology. **Oracle Data Integration (ODI)** is currently positioned as "a fully unified solution for building, deploying, and managing real-time, data-centric architectures in an SOA, BI, and data warehouse environment." While **Oracle GoldenGate (OGG)** provides "real-time, log-based change data capture, and delivery between heterogeneous systems."

Take note that both of these products are complementary to Oracle Streams. For instance, ODI provides advance ETL/ELT abilities in real time across heterogeneous environments. ODI essentially moves and transforms data regardless of the database platform.

OGG brings a strong story related to supporting heterogeneous environments. OGG brings XSTREAM to Oracle Streams. XSTREAM exposes APIs allowing for data sharing between "other systems that include non-Oracle databases, non-RDBMS Oracle products, filesystems, third-party software applications, and so on." OGG and Streams will eventually merge into one product and take on the best of both worlds. Exactly what comes from the merging of OGG and Streams is being worked on by Oracle. At the time this book went to press the direction is Oracle Streams will continue to be maintained. Emphasis and further development will be on OGG. Whatever the final results are, the merging of OGG and Streams will be a new and exciting product.

Glossary

* indicates Oracle Parameter. Please refer to Oracle® Database Reference 11g Release 2 (11.2) Part Number E10820-03 for further details.

Master-to-Slave/Single-Source	A configuration of Oracle Streams where there is one Source and one Target.
MEMORY_MAX_TARGET *	Specifies the maximum value to which a DBA can set the MEMORY_TARGET initialization parameter.
MEMORY_TARGET *	Specifies the Oracle system-wide usable memory.
N-Way Replication	Refer to Master-to-Master/Multi-Source.
OPEN_LINKS *	Specifies the maximum number of concurrent open connections to remote databases in one session.
Oracle Data Guard	An Oracle product specifically for High Availablity. This product handles failover in a gracious manner.

PROCESSES *	Specifies the maximum number of operating system user processes that can simultaneously connect to Oracle.
Propagation (Process)	The Streams process that sends LCRs from Source to Target across a Database Link.
QUEUE	Staging area in both memory and/or tables that contain messages and/or LCRs.
Replication	As related to Streams, the sharing data across multiple database.
Rule(s)	Are used to determine how message and/or LCR are handled.
SCN	System Change Number.
SHARED_POOL_SIZE *	Specifies (in bytes) the size of the shared pool.
Slave Site	The Target site where LCRs are applied.
SPFILE	The dynamic parameter file of the Oracle database.
STREAMS_POOL_SIZE*	
Synchronous	Processes that are blocking. With reference to Streams there are Asynchronous actions related to configuring LOG_ARCHIVE_DEST_N of Downstreams Capture.
Tag(s)	An identifier that relates to a LCR. Tags can be evaluted by Rules to determine how the LCR is to be handled.
TIMED_STATISTICS	Oracle parameter that is recommended to be set to TRUE. This allows for collection of time statistics.
Two phase commit	A commit or rollback of a transaction. An all-commit or all-rollback situation.
UNDO_RETENTION *	Oracle parameter that specifies (in seconds) the low threshold value of undo retention.
Unidirectional	Related to Streams configuration, from a Master Site to Slave Site.
WAN	Wide Area Network.

Summary

This chapter addressed some of the loose ends that are found in all books. We took a look at an Oracle Consulting tool from Oracle Deutschland GmbH, that being Oracle Streams Commander (OSC). Although OSC is not an official Oracle product, you may find it useful when working with Streams. Next, we went into some consideration when combining Streams and RAC. We highly recommend pre-planning and sketching out a diagram before actual configuration. The merging of OGG and Streams will provide for some interesting times.

Index

Symbols

A

B

C

G

GET_COMMAND_TYPE function 189
GET_COMMIT_SCN function 189
GET_COMPATIBLE function 189
GET_EXTRA_ATTRIBUTE function 189
GET_OBJECT_NAME function 189
GET_OBJECT_OWNER function 189
GET_SCN function 189
GET_SOURCE_DATABASE_NAME
     function 189
GET_SOURCE_TIME function 189
GET_TAG function 189
GET_TRANSACTION_ID function 189
GLOBAL_NAMES parameter 88
GoldenGate XSTREAMS. *See* XSTREAMS

H

Heterogeneous configuration
   about 236
   Apply process, configuring 236-238
   Apply process, configuring for Non Oracle
      database 239
   data transferring, via Queue Messaging 239
   Oracle to Non-Oracle communication,
      steps 234
Heterogeneous Services (HS) 234

I

Index Organized Tables. *See* IOT
instantiation
   about 28
   Data Pump, using 29
   levels 29
   methods 29
   SCN settings, factors 30, 31
   steps 28
   tools 98, 99
instantiation tools
   DataPump, using 98
   Instantiation SCN setup, manually 99-102
IOT 27

J

Java Messaging Service. *See* JMS

JMS 57

K

key aspects, conflict detection 51

L

LCR
   about 19, 48
   conflict detection 50, 51
   data, extracting from 50
   information, building 49, 50
   types 52
ListARs.sql 253
ListBNs.sql 253
ListDBs.sql 253
ListParts.sql 253
ListPaths.sql 253
ListPerfFlows.sql 253
ListPerfParts.sql 253
ListPerfS2E.sql 253
LOCK TABLE command
   using 254
LOG_ARCHIVE_DEST_STATE_n
     parameter 88
LOG_BUFFER parameter 88
logging feature, database configuration
   Archive logging 90
   forced logging 91
   supplemental logging 90
   supplemental logging, activating 90, 91
Logical Change Record. *See* LCR
LogMiner, failure points
   _LOG_PARALLELISM parameter 279
   LOGMNR_MAX_PERSISTENT_SESSIONS
      parameter 279
   supplemental logging 278

M

MAA 320
Master-to-Slave/Single-Source 323
Maximum Available Architecture. *See*
     MAA
MEMORY_MAX_TARGET parameter 88
MEMORY_TARGET parameter 88

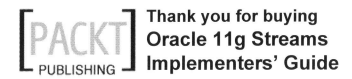
Thank you for buying
Oracle 11g Streams
Implementers' Guide

About Packt Publishing

Packt, pronounced 'packed', published its first book "*Mastering phpMyAdmin for Effective MySQL Management*" in April 2004 and subsequently continued to specialize in publishing highly focused books on specific technologies and solutions.

Our books and publications share the experiences of your fellow IT professionals in adapting and customizing today's systems, applications, and frameworks. Our solution based books give you the knowledge and power to customize the software and technologies you're using to get the job done. Packt books are more specific and less general than the IT books you have seen in the past. Our unique business model allows us to bring you more focused information, giving you more of what you need to know, and less of what you don't.

Packt is a modern, yet unique publishing company, which focuses on producing quality, cutting-edge books for communities of developers, administrators, and newbies alike. For more information, please visit our website: www.packtpub.com.

Writing for Packt

We welcome all inquiries from people who are interested in authoring. Book proposals should be sent to author@packtpub.com. If your book idea is still at an early stage and you would like to discuss it first before writing a formal book proposal, contact us; one of our commissioning editors will get in touch with you.

We're not just looking for published authors; if you have strong technical skills but no writing experience, our experienced editors can help you develop a writing career, or simply get some additional reward for your expertise.

Oracle 10g/11g Data and
Database Management Utilities

Master twelve must-use utilities to optimize the efficiency,
management, and performance of your daily database tasks

Hector R. Madrid   PACKT

Oracle 10g/11g Data and Database Management Utilities

ISBN: 978-1-847196-28-6   Paperback: 432 pages

Master twelve must-use utilities to optimize the efficiency, management, and performance of your daily database tasks

1. Optimize time-consuming tasks efficiently using the Oracle database utilities

2. Perform data loads on the fly and replace the functionality of the old export and import utilities using Data Pump or SQL*Loader

3. Boost database defenses with Oracle Wallet Manager and Security

Mastering Oracle Scheduler
in Oracle 11g Databases

Schedule, manage, and execute jobs that automate your
business processes

Ronald Rood   PACKT

Mastering Oracle Scheduler in Oracle 11g Databases

ISBN: 978-1-847195-98-2   Paperback: 240 pages

Schedule, manage, and execute jobs that automate your business processes

1. Automate jobs from within the Oracle database with the built-in Scheduler

2. Boost database performance by managing, monitoring, and controlling jobs more effectively

3. Contains easy-to-understand explanations, simple examples, debugging tips, and real-life scenarios

Please check **www.PacktPub.com** for information on our titles

Oracle SQL Developer 2.1

ISBN: 978-1-847196-26-2   Paperback: 460 pages

Install, configure, customize, and manage your SQL Developer environment

1. Includes the latest features to enhance productivity and simplify database development

2. Covers reporting, testing, and debugging concepts

3. Meet the new powerful Data Modeling tool – Oracle SQL Developer Data Modeler

4. Detailed code examples and screenshots for easy learning

Oracle Modernization Solutions

ISBN: 978-1-847194-64-0   Paperback: 432 pages

A practical guide to planning and implementing SOA Integration and Re-architecting to an Oracle platform

1. Complete, practical guide to legacy modernization using SOA Integration and Re-architecture

2. Understand when and why to choose the non-invasive SOA Integration approach to reuse and integrate legacy components quickly and safely

3. Understand when and why to choose Re-architecture to reverse engineer legacy components and preserve business knowledge in a modern open and extensible architecture

Please check **www.PacktPub.com** for information on our titles